SONIA SOTOMAYOR

This Large Print Book carries the
Seal of Approval of N.A.V.H.

Sonia Sotomayor

THE TRUE AMERICAN DREAM

Antonia Felix

THORNDIKE PRESS
A part of Gale, Cengage Learning

Detroit • New York • San Francisco • New Haven, Conn • Waterville, Maine • London

GALE
CENGAGE Learning

Thorndike Press, a part of Gale, Cengage Learning.

LIBRARY OF CONGRESS CATALOGING-IN-PUBLICATION DATA

Felix, Antonia.
    Sonia Sotomayor : the true American dream / by Antonia Felix. — Large print ed.
        p. (large print) cm.
    Originally published: New York : Berkley Books, 2010.
    Includes bibliographical references.
    ISBN-13: 978-1-4104-2894-3 (lg. print : hardcover)
    ISBN-10: 1-4104-2894-X (lg. print : hardcover) 1. Sotomayor, Sonia, 1954- 2. Hispanic American judges — Biography. 3. Judges — United States — Biography. 4. Large type books. I. Title.
    KF8745.S67F45 2010b
    347.73'2634—dc22
    [B]
                                                                    2010014335

Published in 2010 in arrangement with The Berkley Publishing Group, a member of Penguin Group (USA) Inc.

*In memory of Margaret Rabb,
poet, mentor, and friend*

And how do the roots know
they should rise up toward the sun?
And later, wave at the air
with such flowers and colors?

— PABLO NERUDA, from
The Book of Questions, "LXXII"

CONTENTS

ACKNOWLEDGMENTS

Writing about Associate Justice Sonia Sotomayor has been rewarding on many levels. I have not only been moved and inspired by her story and those of her mother and extended family but have had the great fortune to meet some of the remarkable people in the law and other professions whose lives have crossed hers. Researching her ancestral background introduced me to a special corner of southwestern Puerto Rico to which I hope to return as often as possible. Of the many places around the world that have become dear to me, I have never experienced the degree of warmth, hospitality, or authentic pride of place I encountered there.

There are many to thank for their support of this work, beginning with my two interpreters in Puerto Rico: Edward G. Contreras Santiago and his uncle, Dr. Edward Santiago, both of Mayaguez. Their generosity and professionalism knew no bounds, and my life is richer for having met them. My thanks also go to Daniel Sanchez and Dr. Jorge Ballester for their translation services, and friends and family who assisted me in many ways, including Timothy Shaner, Christopher Measom, Joseph and Elizabeth Mahowald, Anne Wilson, Bruce Felix, Audrey Schindler, Lily Schindler, Dan Markowitz, and Allen and Myrna Comstock.

I am indebted to those who helped with research, including Elizabeth L. Mo and Boris Milman for their expert work in the New York Supreme Court Law Library; David G. Badertscher, Principal Law Librarian at the New York Supreme Court; Robyn K. Dexter at the U.S. Army Women's Museum; and Erica Chabot in Senator Patrick Leahy's office. Thanks also to U.S. Supreme Court Public Information Officer Kathleen L. Arberg and to Jennifer A. Poggi at the White House.

Although I was not able to interview Justice Sotomayor — she announced after her nomination that she would not grant interviews because she did not want to show favoritism toward particular members of the media — my conversations with dozens of figures in her life have provided the core of this book. It was a particular honor to meet

Tito Baez, whose presence alone taught me much about Justice Sotomayor, and other members of her family who welcomed me into their homes.

I extend an enormous thank-you to all of my interviewees for sharing their insights and experiences. It was a pleasure to meet each of them and I am deeply grateful for their input:

Carlos Baez	Robert H. Klonoff
Mario Baez	Peter Kougasian
Tito Baez	Richard L. Mattiaccio
Brian Brokate	Heather McDonald
Marc J. Citrin	Hugh H. Mo
George H. Cohen	Andrew Oberfeldt
Ruben Diaz Jr.	Tom Ostertag
Jameson Doig	Cesar Perales
Joseph Evall	Jorge Rangel
Ignatio Flores	Benito Romano
John W. Fried	Theodore Shaw
John Garcia	Daniel Silverman
Patricia Gatling	Steven Skulnik
Richard Girgente	Leovigildo Cotte Torres
Veronica Hrdy	Donald B. Zavelo
Isabelle Kirshner	

— ANTONIA FELIX, January 25, 2010

PROLOGUE

Early on a Sunday morning in October, customers wander in and out of Tito Baez's bakery in Mayaguez to buy a *libra,* a freshly baked loaf of bread, and maybe a *dulce* or two. An elderly man in a bright blue shirt stops to shake Tito's hand on his way to the counter. The smell of bread and coffee fills the place. Three young men sit down at the table next to us and speak quietly to each other as we drink our coffee and talk about Tito's cousin, Sonia, and the changes that Puerto Rico has seen since her mother and father left during World War II.

Tito points at an abandoned white building with glass-block windows across the street, where three hundred women used to sew uniforms for the U.S. Army. Like many other factories in this west-coast region of the island, he says, it closed in the 1990s when American companies took their business to less expensive sources in Mexico and the Dominican Republic. The island's heavy loss of manufacturing has never been replaced and is partly responsible for the 15 percent unemployment rate.

The current global recession made another hit on the economy, and Tito has made adjustments to ensure that his long-time customers, each one a friend, can continue to buy their daily bread. The *pastelillo manzane,* mini apple turnovers on the top shelf of the case, cost twenty-five cents each, one-fifth the price of the traditional size. Although everyone is spending less these days, the small-size sweets mean that "they can still get a little taste of everything," Tito says. As I chide him about how difficult it must be to roll up dainty pastries with his large hands, a man walks up and gives him a dollar bill. They exchange a few words, and my interpreter, Edward, tells me that the man was repaying Tito for a loaf of bread he had given him a couple of days earlier. Tito, Edward learns from the man, often gives his customers bread and newspapers and other small things. There is no risk, and there is no reason for anyone to go without bread in the morning. As Edward, a graduate student in English at the University of Puerto Rico-Mayaguez, informs me, bread is a ritual every morning. It is impossible to imagine a day that does not start without it. I can see why: the bread is amazingly white and soft, covered with a delicate crust.

I feel guilty about keeping Tito from his customers, but he stays at our table to answer my questions about his business, the people at the counter, and their hard times. Like other bakery owners, he added a small grill to his kitchen to offer sandwiches and bring in business throughout the day. Over the past thirty years, other shops in the neighborhood have come and gone, but Tito's ingenuity and personable nature have made his place a permanent fixture in this section of town called Yaguez.

When Tito talks about his recent trip to Washington to attend Sonia's installation to the Supreme Court, he squeezes his hands together as if to hold himself in check. His cousin has been a source of pride for a very long time, and her latest accomplishment appears to be overwhelming. She has always remained the same person, he says, no matter how far up she has gone. Everything about her is expressed in her smile, which she gives so easily and which reveals her true nature. Her smile is powerful, he tells me, because it is so genuine.

Everyone with whom I had spoken before visiting Mayaguez — lawyers, professors, and other colleagues in the United States who have known Sonia Sotomayor through the years — had described her in similar terms: warm and generous with an intense focus, seemingly unlimited capacity for work, and New York gregariousness.

The thread that connects Sonia Sotomayor to Mayaguez extends a few miles southeast to a smaller town called Lajas, where her mother, Celina, was born, and back east to San Juan, her father's hometown. The stories that resound within that network have come up in her speeches as she traces the foundations of her success. Whether giving a college commencement address or making remarks at a judicial installation ceremony, she consistently glosses over her accomplishments and emphasizes the story of her mother's rise from unimaginable poverty. Her pride in that story blends ironically and inseparably with the humility and sacrifice of the tale itself.

In a similar fashion, Tito does not advertise that he has a degree in economics but integrates that experience into the running of the bakery. His family has run this *panaderia y reposteria* (bakery and confectionary) for fifty years, and he lived on the same block before moving with his wife and daughter to a more upscale neighborhood called Rio

Hondo. He arrives at work in the middle of night and bakes until the doors open and the first customers come through the unmarked door.

By the time I leave that morning, church has let out, and the foot traffic to the counter is picking up. Tito gives me an avocado as big as a melon, a monster compared to the lime-size ones I know from home. He instructs me to shave off slices and place them on a slice of bread, the best way to eat it. I will take pictures of all the fruit I am given during my visit because I cannot take food on the plane. Tito's avocado will dwarf the green-bordered star fruit, artichoke, papaya, lime, and pomelo lined up on my balcony ledge. It is majestic — firm and green and meant to be layered on bread made from most simple ingredients: flour, water, and salt.

Once I'm back home, the photo will remind me of the forested section of Lajas in which many of Sonia Sotomayor's relatives have lived. A lush green canopy covers much of that place, and standing in the open-air house of one of her relations, near where Celina spent her youngest years, I could practically reach out and pick an avocado. The air was full of birdsong and shiny leaves turning in the wind, much as it was, I imagine, eighty-two years ago, when Celina's story began.

CHAPTER 1
TALKING TO THE TREES

I extracted from the mountain
a luminous perfume.
My infancy twinkled away
in the village of the dew.

— from Francisco Matos Paoli (1915–2000),
"Biographical Summary,"
translated by Roberto Márquez

Moments after President Barack Obama introduced Sonia Sotomayor as his appointee to the Supreme Court at a press conference on May 26, 2009, Sotomayor adjusted the focus to a woman sitting in the front row. "My mother has devoted her life to my brother and me," Sotomayor said, acknowledging the woman with curly gray hair who was sporting a light blue suit. "I have often said that I am who I am because of her, and I am only half the woman she is."[1]

The nominee's rush to spotlight Celina

Baez Sotomayor came as no surprise to anyone who knew the judge or had heard her deliver a speech in which time permitted her to share a sketch of her background. When addressing the 1999 graduating class of Lehman College in New York City, for example, she started off by telling her mother's story, as she suspected it was "simply a variation of the story of many of the parents" in that room. She told them about her mother's birth in Lajas, Puerto Rico, and how she was raised "in a context of poverty that no child in this room will ever have to experience or know."[2]

How Celina Baez found her way out of that poverty and how the family members who remained dealt with conditions on the economically impoverished island reveal the underpinnings of character traits that everyone I spoke to described about Sonia Sotomayor herself. Hearing the stories of Celina's family in their own words drew a direct line between Sonia's ancestry and the generosity, compassion, and authenticity that define her.

Celina's story begins in the village of Lajas in the southwestern corner of Puerto Rico. The youngest of five children, she was born in 1927, twenty-nine years after the island became a U.S. territory after the Spanish-

American War. The family lived in a section of Barrio Sabana Yeguas called Cañitas, a rural area of farms and sugarcane fields just south of the town center. Part of Lajas is nestled in the Southwestern Hills, foothills of the mountain range that makes up 60 percent of the island, and the rest lies in the dry, flat valley below the mountains.

Like other coastal plains surrounding the island, the Lajas Valley during Celina's childhood was covered with sugarcane fields. Her parents' generation had witnessed a radical transformation of the land in the decades after the U.S. takeover: Before the industrialization of the sugar industry, much of the plains had been devoted to grazing. As the Brookings Institution study of 1930 observed, "Thirty years ago, what are today wide expanses of cane were great stretches of green pasture where, during the rainy season, cattle stood shoulder high in the rank forage."[3]

The year Celina was born, sugar made up nearly 60 percent of the island's exports, and the sugar economy would peak in the 1930s. The majority of sugarcane was grown by four big American corporations that bought or leased land from the island's farmers, and the profitability of the business brought millions of dollars of investment to the territory. Even though some of that investment went to projects outside the sugar industry and the U.S. government brought in money for public works such as roads and schools, the sugar boom did not improve the quality of life of the Puerto Rican people. Sugar mills sprang up "as industrial outposts in the countryside," wrote sociologist César J. Ayala, "but no significant development of urban industry or industrial towns took place."[4] Puerto Rico remained overwhelmingly rural and exceedingly poor.

In 1929, the governor of Puerto Rico, Theodore Roosevelt Jr., son of the president, reported that more than 60 percent of the population was unemployed either all or part of the year. The Brookings Institution study spelled out the facts behind the poor conditions for Puerto Rican workers in the midst of the fast-growing sugar economy. The average weekly wage for the working class was $6.71 per family, $3.49 per worker, and $0.85 per person, or about $0.12 per day. Approximately 94 percent of those earnings went to buying food, primarily rice. In his famous report on the sugar industry published in 1941, Puerto Rican reformist Estéban Bird wrote, "Twelve cents per person per day is only four cents more than the food expense required for feeding a hog in the

United States! . . . Twelve cents per person per day is the root of all evil . . . [and] plays a prominent part in a death rate of 575 (per 100,000) for enteritis and diarrhea, 237 for tuberculosis, and 221 for malaria in the sugarcane areas of Puerto Rico."[5]

The year after Celina's birth, a natural disaster brought more misery to the population. Hurricane Felipe cut across the island on September 13, 1928, wiping out whole villages and the territory's entire coffee crop. The official death count from the category five hurricane was three hundred, but some estimates raised that to fifteen hundred, and hundreds of thousands lost their homes. Ten inches of rain hit the southwestern part of the island, and twice as much fell in the northeast; the winds were the highest on record at 150 miles per hour. One of Sonia Sotomayor's cousins recalled that the homes in the Santa Rosa *barrio* were unharmed, but the sugarcane in the fields was flattened.

Hurricane Felipe's devastation ruined lives and futures. That storm and a second hurricane that struck four years later destroyed the coffee industry, which before World War I had been the principle, world-renowned export of Puerto Rico. After the 1928 hurricane alone, coffee production dropped from thirty-two million pounds to five million the following year. Coffee production had already been on the decline, but the hurricanes were the finishing touch. With the rise of sugar production, which was protected by tariffs that made sugar imported into the United States from other countries more expensive came the decline of coffee, which was not protected in the same way. The hurricanes wiped out most of the industry, and the way of life of farmers in the mountainous heart of the island.

Some members of Sonia's extended family worked in the sugarcane fields, including her cousin Rosa's husband, Ignatio, who described the work with a sweep of his arms, illustrating how he used a scythe to cut the bamboo-like stalks that grew over twelve feet high. He would gather the cane and load it in trucks, which would transport it to a mill to be crushed. The very low wages of this work barely sustained anyone, and like the majority of others on the island, Sotomayor's relations suffered all the effects of poverty.

There were natural comforts in Lajas, such as the green canopy that blocked out the sun and the daily rhythm of the rain that came every afternoon, leaving the air fresh for the evening. There was a sense of awe at the elegant gait of the Paso Fino horses as they pranced down the dirt roads. But none of that, not even the pleasant sound of bells coming from the bright yellow church on the town square, could take away the tragedy of being hungry and very, very poor.

Sotomayor told her mother's story for the first time during the induction proceedings of November 6, 1998, that elevated her to the bench of the Second Circuit Court of Appeals in New York. Before an audience of twelve circuit court judges, U.S. Senator Daniel Patrick Moynihan, Senator-elect Charles Schumer, New York District Attorney Robert M. Morgenthau, and many friends, she described the Puerto Rico of her mother's generation:

> Unlike today, the Puerto Rico of my mother's childhood was completely undeveloped and was vastly poorer than any state of the Union. . . . The island's literacy rate was only 39 percent, and while over 50 percent of the population was infected with tuberculosis, malaria and hookworms, only 2 of the island's 77 districts had doctors.[6]

That environment, Sotomayor continued, took its toll on Celina's mother, Pancha Toro, who never left her bed from the day Celina was born. She never recovered her health and died nine years later. Soon afterward, Celina's father, Agustin Baez, abandoned the children and moved up the coast to Añasco. Sonia's cousin Mario "Papo" Baez said that Agustin was "not a family-oriented person."

As the Great Depression exacerbated the already impoverished conditions of the island, Celina and her siblings fended for themselves. Mayo and Aurora, whom Sotomayor described as only slightly older than Celina, assumed the responsibility of raising their nine-year-old sister. Celina went to school, but unable to buy pencils — other than precious ones she and her brothers and sister shared at home — or notebooks, resorted to memorizing her teachers' words. As soon as she came home from school she would repeat what she had learned to the trees, whom she had named after her schoolmates, imagining she was their teacher. Standing among the banana, avocado, lime, and star fruit trees, she used "a stick as a pointer to teach the trees the lessons she had learned for that day," Sotomayor said. "This was her one hour of happiness before she went into the house to work."[7]

Other family members helped the Baez children as much as they could, including their paternal grandmother, Juana. Mayo, who was assisted by one uncle in particular, never forgot it and spent the rest of his life returning the favor to his extended family and others. Carlos Baez, one of Sotomayor's cousins who lives in a neighborhood near Cañitas, grew up surrounded by Uncle Mayo's generosity. Carlos's father was paralyzed and could not work, so when he and his wife started a family, Uncle Mayo bought them a house as a gift.

When her older sister, Aurora, got married, Celina moved with her to San German, a historic town set in the Southwestern Hills overlooking Lajas. Their brother Mayo moved to Mayaguez, the big town twenty-five miles northwest of Lajas, and bought a farm where he grew vegetables and bananas. He and his wife, Maria, continuously gave away produce and money to help out members of his extended family back in Lajas as well as anyone else who needed it. A few vegetables went a long way for a family in those days, Carlos told me.

Throughout the decades, Mayo's kind acts made him a beloved figure in his hometown. When he died in his seventies, "all the town of Lajas felt his loss," Carlos said.

The sugar-dominated economy, below-poverty-level wages, hurricanes, and economic depression that plagued Puerto Rico during Celina's childhood created the "context of poverty" Sotomayor referred to in her speech. After the outbreak of World War II, however, Celina discovered an opportunity that would lift her out of her desperate circumstances. Conditions were still severe when she reached her teenage years. Writing about Puerto Rico in 1941, John Gunther described the unsafe water supply, lack of classrooms that left more than half the children out of school, rampant malaria, and an infant mortality rate four times that of the United States. "It would be lamentable enough to see this anywhere," he wrote, "but to see it on American territory . . . in a region for which our federal responsibility has been complete for 43 years, is a paralyzing jolt to anyone who believes in American standards of progress and civilization."[8]

Celina's opportunity to make a dramatic change came to the island in the spring of 1944. That year, the Women's Army Corps (WAC) began a program of recruiting Puerto Rican women to help fill the much-needed ranks of noncombat personnel. Twenty-two thousand Puerto Rican men, who were eligible for the draft under the 1917 Jones-Shafroth Act that granted Puerto Ricans U.S. citizenship, had already been called up to serve.

The U.S. Army authorized the WAC to enlist two hundred women from Puerto Rico. This directive came only after personnel shortages in the Army's Transportation Corps and Medical Department demanded it; other than blacks, very few minorities were recruited into the WAC. At its peak during the war, the Transportation Corps incorporated five thousand WACs in its offices and installations at the eight major ports of embarkation, where the final preparations of loading personnel and materials onto ships and aircraft were made. Under orders to replace general servicemen with WACs and civilians, the Transportation Corps relied heavily on the women because civilian labor was hard to come by in the port cities of New York, Boston, Hampton Roads, Charleston, Los Angeles, San Francisco, Seattle, and New Orleans. The ports were so busy that the installations in New York and San Francisco enthusiastically accepted the all-WAC bands that had been cut from WAC training centers and sent them out on small boats to welcome the troops.

In spite of fears about the "possible language difficulties" of Puerto Rican recruits, the army needed more staff in the ports and a four-woman recruiting team was shipped to the island in April 1944.

The recruitment group, consisting of one WAC officer and three enlisted women, distributed applications and received an overwhelming response from more than fifteen hundred women who wanted to join up, including seventeen-year-old Celina Baez. News about the recruiters had reached every corner of the island, including San German, where an announcement in the newspaper got Celina's attention.

Many applicants were rejected near the beginning of the selection process after failing to pass the aptitude test. A good portion of the others were taken out of the pool "because of family objections."[9] Celina made the cut after taking the test but not until dealing with a second hurdle. Like the army officials who were suspect about bringing women into the ports of embarkation, Celina's siblings feared that the U.S. Army was far too rough a place for their little sister. "They were not happy with her decision to join the army because she was the youngest," said Carlos Baez. "They thought the army may be dangerous for a woman."

Celina had her way, however, and was sworn in with the rest of the small unit. Even though the recruiters had been sent to the island to build a two-hundred-woman unit, they left the island with only about a hundred. The first group of fifty-one left for Miami on October 6, 1944, and were then taken to Fort Oglethorpe, Georgia, for processing and basic training. The remaining fifty joined them two weeks later. About 40 percent of Celina's fellow recruits were college graduates, and many of them were teachers or office workers.

Unlike other WAC recruits of Hispanic descent, all of whom were integrated into units with the white WACs, the Puerto Rican unit remained intact throughout the women's enlistment, training, and assignment because of their lack of facility in English. Aside from that, Celina's small unit "presented no notable problems" and would have been able to contribute even more had they spoken English.[10] Army officers were unable to give them assignments that matched their bright intelligence solely because of the language barrier.

Fort Oglethorpe in northwest Georgia had been devoted solely to WACs since September 1943 and was the third of five WAC training centers set up during the war. Celina entered a highly active installation in which a thousand women per week went through a four-week basic training course and were then assigned to duties stateside or abroad. Celina and her unit were inducted into an army regimen of marching drills, calisthenics, inspections, specialized office or equipment training, vaccinations, barracks cleaning, kitchen duty, and three big meals a day at the mess hall with women from every region of the country.

As explained in the WAC manual published by the Des Moines Training Center, the purpose of the corps was "to make available the knowledge, skill, and special training of the women of our nation for the war effort." To reach that goal, the training center would teach corps members "how to salute, how to march, how to look like a soldier, how to handle a gas mask, and how to make a bed the Army way." Learning how to handle a gas mask would include a couple of trips into the tear gas chamber, and learning to march would take drills on an almost daily basis. "Those of you with specialties will be encouraged to use them; the others will learn specialties." And last but not least, WAC pay was $50 a month.[11]

A Texan woman named Concepcion Alvarado Escobedo who underwent basic training at Fort Oglethorpe said she was "disciplined twenty-four hours a day." She learned to make her bed so a quarter would bounce off it, and never quite got used to being shouted at. "They would yell at you, as if you couldn't hear. They would yell right in front of your face and have you shaking in your boots," she said.[12]

No scene, from the barracks to the marching drills to the classrooms and office training, could have been more remote from Celina's corner of Lajas. "I can only imagine the culture shock she must have felt as a youth," Sotomayor said, "somewhere between childhood and womanhood, trying to work in the South with a Spanish-only grammar school education." Without any experience in an office or with telephones, Celina had to learn everything from scratch. "She has told me that the first time she picked up a telephone and received a call [for] her sergeant," said Sotomayor, "she thought she had to hang up the receiver to find him. You can imagine the dismay of the sergeant when he arrived only to find a dial tone."[13]

The women in Celina's unit were not alone in mingling with other cultures for the first time. Memoirs of women who trained at Fort Oglethorpe reveal some prickly exchanges between northerners and southerners about each other's dialects and manners, but one woman from Florida recalled being fascinated with the language of the Puerto Rican unit: "It is quite amusing to go into a company with a large number of these girls and hear them talking in Spanish," the recruit wrote in a letter home. "They talk so fast and with the most expression on their face and in their eyes. It is very interesting to listen and to look at them talking."[14]

After completing basic training, the Puerto Rican unit was assigned to work in the military offices at the Port of Embarkation of New York City. The administrative work at the port involved organizing shipments of soldiers and hundreds of thousands of supply items to Europe. Women's Army Corps members fulfilled all the functions that kept the port running smoothly, from clerical and secretarial work to taking roll call when the men walked down the gangplank and escorting them to their trains.

Not everyone up the line of command was convinced that WAC detachments belonged in the ports. "Early pessimists feared that ports of embarkation were no place for WACs," wrote military historian Mattie E. Treadwell, "who would undoubtedly be invalided by the rough physical work or seduced by the transient combat troops."[15] In spite of those concerns, the army vigorously stepped up WAC recruiting to install at least one WAC detachment at each port of embarkation.

The WACs did not report any difficulties such as lack of respect when working with the troops. On the contrary, one report stated, "Directions given [by WACs] to troops debarking were cheerfully obeyed for the men 'just wanted to hear them talk.' "[16]

Celina's unit was "successfully employed" at the port offices in New York, and their numbers made up a small but significant fraction of the approximately hundred thousand Puerto Ricans who served in the war.[17]

The hardships of Celina's childhood did not engender bitterness or fearful self-centeredness. She and her siblings kept alive the generosity that had helped them survive and brought it into the next generation. The sense of responsibility for family and community that motivated Celina's brother Mayo would become evident in the way Celina worked three jobs to ensure a good education for her children. It would carry on in Sonia Sotomayor's commitment to mentoring young people and serving the disenfranchised through her pro bono work and in the way her cousin Tito treats his longtime customers.

Sotomayor's consistent practice of pointing to others when crediting her success also echoes the character traits expressed by her family. When sharing her mother's story with the distinguished audience at her appeals court induction ceremony, she allocated most of her remarks to thanking the dozens of people who supported her at various stages of her career. She pointed out that the media's coverage of her new federal court appointment "failed to appreciate . . . that despite economic hardship, it was not so hard for me to succeed because I had the example of guidance of a truly remarkable woman, my mother." When she began to speak about Celina, she referred to her mother's life as "truly the most interesting story I know."[18]

The extent to which Celina would bring her siblings' and other relatives' qualities to her own family and community form a compelling part of her personal history. "My mother is so humble and unassuming that she does not perceive herself as a special person in any sense," Sotomayor said, "and she speaks about the burdens in her life in fragments and only sparingly. A close friend of mine once remarked, however, that the more interesting part of my life is really the story of my mother's life."[19]

Celina's childhood in Puerto Rico is a small fraction of that story, the section that offers a glimpse of a family whose confrontation with poverty brought out a commitment to assist other people. Celina's determination to strike out on her own from a small village to a country with a different language and in which she had no friends or relatives illustrates the passion and independence that she most definitely passed down to her kids. Her spirited personality recalls a line from famed Puerto Rican poet Julia de Burgos: "I am life, I am strength, I am woman."[20]

Celina's ability to forge a strong sense of self in her children would guarantee their success. The consideration that she and her family members extended to others would be imprinted on them as a commitment to service. And Celina's strong-willed, uncompromising approach to improving her life would make them just as strong.

CHAPTER 2
THE BRONXDALIANS

Each person enters the world called.

— James Hillman

The Puerto Rican unit of the Women's Army Corps remained on duty in New York after the war ended in August 1945. By then known as the Transportation WACs, Celina Baez's unit was vital to the operation of the port as it processed millions of soldiers coming home.

The Puerto Rican population in New York had been steadily increasing in the 1940s, and the numbers rose dramatically during and just after the war. The army brought Celina to New York during that booming period known as the Great Migration: Between 1940 and 1950 the Puerto Rican population in New York City increased from 61,463 to 612,574. Attracted to the expansive job market in the industrial cities of America's northeast, Puerto Rican workers found higher wages than those they left behind on the island. Approximately 80 percent of the Puerto Ricans coming to the mainland settled in the greater New York area, especially in the East Harlem and Lower East Side neighborhoods of Manhattan and the Williamsburg section of Brooklyn.

While stationed in New York, Celina met Juan Luis Sotomayor, whose family had migrated from San Juan to the mainland during the war. Juan came from the Santurce district of Puerto Rico's capital, the northernmost and most populous part of the city that borders the Atlantic Ocean, where he had worked in an auto repair shop. He found work in New York in a tool-and-die factory, which, even though he did not speak English and had only a third-grade education, probably provided him with a much better salary than he had made back home.

Studies of migration from Puerto Rico found that "migration to the mainland offered the prospect of upward movement for those with lesser skills or work experience,"[1] and Juan Sotomayor's shift from auto repair to the tool-and-die trade was most likely an upward move. Toolmakers work from blueprints to create one-of-a-kind tools for producing objects, such as molds, block dies that work with a punch press, and cutters that fit on lathes. (My dad was a tool-and-die maker who designed molds for making toy truck windshields and many other parts — we proudly displayed his prototype tools and parts at home in a glass jar.) Moving to an industrialized part of the country where toolmakers were in high demand gave Juan the opportunity to learn a highly skilled job.

Shortly after Celina was discharged from the army in 1946, she and Juan were married and settled in the South Bronx. By that time, the Puerto Rican population of that section of the city was also expanding significantly; in another couple of years, about seventy-two thousand Puerto Ricans would have moved to the borough. Even though she could have easily found a job that didn't require English, Celina set out to get a high school equivalency credential. Only with that document, and the excellent English skills that went along with it, would she have a wide range of options for making the most productive life possible for herself and her family.

Celina enrolled in the General Education Development (GED) test program at James Monroe High School in the South Bronx. The GED test, administered at that time by the Veteran's Testing Service, was a high school equivalency opportunity launched in 1942 to help military personnel without diplomas qualify for jobs and postsecondary education. The test was given in English only, so she had no choice but to improve her language ability to master the social studies, science, mathematics, reading, and writing areas of the exam. It is a testament to her self-determination that she mastered English and developed the study habits that allowed her to pass the seven-hour test that only 60 percent of graduating high school seniors pass on their first attempt.

With GED in hand, Celina got a job as a telephone operator at Prospect Hospital in the Longwood section of the South Bronx. She committed herself to the entry-level position with the same disciplined and hard-working approach that had allowed her to absorb the equivalent of four years of high school, and her efforts did not go unnoticed. "At that hospital," Sotomayor said, "my mother was always a tireless and energetic worker, and the owner soon recognized her potential and encouraged her to get a practical nurse's license."[2]

Celina's ambition would eventually take her down that path, but not until she and Juan had started a family. Their first child,

Sonia Maria, was born on June 25, 1954, and shortly afterward Celina began studying to be a licensed practical nurse (LPN). While she concentrated on this goal, she and Juan made plans to move out of their tenement apartment into one of the public housing projects springing up throughout the Bronx. The federal government built sixteen projects in the Bronx between 1950 and 1959, and when Sonia was three years old, the family moved into one called the Bronxdale Houses. Construction had begun two years previously and some of the buildings were still unfinished when they moved in. The twenty-eight apartment buildings, each made of red brick and built seven stories high, spread out over about thirty-one acres of the Soundview section of the South Bronx.

Even though she was just a toddler when the family moved, Sonia Sotomayor remembers the emotional impact of seeing the apartment in Building 28 for the first time. Her description leads us to envision the neglected condition of the family's former tenement building:

It had just been freshly painted and there were lights everywhere and the floor was clean. It was the cleanest apartment I had ever seen in my three years of living. And the memory was so overwhelming of walking into this pristine environment and realizing that this was going to be our new home. It overwhelmed me.[3]

She remembers pedaling her tricycle over those clean floors and into her bedroom that day and the moment when her tricycle made a scratch on the wall. "I was absolutely heartbroken that I had marred this environment," she recalled. "I thought my mother would kill me and I hid under the bed."[4]

For many, public housing often conjures up images of violent, crime-ridden urban decay, but in the 1950s, projects like the Bronxdale Houses were respectable working-class enclaves filled with the families of World War II veterans. They were well-kept, affordable, and desirable addresses with carefully landscaped grounds that provided spacious and child-friendly outdoor spaces. With rents that averaged about $51 a month, the projects were alternatives to cramped and poorly maintained tenements, and it was difficult to land one of the apartments if you had a drug abuse record, were unemployed, or were a single parent.

As Fordham University historian Mark Naison explains, there was no stigma attached to living in the projects in those years, but "to the contrary, many residents took tremendous pride in the beauty of their surroundings." The projects were not only designed to be attractive green oases in the city, but family oriented with playgrounds, community centers, and schools located within walking distance.[5] Like the tens of thousands of others who made a similar change that decade, moving to the Bronxdale Houses was a step up for the Sotomayor family.

According to Bronx Borough President Ruben Diaz Jr., who grew up across the street from Sonia's building a few years after the Sotomayors left, there was a name for people from the Bronxdale Houses and the blocks surrounding it. "If you were from that area and hung out in Bronxdale," he said, "you were a Bronxdalian."

Besides the move, the other major event Sonia experienced at age three was the birth of her brother, who was named after his father. By the time Juan Luis Jr. was born, Celina had already passed her exams and was working as an LPN at Prospect Hospital. In a short span of years she had elevated herself from a menial office job to the first tier of professional nursing — and become the mother of two. As an LPN, she brought

46

her work ethic and caring personality to dispensing drugs and setting up IVs, monitoring patients' vital signs, and applying first aid to minor injuries. Her daughter recalled that by the time Juan was born, Celina "was one of the most respected nurses in the hospital."[6]

Each step of Celina's upward trajectory was based on education, the strongly self-motivated kind. She was her own example of the rewards of training and study and decided early on that her children would get the best education possible. "My mom believed that education was the key to everything in the world," Sotomayor said. "If you became educated you could do whatever you wanted and accomplish whatever dreams you had."[7]

Public school would not be good enough for Celina and Juan's children, and fortunately their apartment was situated very near an excellent private Catholic school, Blessed Sacrament. The household budget would be squeezed to pay the tuition for Sonia and, three years later, Juan, so Celina increased her hours at the hospital to meet those costs. In 1959, Sonia donned a green-and-navy-blue-plaid uniform and entered kindergarten in the beige-brick classroom building behind Blessed Sacrament Church on the corner of Beach and Gleason Avenues. Twelve hundred boys and girls attended the school, with about two hundred entering and another two hundred graduating every year; all were taught by the Sisters of Charity.

During her years at Blessed Sacrament, Sonia's home life revolved around family gatherings and socializing with close-knit neighbors. Half of the families living in the nearly fifteen hundred Bronxdale apartments were either black or Puerto Rican, and the white population consisted mostly of Italian, Jewish, and Irish residents. When she wasn't working, Celina could visit with neighbors through the open doors as the women made dinner in their kitchens or sit outside with them to watch the children in the playground. The buildings were bright and safe; no one worried about leaving their bicycles or baby carriages in the lobby downstairs and the kids ran freely from apartment to apartment. [8]

Unlike some projects built in that era, the Bronxdale Houses featured glass-enclosed, visible lobbies that would make them more crime resistant when the neighborhood started to change.[9] But when Sonia and her brother were students at Blessed Sacrament, the kids enjoyed the freedom of having the run of the projects.[10] Celina's best friend, a neighbor named Ana, babysat Sonia and her brother in the hours before she and Juan got home from work.[11]

The weekends belonged to the entire extended family. Sonia's cousins, aunts, and uncles all met at the home of Sonia's paternal grandmother, Mercedes Ortega, the family matriarch in the Bronx. They feasted on traditional Puerto Rican dishes, and Sonia developed a taste for some of the more unusual ones such as *morcilla,* pigs' intestines; *patitas de cerdo con garbanzo,* pigs' feet with beans; and *la lengua y orejas de cuchifrito,* pigs' tongue and ears. While the adults played dominoes or danced the *guaguaco* and merengue in the living room, the children played *loteria* (bingo), placing chickpeas on their cards as Grandmother Mercedes called out numbers. In those hours surrounded by her family, Sonia recalled, her "Latina soul was nourished."[12]

In the summers, the whole group would spend entire days picnicking at Orchard Beach, the "Riviera of New York" on Long Island Sound.[13] One family outing photo shows Sonia, looking about eight years old, smiling beneath a white hat that sports a tall red feather, while her father's hands rest proudly on his five-year-old son's shoulders.

And some weekends they took in a game at Yankee Stadium in the Concourse section of the South Bronx, about four miles west.

There was a lot for families to do in the Bronx that didn't cost very much. Even though both of Sonia's parents had to work, new clothes were scarce, and they lived sparingly, Sonia did not feel they lacked for anything. "I never perceived myself as a poor child," she said.[14]

For all the socializing the family did throughout Sonia's earliest school years, Sonia did not display the outgoing and gregarious personality that would define her as an adult. Not until she was eight years old did her parents learn why she was such a quiet girl, often tired, listless, and uninterested in school: that year she was diagnosed with type 1 diabetes. The autoimmune illness had been destroying her pancreas's ability to create insulin, without which her cells could not access the energy-giving glucose locked inside her bloodstream. The diagnosis and subsequent treatment saved her from the life-threatening effects that would occur if the disease had gone undetected. And once Sonia fell into the daily treatment regimen she became a different child. Her brother described it as a "seminal change."[15]

Sonia began to engage in the world in a

much more energetic way, but her awareness of her chronic disease came with a price
beyond the daily round of blood monitoring
and insulin injections. In those days, when
the condition was typically called juvenile or
insulin-dependent diabetes, the prevailing
assumption was that it could take decades
off a person's life. There was also a risk of
developing eye, kidney, heart, and other
problems when she got older, and these messages would have a profound impact on how
she approached her goals when she became
a young adult.

Having a nurse for a mother helped when it
came to forming diligent habits to control the
disease. Treatments were less sophisticated
in the 1960s, but the clean bill of health and
excellent medical history that Sonia's physician would report about her decades later
revealed that she did everything right from
the beginning. Reports of her lifelong diabetes management would become a source of
great inspiration to diabetics throughout the
country when she stepped into the national
spotlight in 2009.

The second crack in Sotomayor's childhood picture came when her father, at age
forty-two, succumbed to the heart problem
that had plagued him for years. The U.S.
military had turned him down for service

during World War II because of it, and a year after Sonia was diagnosed with diabetes he had a heart attack. One moment he was standing in the kitchen and the next he was on his way to the floor, clutching his chest. He died the next morning at the hospital. Juan's sudden death was a devastating blow to the close-knit family. A year of diabetes treatment had increased Sonia's energy by that time, and she had become a more outgoing girl, but her father's death made her seek out more private time, especially with books.

Like Celina, Juan Sotomayor had envisioned his children attaining anything they could dream up. At such young ages, they already had a lifetime of greater opportunity than he or his wife had had when they left Puerto Rico. He saw in them the unfolding of the American Dream and had reminded Sonia of that every time he said, *"Algún día, usted va a ir a la luna"* (Someday, you're going to go to the moon).[16]

After Juan Sotomayor died, Celina moved the family to a smaller apartment in Building 24 of the Bronxdale Houses. The two children shared a room, and the windows in Apartment 2F had a direct view of Blessed Sacrament and the street leading to it.

As a single mother, Celina ran a tightly ordered household, and Sonia was allowed to play with friends in the building only after she finished her homework and chores. Anxious to escape into books, some of her favorites were Carolyn Keene's Nancy Drew mysteries, which she had been checking out from the library for the past couple of years. Sonia and her friends swapped the books and talked about the clever ways Nancy could connect the dots of a mystery. Sonia, like generations of girls before and after her, could not get enough of Nancy's self-possessed and independent personality. Solving mysteries was much more important to Nancy than her boyfriend's silly ideas about getting serious. And the teenage character had an emotional wound with which Sonia could identify — the loss of a parent — forming a personal connection. Poet Meghan O'Rourke, who reflected on her own obsession with Nancy Drew mysteries in a *New Yorker* essay, suspected that the whodunit structure of the books addressed two basic aspects of childhood: "The mystery formula elegantly embodies children's two conflicting impulses: the search for order and security, and the appetite for novelty and risk-taking."[17]

For a while, Sonia was crazy about the idea

of becoming a detective, but when she was diagnosed with diabetes she was told that it would be too strenuous a career for someone with the disease. By that age, however, she had become strongly attached to her dream and felt unsettled when she had to let it go. "I became very disappointed about not having a life plan," she said.[18] Her sense of urgency about establishing a career path so early in life brings to mind the calling that James Hillman claims is present in every child. Hillman, a Jungian analyst and author, maintains that all children are aware of "a uniqueness that asks to be lived and that is already present before it can be lived."[19] He calls this idea — that each person comes into the world with something to do and to be — the "acorn theory." By age eight, Sonia was evidently aware that she had a unique destiny to fulfill, and when the first obstacle appeared it distressed her. But, according to Hillman, a calling never lets go, and it did not take long for Sonia to reconnect with her dream.

Sonia soon discovered that there were other crime-fighting roles equally impressive as detective work but (allegedly) less physically demanding. Watching *Perry Mason* on Thursday nights brought her dream back into focus.

Sonia watched the show religiously and forced her little brother to watch it with her. Sharing the excitement as Mason pieced together a case was apparently half the fun. Over the course of an hour, the LA defense attorney, played by Raymond Burr, set out to prove the innocence of his client who had been charged by tough district attorney Hamilton Burger. Sonia also set her brother down on Friday nights to watch *Judd for the Defense,* another legal drama that starred Carl Betz as Texas criminal defense lawyer Clinton Judd. Unlike *Perry Mason,* set in one city, this show had Betz careening all over the country as he represented his wealthy and eccentric clientele. But it was *Perry Mason* that defined Sonia's dream. From the serious, one-two punch opening theme to the final courtroom scene, Perry Mason inspired a generation of young people, including Sonia Sotomayor, to go into law. "I was going to college and I was going to become an attorney, and I knew that when I was ten," she said.[20]

However, shortly after that, the plot line of one particular episode took her goal a "quantum leap" higher, she recalled. The prosecutor's role was "a wonderful occupation," but the person in the courtroom who had the power to dismiss the case when the defendant turned out to be innocent had an even more impressive job.[21] "I realized that the judge was the most important player in that room," she said.[22] Something clicked when she observed that every time Mason "wanted to do something," he had to ask the judge for permission.[23] Every week, the proceedings in the courtroom scenes revolved around the person on the bench, the robe-clad referee, the judge. "That was what I was going to be," she said.[24] From that moment, she aligned herself with her calling for a life in the law and never deviated from it.

Reading about sleuths and watching TV lawyers fueled Sonia's passion for the field, but these entertainments also helped her escape from the darker realities of life after her father died. When Ana or Grandmother Mercedes could not babysit, Sonia was left with one of her aunts who worked in a sweatshop. The seamstresses were confined in a room with blacked-out windows and little ventilation, and Sonia recalled trying to stay close to the door on those long days. "I struggled all day to get to the door to smell some fresh air and see light," she said. "Titi would vigilantly chase me away from the door all day long. Little did I know then that the shop and its employees were hiding themselves from the police."[25]

In postwar New York City, Puerto Rican women made up half of the skirt-making workforce and were a major source of labor in the garment industry. Sewing and needle-work industries had been a large part of the economy in Puerto Rico, and their work was in demand on the mainland. But women like Sonia's aunt who worked in the nonunion shops and sweatshops made a fraction of union wages, typically less than a dollar an hour, sewing for long hours under inhumane conditions.

Those grim childhood memories are mixed with Sonia's recollections of Saturday after-noons at the movies watching the slapstick comedy of Cantinflas, the "Charlie Chaplin of Mexico," and listening to merengue "and the heart-wrenching Spanish love songs that we enjoy" at family gatherings.[26] There were lazy summer afternoons hanging out on the front steps of Blessed Sacrament with her girlfriends, always within view of the second-floor windows in Building 24 down the street. Throughout the year, she met many of the same friends every week at St. Athanasius Roman Catholic Church, across Bruckner Boulevard on Tiffany Street, where the Sotomayors attended ten o'clock Sunday mass.

And there are memories of the summers

when Celina flew Sonia and Juan to Puerto Rico to visit their aunts, uncles, and cousins in Mayaguez and Lajas. They would drive out to Cabo Rojo on the west coast, one of the islanders' most beloved vacation destinations, and take the little boat across the sparkling water to Isla de Ratones, Mouse Island. Sonia and her cousins ran along the perfect sandy beach and swam under the sun.

Flights to Puerto Rico were inexpensive in those days, but one expenditure that Celina did splurge on was a set of the *Encyclopaedia Britannica,* a virtual library in those days. They were the only family in the Bronxdale projects to have them, and although their lifestyle was spare in many ways, Celina's emphasis on education motivated her to take on the considerable expense. "She had almost a fanatical emphasis on education," Sonia said. "We got encyclopedias, and she struggled to make those payments."[27] The encyclopedias were very costly for someone on an LPN's salary, and they were treated with an almost reverential respect, like the other books in the house. "Books were my mother's priority; they came before clothes," Sonia said. "I was a student in law school before I could bring myself to mark a book — that's how precious books were to us."[28]

Most of the books Sonia and Juan read, including Sonia's Nancy Drew mysteries, came from the nearby Parkchester branch of the New York Public Library; Sonia never stepped foot in a bookstore until her college years.

Sonia and her brother used the twenty-four-volume encyclopedia to plagiarize "many a school report," [29] she said, and spent hours poring over the images such as colorful anatomy transparencies, maps, and "beautiful pictures of almost anything you wanted to know about."[30] In a speech at Lehman College, she told the students how special those books were for a generation raised before the Internet and color television:

> When I was growing up, the Encyclopedia was a home library. . . . Most of you can't imagine what it was like — the days before color TV — to open up those wonderful books and stare at those beautifully colored and educational pictures. Despite the enormous financial burden that purchase placed on my mother, we had those wonderful books.[31]

Celina proved that education was her number one priority by investing in the best home encyclopedias money could buy. Talking about the value of education was one thing, but allotting a portion of the month's hard-earned income to it sent a powerful message. A lot was expected of Sonia, and Celina was not the only woman in the family who entrusted herself to her future.

"The females were expected to achieve more," her brother recalled. When Sonia's aunts and Grandmother Mercedes decided that Sonia was spending too much time reading Archie, Casper the Ghost, and Richie Rich comic books, they arranged a family meeting with Celina to express their concerns that this light reading may be corrupting her daughter.[32]

As Sonia moved into the higher grades at Blessed Sacrament, she became more confident about expressing her views and was always eager to talk and debate about current events. She was comfortable with her interests, which stretched far beyond the projects and parochial school, and when she spoke about things that intrigued her, she spoke with genuine feeling. When she presented her view of any number of issues and events, recalled her childhood friend Jeanette Valdespino-Torres, "she really felt whatever it was."[33]

Her confidence also played out in the way she watched over her brother. When older kids picked on or bullied him, she came to his defense and got right into the mix. As the South Bronx grew into a tougher place in the late 1960s, Juan had more problems out on the streets — his bicycle was stolen, and he was mugged repeatedly. "My sister always had to come over and diffuse situations," Juan said.[34] Like a natural diplomat, she tried negotiation first and, if words didn't work, would "move on to step two," he said.[35] "I distinctly remember one episode where I was surrounded by kids," he said, "and she came over saying, 'Listen, if you're going to beat him up you got to beat me up, too.'"[36] While some friends would call her strong willed and confident, her brother cut to the chase: "My sister was tough as nails."[37]

Father Marty Dolan and Father Vinny Gorman, two of the priests at Blessed Sacrament, were committed to teaching the children from such varying ethnic and cultural backgrounds to get along and to introducing them to wider New York. In 2009, Father Gorman remarked on the "fine education and moral standards" imparted by the school and expressed his pride that Sonia "is one of us." According to Paul LaRosa, a television producer and author who attended the school at the same time as Sonia: "If you went to Blessed Sacrament you got a major league Catholic education." He recalled that Father Dolan, who died in 1990, "had a great spirit about him" and a wonderful sense of humor.

"Father Dolan was one of the best, a great guy," LaRosa said. "He spent many weekends taking students on various outings to make our worldview larger than just the Bronx and the projects." LaRosa, who grew up in the Monroe Houses in the South Bronx, considered the trips necessary for city kids whose experiences were confined to their neighborhoods and school. "Father Dolan was showing us the world outside the Bronx, and teaching us how to get along, boys and girls, Irish, Italian, Latino and African-American," he said.[38]

When Sonia was not at school, there was a time to play and a time to work. Celina motivated her children to be fully committed to everything they did and never settle for mediocrity. "She kept saying, 'I don't care what you do, but be the best at it,'" Sonia said.[39] She internalized that high standard of performance very young. The thoroughness and focus she brought to her schoolwork and first jobs hinted at the reputation she would gain later as the hardest-working person in a variety of professional environments.

Sonia's first part-time job was at Zaro's

Bakery about ten blocks away from home, where she worked so hard, her brother recalled, she was a tough act to follow when he got old enough to start working there. Sonia worked in a larger retail setting at the United Bargains store the summer she was fifteen years old. By then, commuting around the South Bronx had become a hazardous business. The transformation that swept through the area in the late 1960s brought armed gangs and drug dealers to the carefully maintained Bronxdale Houses and the neighborhoods around it. Over the next two decades, the projects that people of Celina's generation had competed to get into became the last place anyone wanted to live. In the late 1960s, Celina began looking for a better place to live. In the meantime, she was vigilant about keeping her children out of harm's way.

"She was a protective lioness," said Juan. He was afraid of running into bad company and his mother feared that he and Sonia would somehow get caught up with them. A few of the local delinquents had evolved into a full-fledged drug-dealing gang called the Black Spades, and the sight of them ignited his mother's worst fears. "My mother was going to make sure we never went down the wrong side," Juan said.[40]

In eighth grade, Sonia took the Catholic High School entrance exam and finished her last year at Blessed Sacrament with the highest grades in her class. She was accepted to Cardinal Spellman High School, one of the top high schools in the city located about five miles north of the Bronxdale Houses. At that time, the school was approximately 90 percent white, with students from predominantly Italian and Irish families, and 10 percent black and Hispanic. Although the school had been founded in 1959, the permanent building had been open only six years when Sonia enrolled as a freshman in 1968.

The student body was divided into the Boys' and Girls' Departments, which had separate principals, faculty, and classrooms. The boys were taught by priests and male laypersons, and the girls by nuns and female non-clergy, but both genders participated in school activities and ate together in the cafeteria. Sonia left the house every morning in her uniform skirt and navy blue blazer marked with the school crest that read, *Sequere Deum* (Follow God).

One of Sonia's classmates, Theodore Shaw, recalled the strict rules they confronted when they started as freshmen together. The styles of the times were not tolerated: a boy's hair could not extend below the collar of his shirt, and if his sideburns were too long he would be hauled into the dean of discipline's office to get them shaved off and then be thrown into detention after school. (Shaw felt it was unfair to the white students that he and his black friends could wear afros "that could blot out the sun" but not grow downward to their collars.) This was the era of miniskirts, and many of the girls rolled up their skirts at the waist to shorten them, only to be ordered by the nuns to roll them back down when they got inside the school.

Regulations aside, Cardinal Spellman's rigorous academics prepared many of the students for college and professional schools. Shaw, who went on to make a career as a civil rights lawyer with the NAACP and is now a professor at the Columbia University School of Law, recalled that Sonia was "academically and intellectually focused," a student who developed a reputation as one of the top scholars at the school. "Everybody knew that," he said. Shaw grew up in the Castle Hill Projects near the Bronxdale Houses and observed that Sonia had a well-ordered life that kept her close to home. "She was not somebody who grew up on the streets, hanging out," he said.

In the winter of 1970, halfway through Sonia's sophomore year of high school, Celina could no longer tolerate the decline of the neighborhood, and she moved the family out of the South Bronx. There was too much gang activity, too many drugs, and too many hazards as landlords burned down their tenements and apartment buildings to collect the insurance money. The war-ravaged look of the area signaled the end of the projects as a safe haven for working-class families — at least for a time.

Ruben Diaz Jr., who grew up next to the Bronxdale Houses in the 1970s, lived through some of the worst years of the neighborhood. "When I was a boy and a teenager, you saw a lot of buildings burned and leveled," he said. "You saw rubble and brick all over the place." That image of the Bronx is the one indelibly printed in many people's minds, especially after sportscaster Howard Cosell's famous line from Yankee Stadium during game two of the 1977 World Series. As an elementary school near the stadium burned, a helicopter-mounted television camera panned to the scene. "There it is, ladies and gentlemen," Cosell said, "the Bronx is burning."[41] That was the Bronx the Sotomayors left for an altogether different one in the north.

Celina moved the family up to Co-op City,

a massive new project in the northeast section of the borough that had opened two years earlier. Designed to provide low-cost ownership for middle-income New Yorkers, the city-within-a-city is still the largest apartment development of its kind in the United States. Its thirty-five towers, several of which are thirty-three stories high, contain a total of 15,372 units and are clustered across three hundred acres along with four schools, three shopping malls, a post office, fire station, library, playgrounds, "Educational Park with its own planetarium and swimming pools," and other amenities.

Co-op City, which dominates the North Bronx skyline between the New England Thruway and the Hutchinson River, was another big step up for the Sotomayors.

If the Bronxdale Houses were built for the poor who were on their way up, Co-op City was built for those who were ready to settle in a new middle-class section of New York. Celina bought a two-bedroom apartment, which typically sold for about $2,025 down and $116 a month. According to a promotional brochure from that time, each apartment had "maximum light and privacy" and some had terraces and dining rooms. All the apartments had foyers, "light, cheerful kitchens with large refrigerators, ranges, wood-grained plastic-finish cabinets" and "dramatic panoramic views of park and marine surroundings. . . . All spread over beautifully landscaped terrain."[42] Most important, Co-op City was in a safe section of the Bronx and, coincidentally, practically next door to Cardinal Spellman High School. A fifteen-minute city bus ride from the grounds took students one block away from the school.

Celina took the smaller of the two bedrooms in the new co-op apartment, and Sonia and Juan shared the other. Even though Co-op City was a safe, middle-class place, Sonia and Juan were instructed to go home after school and stay there until Celina returned from the hospital. "They had their rules," one neighbor remembered. "Basically no one was allowed out of the house until she came home from work."[43] Friends came over for the rice and beans Celina left for them, and the apartment was rarely quiet. It was a welcoming home with teenagers, relatives, and neighbors always at the door. Even though the family's building was much larger than the one they left in Soundview, Celina became close to several of her new neighbors. As a single mother working long hours six days a week, she never seemed to be short on time for someone who needed help, nor did she ever talk about how difficult it was to make ends meet or find enough time to sleep. Instead, she became the unofficial nurse in her small corner of Co-op City and spent quality time caring for those who didn't have anyone else. When one of her neighbors was sick with cancer, one friend remembered, Celina got up early to bring her breakfast before she went to work.

People came to Celina with all kinds of medical issues, and she was always ready to take a child's temperature or check someone's blood pressure. "Whoever was sick rang the doorbell," according to one of her longtime neighbors Dinorah Tirado. Dinorah herself had no qualms about asking Celina to help with minor medical emergencies, such as taking out her cat's stitches.[44]

Celina's compassionate nature made an even deeper impression on Sonia than her tireless work ethic. Sonia has described her mother as the most generous, giving person she has ever known:

My mother gives unselfishly, giving what she cannot spare, and always without expecting anything in return. I cannot name all of the people who have relied upon my mother to come to their homes without pay to give them shots, to change their dressings, to intubate them, or simply to bathe them during their illnesses.[45]

Celina had good job security at Prospect Hospital, which was a busy place in the 1970s, serving the low-income population of the South Bronx. But she had enough experience on the nursing staff to know that her pay as an LPN would never be enough to support herself after Sonia and Juan graduated from high school and their Social Security death benefits ran out. The best solution, she figured, was to become a registered nurse and receive the better pay, benefits, and continuing opportunities for advancement that went along with the profession. Going back to school for a nursing degree was a good strategy for the long term, but in the meantime it would require an enormous sacrifice of everyone's time and energy. At that point, Sonia was a junior and Juan had just started high school, so Celina needed to start a nursing program soon to be better employed by the time they went to college. The three of them sat down for a family meeting and Celina explained that she did not want to depend on them in the near future but was ready to go back to school if they were willing to help. "She wanted to give us the freedom to pursue our own lives," Sonia said. She and her brother had no problem with the plan, even though it meant they would have to spend more hours working on weekends and during summer vacation to make up for Celina's lost income while she was going to school. [46]

Celina enrolled in the RN program at Hostos Community College in the South Bronx, a division of the City University of New York (CUNY) that offered an associate degree in registered nursing and prepared graduates for licensure. The school, which had just opened, was the product of efforts by Puerto Rican and other Hispanic leaders who had worked for years to convince the city to establish a college designed to meet the needs of the South Bronx. When Celina enrolled, the school was housed in a former tire factory at 475 Grand Concourse.

Studying all evening after coming home from work, Celina's example raised the bar even higher for her children. Sonia and Juan were 100 percent behind her decision to drop most of her working hours at the hospital to attend college full-time. She worked on Saturdays and Sundays, took out loans, and depended on the part-time jobs that Sonia and Juan gladly took on. "It was no sacrifice at all for my brother and me to help my Mom go to school," Sonia said.[47]

Celina arranged for Sonia to work part-time at the hospital, and in spite of that new commitment, Sonia kept up her grades and was one of the top students in her class.

Throughout Sonia's junior and senior years, she and her brother studied side by side with their mother at the kitchen table. Celina's devotion to getting her degree made a strong and lasting impact on them. "My mom was like no student I knew," said Sonia. "She got home from school or work and literally immersed herself in her studies, working until midnight or beyond, only to get up again before all of us."[48] Celina earned A's in all her classes — biology, pharmacology, psychology, and other science and clinical nursing courses, which led to her passing all five parts of the licensing exam on the first try. "With an example like that," Sonia said, "my brother and I had no choice but to do well in school."[49]

Celina returned to Prospect Hospital as an RN and spent the rest of her career there until the hospital closed in 1985. Two years into her new status, she was promoted to emergency room supervisor, and the 168-bed hospital continued to serve one of the poorest neighborhoods in the Bronx. Medicaid paid for the care of about 65 percent of the patients, and 15 percent of the hospital's income came from Medicare assistance for the elderly. People in the neighborhood praised the hospital for its very affordable care — it ranked as the nineteenth least expensive among New York's ninety-nine hospitals in 1977 — and its commitment to the community.

Working a few hours every week at Prospect Hospital when she was in high school exposed Sonia to poverty-stricken people at their most vulnerable. The hospital was housed in a light-brick building on the corner of Kelly and East 156th Street that had been built in the 1960s, but the conditions around it had deteriorated horribly. Working in the hospital taught her not only about the degree of suffering in the city but about the lengths her mother would go, including moving the family to a safer part of the Bronx, to provide the best life she could for all of them.

At school, Sonia participated in school government and put in long hours as a member of the Cardinal Spellman debate team. She stood out in a school filled with exceptional people, and friends like Ted Shaw already considered her an "intellectual powerhouse." Looking back on those years, Shaw said:

Sonia was a leader at Cardinal Spellman. . . .

She was studious, independent-minded, mature beyond her years, thoughtful, and was comfortable in her own skin and proud of her community and her heritage. She did not run from who or what she was and is. Still, Sonia was not one to be easily swayed by peer pressure, fad, or the politics of others around her. She approached any issue from the standpoint of a fierce intellectual curiosity and integrity.[50]

The rules at Cardinal Spellman were beginning to relax by Sonia's senior year. In the early 1970s, the school ended its gender segregation system and went co-ed. Times were changing inside school and out.

Sonia's class came of age during a historically turbulent four-year period that saw massive demonstrations against the Vietnam War, the assassinations of Martin Luther King Jr. and Robert F. Kennedy, and the shootings at Kent State. It was also the era of Woodstock and Neil Armstrong's walk on the moon and, for Sonia, falling in love for the first time.

She and Kevin Noonan were both very smart, obviously going places, and known as a serious item throughout the school. Kevin was one of the cool white guys, according to Ted Shaw. "Kevin was part of a clique;

these people were pretty cool because of the music they listened to, the way they talked," he said. Sonia's boyfriend wore his hair dangerously long, at least by Cardinal Spellman standards, and wore a very hip 1970s look. Even though Sonia was in love, she did not get distracted from her classes, debate meets, or work with the Latino organization ASPIRA. Kevin also focused on college and studying for entrance exams.

When it came time to think seriously about applying for college during her senior year in high school, Sotomayor sidestepped state schools and aimed for the top. Her only concept of Ivy League schools came from *Love Story,* the hit movie starring Ali MacGraw and Ryan O'Neal as Radcliffe and Harvard graduates, but she knew she wanted the best she could get.

She traveled to Boston to take an interview with an admissions counselor at Harvard, and for the first time she felt she'd been written off. "She sensed that the woman was condescending to her," said Sotomayor's friend Dawn Cardi. "It made her feel she wouldn't be welcome there." When Sonia got home, she told her mother she was no longer interested in Harvard.[51] Instead, she was guided to Princeton by a friend who had graduated a year ahead of her and was attending the university. As would happen several times in her future, a mentor introduced her to an extraordinary opportunity.

Sonia Sotomayor performed her final high-profile achievement at Cardinal Spellman during spring commencement 1972, when she delivered the valedictory address. Contrary to reports that came out thirty-seven years later when she was named to the Supreme Court, she earned that honor by winning a speech competition, not by holding the highest grade point average in the class. "They offered the opportunity to make the speech to people who were willing to try out," said Angela Longerew, a fellow 1972 Cardinal Spellman graduate. "In this way, even if you did not rank first you had an opportunity to make the valedictory address." Longerew, speaking in an interview on National Public Radio in May 2009, explained that she graduated with the top GPA that year, but did not hold any animosity toward the White House's remarks.[52]

Sonia would leave the Bronx that fall, but never severed her ties to the borough. The experiences that formed her identity are deeply imbedded there, and when the press described her impoverished past during her nomination to a federal judgeship in 1998, she corrected them in a speech during her induction ceremony. "Many newspaper articles have described me as coming from humble beginnings," she said. "That description is woefully misleading." What the press missed, she said, was "that despite economic hardship, it was not so hard for me to succeed because I had the example and guidance of a truly remarkable woman, my mother."[53]

The Sotomayors' continuous rise to better neighborhoods, from a tenement in the South Bronx to the Bronxdale Houses and then Co-op City, was paralleled in Celina's journey of consistent and tireless self-improvement through education. Her double message about the virtues of education, expressed in the sacrifices she made to pay for private school tuition and through her own example, set Sonia and Juan on their own paths of achievement. But true to the humility that marks her family, Celina does not easily take credit for that.

In 2009, when reporters asked Celina to respond to her daughter's moving remarks about the role she played in her accomplishments, Celina was typically understated:

"I don't know what I did," she said. "I was just there."[54]

CHAPTER 3
PRINCETON

I wonder if I've been changed in the night?
Let me think: was I the same when I got
up this morning? I almost think I can remember feeling a little different. But if I'm
not the same, the next question is, Who
in the world am I? Ah, THAT'S the great
puzzle!

— from Lewis Carroll, *Alice's Adventures
in Wonderland*

Sonia Sotomayor's Latina soul was nurtured
in the Bronx, but her Latina identity was
forged during her first four years away from
home. In the autumn of 1972 she entered
Princeton University as one of only a handful
of Hispanics and women, and experiencing
life as a minority for the first time affected
her deeply. "My days at Princeton were the
single most transforming experience of my
life," she told a Princeton Women's group

in 2002. "It was at Princeton that I became truly aware of my Latina identity — an awareness that has shaped the course of my life."[1]

A Cardinal Spellman classmate became the guiding force that led her to Princeton. Kenneth K. Moy, her debate team colleague and friend, was one of the regulars around the Sotomayor's kitchen table for meals and discussion about the events of the day, including the war in Vietnam, where some of their friends had been deployed. Kenneth was one year ahead of Sonia and during his freshman year at Princeton he encouraged her to apply. The son of Chinese immigrants, he did not spare her the truth about the challenges she would face as an outsider among the largely white male population. "I told her I don't want you to come here with any illusions," he said. "Social isolation is going to be a part of your experience, and you have to have the strength of character to get through intact."[2] It was also Kenneth who told her she could apply for scholarships as financial aid.

Sotomayor readily admits that she entered Princeton through affirmative action, but a close look at admissions policies at the time reveals that she had to make an extraordinarily positive impression on the admissions committee to pass through the rigid policy guidelines. As Jerome Karabel discusses in his book about admissions policies in the Ivy League, Princeton began recruiting Puerto Rican students in the 1968–1969 academic year and admitted its first class of women in the fall of 1969. In 1972, Sonia's class of about 1,127 entering freshmen included 22 Latino, 15 Chicano, and 113 black students. The new policy for admitting women, which ensured that men would not be turned away to make room for women, put another constraint on her odds: "In 1970," Karabel wrote, "with a 'fixed ratio' of 4 men for every woman, this meant that only 14 percent of the female applicants were accepted, compared to 22 percent of men."[3] That policy alone made every woman at Princeton a more elite selection.

The affirmative action policy looked beyond her Standard Aptitude Test (SAT) scores, which were lower than those of her white colleagues, and took into consideration her grades and achievements at Cardinal Spellman. As Jay Mathews explains in his essay on academic bias, colleges and universities in the 1960s and 1970s "began to give preference to some minority students who had lower test scores than whites but whose high school grades and personal qualities suggested that they would benefit from a demanding academic environment." Princeton's admissions office was evidently convinced that Sotomayor met those criteria.[4]

During her remarks at a Practicing Law Institute (PLI) panel discussion in the early 1990s, after Sotomayor had become a federal judge, she was extraordinarily forthcoming about her affirmative action placement at both Princeton and Yale Law:

I am a product of affirmative action. I am the perfect affirmative action baby. I am a Puerto Rican born and raised in the South Bronx from what is traditionally described as a socio-economically poor background. My test scores were not comparable to that of my colleagues at Princeton or Yale, but not so far off the mark that I wasn't able to succeed at those institutions. But if we had gone through the traditional numbers route of those institutions it would have been highly questionable whether I would have been accepted with my academic achievements in high school.

I was accepted rather readily at Princeton and equally as fast at Yale. But my test scores were not comparable to that of my classmates and that's been shown by statistics. There are reasons for that, there are cultural biases built into testing. And that was one of the motivations for the concept of affirmative action, to try to balance out those effects.[5]

Sotomayor highlights the point that her test scores were not included in the university's decision. The very low number of women and minority recruits at Princeton, however, shows that she had an abundance of other academic experiences and qualities that made her stand out from other applicants.

Her sensitivity to the test issue may have arisen because of all the attention given this topic over the years in terms of merits and affirmative action. The question of whether the SAT is a fair predictor of college performance has been studied for decades. Many colleges made the test optional in the 1990s after considering that it denied equal opportunities to minorities and low-income students, and in 2001, University of California President Richard C. Atkinson recommended that the universities in his system drop the SAT requirement due to the advantages he believed it gave higher-income students. The fact that twelve-year-old children in private schools were already studying verbal analogies to prepare for the SAT, he said, gave them a distinct advantage over low-income students who could not afford private school or tutoring. Just as damaging, he claimed, the test prep put the classroom focus on test taking rather than reading and writing skills.

The University of California did not drop the SAT, but Atkinson's challenge ultimately led to a revised version of the test that was released in 2005. Another call for change leading up to the revision came from former Educational Testing Service research psychologist Roy Freedle. He added fuel to the debate in 2003 by reporting that African Americans did better on more difficult questions on the test than whites. The more difficult questions used harder, but less ambiguous vocabulary, while the easier questions used common words that may have a different meaning in minority neighborhoods. Even though the test was revised, administrators continued to find fault with it, and by 2009, 830 four-year colleges no longer used SAT or the American College Testing exam (ACT) to make admissions decisions.

When Sotomayor entered Princeton, there were only two Hispanic federal judges on the bench (in addition to four in Puerto

Rico's courts). As William G. Bowen and Derek Bok discuss in their study of race and university admissions, universities across the country recognized the need for more minorities in government, business, and all the professions. The authors made a claim for affirmative action, emphasizing the importance of race in deciding which applicants merit admission. "Taking account of race," they wrote, "helps institutions achieve three objectives central to their mission — identifying individuals of high potential, permitting students to benefit educationally from diversity on campus, and addressing long-term societal needs."[6] Sotomayor is the self-described poster child of that mission.

Her first week at Princeton, Sonia was so overwhelmed by her new surroundings that she secluded herself in her dorm room. Over the next four years she would become more at home among the gothic buildings with their grand arches; the forested grounds covered in elm, white pine, and red oak; and walkways along which so many leaders, scientists, and artists — and future supreme court justices — had strolled. But that first week, everything was alien to her — even the pastoral sounds of the campus became a source of edgy fixation. "I grew up in the inner city," she said. "That entire first week,

I heard a cricket sound in my room. I became obsessed with that sound."[7]

Every night, before her Mexican-American roommate Dolores came home from the library, Sonia tore apart her room in search of that cricket. The only one she had ever seen was the cartoon Jiminy Cricket in Disney's *Pinocchio,* so she didn't know what she was looking for other than something with "long legs." That weekend, her boyfriend, Kevin, came down from Westchester for a visit, and she told him there was a cricket hidden somewhere inside. "He roared with laughter," she said. "He explained to me that the cricket was outside the room, on the tree whose leaves brushed up against my dorm room window. This was all new to me: We didn't have trees brushing up against windows in the South Bronx."[8]

Her memories of those first strange days also include sitting outside the gym during class registration day and meeting a woman from Alabama with an "unusual and lovely accent." Sonia listened to her story about all the family members and friends who had attended Princeton before her and sensed the gulf that separated their experiences. Then her roommate, Dolores, and Puerto Rican friend Theresa approached them, talking loudly, "as is sometimes our wont," Sonia said. The southerner remarked about how wonderful Princeton was to bring together all these strange people. "How ironic," Sonia recalled. "Here I thought she was the strange one!"[9]

During her freshman year, the discomfort she felt in the unfamiliar environment and estranged from her lifelong support system was intensified by a wake-up call about the level of her academic work. She had excelled at both of her schools in the Bronx, but her education did not compare to that of most of her colleagues at Princeton. Halfway through her first semester, when she received a C on a midterm paper, she discovered that her writing was severely under par. She had had "enough natural intelligence" to get through the first twelve years of her education, she said, but to get on an even playing field with her classmates at Princeton, she would have to go back to square one and revamp her writing skills. "I found out that my Latina background had created difficulties in my writing that I needed to overcome," she said.[10]

That humbling revelation, along with the isolation she felt, made her somewhat withdrawn throughout her freshman year. Encountering WASP culture for the first time, she learned that her classmates' lives were filled with tennis lessons, prep schools, skiing trips, and European vacations, while other than her family trips to Puerto Rico, she had barely stepped outside the Bronx. "The chasm I felt between us felt enormous," she said.[11]

"Sonia was at first seemingly meek, quiet, and brainy," recalled one of her classmates, Joseph B. Schubert.[12] Even though she felt intimidated those first few months and rarely raised her hand in class, she did not retract from the challenges that presented themselves but tackled them head-on. Her friends recognized early on that she was driven, and that "part of that drive stemmed from a need to prove that she was equal to those from privileged backgrounds," Schubert said.[13]

Sotomayor's confidence, even when shaken, allowed her to confront an obstacle with forceful determination. This, combined with her intellect and work ethic, created a formula for developing all the potential Princeton initially recognized in her. In the second semester of her freshman year, she made an appointment with her Contemporary Latin America course professor to discuss all the red-ink marks on her paper. That meeting turned out to be a pivotal moment in which she found the mentor who would help her transform as a writer and scholar.

The professor, Peter Winn, recalled that even though she was not "polished or cool" that first year, she was remarkably self-contained for her age. "There was something centered about her that was unusual among first-year minority students at Princeton," he said. During that first meeting, they discussed the big gap between her skills, especially in writing, and those of students who came from elite high schools. "She was determined to close the gap," Winn said. "That became our project."[14]

In that first meeting, Professor Winn explained that the crux of her problem with written English involved the fact that Spanish was her first language. Her writing reflected some of the fundamental differences between the two languages, such as syntax. "Where she had written 'dictatorship of authority,' I had scribbled 'authoritarian dictatorship,'" Winn said. They went through more of those grammatical disparities in her paper, and by the end of the hour Sonia understood the principles behind her mistakes. It was a revelation, a light bulb moment for her. From that day, she worked closely with Winn on all the essays she wrote for his classes and sought out the same type of help from other professors.[15]

Sonia was a history major, and that same semester she took History 382, which covered twentieth-century U.S. history. She was not prepared for the rigorous approach to reading comprehension and writing that a course at that level required. Students typically took three-hundred-level courses in their third or fourth years, so the content, professor's expectations, and quality of her classmates' work made the class enormously demanding. Working with Professor Nancy Malkiel, who is now the dean of the undergraduate college, became another early formative experience. Sotomayor arrived at Princeton "with high intelligence and a great ability," Malkiel said, "but without a very sophisticated grounding in the study of history." Throughout that semester, she would spend many hours helping Sonia "develop the skills of critical reading of primary and secondary sources, analytic writing and historical interpretation that she would then practice regularly as a history major at Princeton."[16]

Sonia's skills steadily improved with each passing semester as she routinely and meticulously went over the notes and corrections professors like Peter Winn made on her papers. While he felt the time he spent marking up most student papers was "largely wasted," Winn was gratified by the attention Sonia brought to each of her essays. "In each paper," he said, "I would focus on a different shortcoming: Spanglish, tenses, passive voice. Taking such constant criticism could not have been easy, but Sonia kept coming back." She took four classes from Winn and selected him to be her senior thesis adviser.[17]

Sonia's self-motivated work on her writing produced results, and as her grades went up she developed more confidence in and outside the classroom. Finding a new support system was another vital experience in her freshman year that became part of the groundwork for the remarkable strides she would take over the next three years. After long weeks of recruiting efforts, the Puerto Rican student organization Acción Puertorriqueña finally convinced her to join. "Sonia had to be persuaded to join us," said Margarita Rosa, who was a junior at the time. "We were a ragtag-looking bunch, and she was always methodical in her decision making."[18] Rosa and her friends observed that Sonia used that approach consistently as she became more active in campus organizations. "She was slow to join things," Rosa said. "She sized things up for awhile before she decided to become a part of something."[19]

Acción Puertorriqueña provided the nurturing camaraderie that Sonia so deeply missed when she entered the school. That organization, along with the Third World Center, made all the difference in her Princeton experience. Both groups "provided me with the anchor I needed to ground myself in that new and different world," she said.[20]

The Third World Center, housed in the Osborn Field House and formed one year before Sonia arrived, was an activity center for minority students. A Princeton publication described this home away from home for students like Sonia as a setting in which to "create a forum for greater awareness and understanding among people of differing cultural backgrounds."[21]

Sonia was cochair of Acción Puertorriqueña by the spring semester of her sophomore year, and she made her first mark as a student leader with a carefully prepared complaint for the group to present to a federal agency. In April 1974, she revealed her plan to charge Princeton with a "lack of commitment" in hiring Puerto Rican and Chicano administrators and faculty and in recruiting students from those same minority groups. She proposed putting those charges into a complaint to be filed with the New York office of the Department of Health, Education and Welfare (HEW). "No one knew she was working on the HEW complaint," said Joseph Schubert, "until it was polished to her high standards. Then she set out to convince the rest of us of its merits." Some students thought it was an inappropriate tactic, but Sonia gradually convinced other student leaders that "it would be a visible and political statement, and would enable us to gain some political leverage in bargaining with the administration," Schubert said.[22]

Sonia persuaded student leaders in Acción Puertorriqueña and the Chicano Organization of Princeton to join together in the action and file the complaint. The announcement about their action made headlines in the *Daily Princetonian*. In an article titled "Latin Student Groups Assail University Hiring Performance," Sonia explained that student groups had tried to dialogue with administration for four years about the fact that there were no Latinos on the administration or faculty, but with no results.

Sonia's HEW complaint included charges that:

- Princeton's Affirmative Action plan did not specify positions available to Spanish-surnamed groups or a timetable of goals, which were provided for other minority groups.

- Attempts to locate qualified Latinos consisted solely of contacts with one foundation and one Chicano student.
- The university had made no attempt to contact Latino organizations, which had lists of available professors and administrators in the New York–New Jersey area.
- No regular university course "even alludes to" Puerto Rican or Chicano culture, and there were no qualified faculty members to teach it.
- Out of the large concentration of Latinos in the area, disproportionately few held secretarial, janitorial, or other staff positions at the university.[23]

The story about the charges also appeared in a brief article in the *New York Times* on April 23, in which Sotomayor stated, "Princeton is following a policy of benign neutrality and is not making substantive efforts to change."[24]

One month later, Sonia followed up with a letter to the editor of the *Daily Princetonian,* in which she said the complaint from the Puerto Rican and Chicano students was "charging the university with an institutional pattern of discrimination." The editorial, published on May 10, 1974, contained comparative population figures:

The facts of the complaint are these: 1) There is not one Puerto Rican or Chicano administrator or faculty member in the university; 2) There are two million Puerto Ricans in the United States and two and a half million more on the island itself. Yet there were only 66 Puerto Rican applicants this year, and only 31 Puerto Rican students on campus. While there are 12 million Chicanos in the United States, there were only 111 Chicano applicants and 27 students on campus this year; 3) Not one permanent course in this university now deals in any notable detail with the Puerto Rican or Chicano cultures.[25]

The facts, she wrote, reflected "the total absence of regard, concern and respect for an entire people and their culture. In effect, they reflect an attempt — a successful attempt so far — to relegate an important cultural sector of the population to oblivion." The role of a university, she added, is to be a "vanguard of societal ideas and changes," and only by becoming more representative of U.S. residents will it be able to "instill in a society a respect for all people — regardless of race, color, sex or national origin."[26]

Sonia's strategy to address the university's policies through an HEW complaint had astounding results. The administration authorized a new class on Puerto Rican history and politics and vamped up its efforts to recruit Latino faculty and administrators. The entire campus recognized Sonia as a student leader and someone to watch. Then Princeton President William G. Bowen described Sonia as a standout student whose multifaceted abilities would be highly recognized upon her graduation. "You couldn't help but notice a student that exceptional," he said.[27] Her success in motivating the university to move more quickly on revising its hiring policies is one of her greatest legacies at Princeton. Bowen recalled that the university "did quite a bit better — in fact, a lot better — along these lines before the petition was ever actually reviewed or handled in the government."[28]

The impact of Sonia's complaint still resonates at the university. "Now it is a given that Princeton has Latino role models at all levels of faculty, administration, and student body," said Joseph Schubert.[29]

In the wake of the HEW affair, Sonia and a group of fifteen Puerto Rican, other Latino, and white students enlisted Professor Winn to head up the new seminar on Puerto Rico. "Sonia envisioned the seminar as a step toward a Latino studies curriculum at Princeton, taught by Latino faculty," Winn said.[30] That vision would take longer to unfold than would the hiring of Latino faculty throughout the curriculum — Princeton did not launch its Latino Studies Program until 2009. But the first seminar planted the seeds for change. The course consisted of a research project about the Puerto Rican community in Trenton, New Jersey, just thirteen miles away. The project involved "mapping the community, analyzing its demographics and developing oral histories of selected families, teaching them how to study communities like their own," said Winn. As a final paper, each student created an oral history of his or her own family, and Sonia would treasure hers many years later as the only recorded history of deceased extended family members from Puerto Rico.[31]

The students also explored what it meant to be a Nuyorican (pronounced *new-yoh-REE-ken*), or New York–born child of parents who had migrated from the island, versus someone born on the island and debated whether Puerto Rico should remain a U.S. commonwealth, become the fifty-first state, or become independent.

At the same time, Sonia started a program for students to volunteer as translators at the Trenton Psychiatric Hospital. During her own volunteering at that facility, she saw the critical need for Spanish-speaking patients to communicate with doctors and staff. Setting up a program gave Princeton's Spanish-speaking students the opportunity to make a difference in the local area.

In the second semester of her sophomore year, Sonia brought up another high-profile controversy as a member of the student advisory committee involved in hiring a new assistant dean of student affairs. The small committee consisted of Sonia, three blacks, and a Chicano. Dean of Student Affairs Adele Simmons was responsible for making the final decision, and she hired a minority, Luis Garcia. But the student committee wrote a complaint letter about how the process was handled. "The dissatisfaction had nothing to do with the choice itself," Sonia told the student newspaper in September 1974. "Most of the students were pleased with Mr. Garcia. The dissatisfaction was with the amount of student input." [32]

The complaint letter pointed out concerns the students had over the treatment that minority applicants received, stating that they appeared to be subjected to closer scrutiny than those for a nonminority placement, and no Asian or American Indian prospects were brought in for consideration. The students expressed their frustration that Dean Simmons selected the committee members rather than allowing Acción Puertorriqueña, the Association of Black Collegians, or the Chicano Organization of Princeton choose the selectees.

Dean Simmons made her selection without responding to the complaint or waiting for the committee's formal recommendation, which frustrated Sonia and her colleagues even more. "We were token students, period," she said. "The decision was made without consulting us."[33]

Sonia's shy freshman persona had been short lived, and by the end of her sophomore year, she had matured into an assertive and well-spoken student who not only held her own but stood out among her classmates. She was not a radical, but a moderate activist who explored how legal actions — in her case making a formal complaint to a government agency — could be used to bring about social change. She became involved in more student activities, such as serving on the university's Discipline Committee, which dealt with student violations of academic work. She found a practical way to be part of the solution in bringing more diversity to the university by taking a work-study job in the Admissions Department, which sent her out to high schools to recruit Latino students. (She also worked in the cafeteria, donning the uniform blue shirt and bow tie to serve students as they filed by the steam tables.) And in addition to those interactions throughout the school, her background brought unique perspective to her classes.

In Jameson Doig's senior-level public policy class, The Politics of Economic and Social Control, for example, she enriched discussions by bringing the perspective of someone "who had grown up in an inner city in a poor area," Doig said.

Meeting three times a week in a semicircular, stadium-style classroom, more than half of each class period was devoted to student discussion. "I always taught with Morton Friedman's book, *Capitalism and Freedom,* in which he says it's best to have government do very little," Doig said. "I used that as a standard against which to study various policy areas — housing, prisons, education, environmental regulation and a couple of others. The students who took the course tended to be attracted to it because it gave them an opportunity to understand the libertarian perspective Friedman had."

Professor Doig started each class period with a fifteen- or twenty-minute presentation and then encouraged the students "to respond, to disagree or in other ways to present their views." Sotomayor, he recalled, was thoughtful, articulate, and expressed her views or, in some cases, the reservations she had about Friedman and some of the other more libertarian people whose readings he assigned. Among the social control topics discussed in the class, police brutality was of greater concern to those like Sonia who were familiar with the problems in crime-ridden areas. "She was an articulate person in expressing concerns about that kind of misbehavior and in suggesting ways that one could reduce problems of police and public housing violence," he said.[34]

The majority of the students who took the course planned, like Sotomayor, to go to law school. "It is a course that has that kind of wide attraction for people who want to try to figure out how to bring about change, and law is the way that most folks go," he said. The quarter who did not go that route went into government work or education, he recalled, and he would rather have seen the percentages reversed. "I didn't encourage law because I thought it attracted a greater amount of bright minds than it deserved," he said.

The skills Sonia had developed by the time she entered Doig's class had not come easily but were the result of intensely focused, self-motivated effort. The summer after her freshman year she committed herself to catching up on some of the reading and grammar she had missed in her early education. At the beginning of vacation — which would be a working one at Prospect Hospital — she indulged in a shopping trip. "I took the subway to Barnes and Noble on Fifth Avenue," she said, "my first trip to a bookstore, to buy the classics so I would know what everyone was talking about."[35] Those books included Jane Austen's *Pride and Prejudice*, Mark Twain's *Huckleberry Finn*, and Lewis Carroll's *Alice's Adventures in Wonderland*. She also drilled through the exercises in a set of grammar books written for grades one through eight.

During the school year she socialized with her friends from Acción Puertorriqueña and the Third World Center and also had occasional visits from Kevin, who was attending the State University of New York. Some weekends she babysat a godchild from the city in her dorm room while she studied. Her mother also came down, especially for Princeton events, but from time to time other forces kept her away. After Sonia left, life went on in her Co-op City apartment as usual, including constant knocks on the door for Celina's help. One day Celina told Sonia she had to cancel her upcoming visit to Princeton to take care of an elderly man in the building. "Although he was a complete stranger to our family," Sonia said, "he needed someone to give him his daily medications." The man was very ill, had no family to call on, and had heard about Celina through the building grapevine. As a last resort, he knocked on the Sotomayor's door and asked for help. "My mother would not leave him in his dying days," said Sonia, "not even for a weekend with me."[36]

In her final year, Sonia developed an idea for her senior thesis from the Puerto Rico seminar that she and her fellow students developed with Peter Winn. With Winn as her thesis director, she wrote a 180-page paper about Luis Muñoz Marin, leader of the Popular Democratic Party in the Puerto Rican senate in the 1940s and first elected, rather than U.S.-appointed, governor of Puerto Rico. Although he initially supported the idea of island independence, Muñoz Marin came to believe that commonwealth status was the most economically feasible direction. His sweeping economic development program called Operation Bootstrap industrialized the island, and when he was elected governor in 1948, he geared the island toward commonwealth status. He helped draft the island's Commonwealth Constitution of 1952, which was a step toward self-governing but did not represent any substantial change in the relationship between the island and the United States.

In presenting Muñoz Marin's story and the island's struggle with its status, Sonia stated in the preface that she had a "bias toward independence" but that her study was not based on that bias, nor did it reflect it.[37] In addition to her overview of the long-standing debate over the options of statehood, limited autonomy, and independence, Sonia describes the effects that statehood could have on the island's culture. "The experiences of Alaska and Hawaii since statehood with cultural destruction has been indicative of the cultural loss Puerto Rico would eventually face if statehood were chosen," she wrote. Since becoming a commonwealth, "there has been a gradual deterioration of the Spanish language among the Puerto Rican populace and a growing Americanization of the island."[38]

Peter Winn considered Sonia's thesis "extremely ambitious and one of the longest I have supervised, but it was the best paper she had ever written." Reflecting on the paper in 2009, he continued:

> I read it again recently, and I would still give it an A. It is clearly conceptualized, solidly researched, incisively analyzed, persuasively argued and very well written, with pithy summaries of her arguments that she could still be proud of today — whether in a published article or a judicial opinion.[39]

The thesis received an honorable mention from the History Department, an honor that capped off two years in which she had received A's in most of her classes and distinguished herself as a student leader committed to service. In her senior year, she made the ranks of Phi Beta Kappa, the honor society that represents the top 10 percent of high-achieving college seniors. And her most outstanding honor came in the form of the M. Taylor Pyne Prize, awarded to one or two seniors each year. President William Bowen, who was among the group that made the prize decision in 1976, explained that it is "the highest prize Princeton bestows on undergraduates, given to a student with a record of excellent academics." But the award required more than outstanding grades, he said. "It's for leadership, it's for being a responsible citizen of the university community, and she had it all. She had, as they say these days, the full package."[40]

The Pyne Prize cowinner that year, J. David Germany, was an economics major who had won two previous honors for holding the highest grades in the university his freshman and junior years. He went on to get a Ph.D. in economics at MIT and served as an economist at the Federal Reserve and President's Council of Economic Advisors before launching a career in investment banking.

Sonia had recognized deep gulfs separating her and her Princeton classmates during her first year, but the gap that stretched between the beginning and ending points of her development over four years was equally vast. "The kid who didn't know how to write her first semester," as she described herself, who journeyed Alice-like to the strange land that helped her claim her identity, became the most highly honored Princeton graduate.[41]

Sonia's ability to grow and flourish at Princeton in spite of the alienation she felt would come into play again at Yale. Her friends and professors witnessed the development of her identity into a confident Nuyorican who could appreciate her heritage rather than shrink from it when integrating into the larger world. Her mentor Peter Winn recognized that at Princeton Sonia "learned to build coalitions, to persuade others to live up to their values and to use the law as an instrument of social change," and to be a leader who was "interested in policy, not posturing." At Princeton, she built her confidence and learned to be a critical thinker, "and her skills became equal to the best of her generation," Winn said.[42]

As she continued her education and moved into her career, Sonia accomplished everything her Princeton experience predicted she would. But for all her achievement and ascension to higher and higher levels of her field, she never completely lost the sense of not quite fitting in that was such an affecting part of her experience at Princeton. "I am always looking over my shoulder, wondering if I measure up," she said decades later.[43]

CHAPTER 4
YALE LAW

In a professional sense I was present at "the creation," at the beginning of Sonia's luminous legal career.

— José A. Cabranes, U.S. Circuit Judge, United States Court of Appeals for the Second Circuit

In her final semester at Princeton, Sonia Sotomayor took a day trip to New Haven, Connecticut, with a friend who had an appointment at Yale University. Her classmate was writing his senior thesis on the history of Puerto Rican citizenship and had arranged to meet José Cabranes, the renowned thirty-five-year-old Puerto Rican lawyer who had recently become Yale's general counsel. The student had scheduled an interview to discuss Puerto Rico's constitutional history with Cabranes, who, as former head of the Commonwealth of Puerto Rico's office in

Washington, D.C., and counsel to the governor of Puerto Rico, had an extensive background in the island's political history.

During the meeting, Sonia engaged in lively conversation with Cabranes, and their discussion soon dominated the lunch meeting, which stretched to three hours. "My poor friend," she recalled later, "he spent all that time listening to José and I dissect the Puerto Rican colonial spirit."[1]

A professor at Princeton had already spoken to Cabranes about Sonia, telling him that she was a fellow Nuyorican whom he simply had to meet. They had similar backgrounds in that Cabranes was born in Mayaguez, where Sonia had spent summer vacations visiting her relatives. Cabranes was five years old when his parents, both teachers, moved to the South Bronx. His father, who was also a social worker, became the director of a settlement house for newly arrived Puerto Rican migrants. Cabranes attended New York public schools, Columbia University, and Yale Law School, and then received a fellowship to Cambridge, where he studied international law. While Sotomayor was at Princeton, Cabranes was administrator of the Office of the Commonwealth of Puerto Rico in Washington, D.C., and special counsel to the fourth governor of

Puerto Rico, Rafael Hernández Colón.

During that first meeting with Sonia, Cabranes spoke to Sonia at length about a study he was working on about the history of Puerto Rico and promised to hire her as a summer research assistant after her first year at the law school. The product of that research, which Sotomayor helped Cabranes conduct with two fellow law students from Yale and one from Rutgers University Law School, was a 101-page article in the *University of Pennsylvania Law Review* titled "Citizenship and the American Empire: Notes on the Legislative History of the United States Citizenship of Puerto Ricans," published in 1978. Yale University Press published the work in book form the following year.[2] [3]

Meeting Cabranes, the most prominent Puerto Rican attorney in the United States as well as Yale counsel and professor who would become one of her most influential mentors, was only a sideline of Sotomayor's defining spring and summer of 1976. On August 14, she and Kevin Noonan were married at St. Patrick's Cathedral on Fifth Avenue in New York City. The prestigious setting — St. Patrick's is the largest Catholic Gothic cathedral in the United States and seat of New York's Roman Catholic diocese — was the site of the nationally televised funerals of Senator Robert F. Kennedy and Cardinal Francis Joseph Spellman when Sonia was growing up.

Sonia took Kevin's last name in a traditionally Spanish way and was known after the wedding as Sonia Sotomayor de Noonan. With Sonia entering Yale in Connecticut and Kevin working on a Ph.D. in molecular biology at Princeton, they would continue to have a long-distance relationship.

Sonia would spend most of her time over the next three years in the massive Sterling Law Building at Yale, a Gothic complex that takes up an entire city block and was patterned after King's College, Cambridge. The English courtyard, rich wood floors and walls, soaring stained-glass windows, ornate spires, and gargoyles are the epitome of Collegiate Gothic. Even if she never left the library, with its long, polished tables, soaring ceilings, hanging lamps, and nearly one million books, Sonia would be able to recognize that she had entered into one of the most elite and beautiful institutions in the academic world.

Yale Law School, unique for its tradition of small class sizes and honors/pass/low pass system versus grades, organizes all first-year students into groups of twelve to fifteen. Each group takes the same classes together, and all of those classes are ungraded, to be followed by the pass/fail system over the next two years. (Yale and Berkeley Law stood out with an alternative grading system for decades, while Stanford and Harvard made the change to a pass/fail system in 2008 and 2009, respectively.) One of Sotomayor's Yale colleagues remarked that the philosophy behind Yale Law's honors/pass system — to engender a spirit of cooperation — was effective from the beginning. "The nice thing about Yale Law School is that a great deal of effort is made to make it not a competitive experience," said Peter Kougasian, who was in Sotomayor's small group. "Our torts professor, Guido Calabresi, gave us a little speech in our first semester, 'You're all going to pass, help each other.' That set the tone."

Sonia's group formed a strong bond, helping each other grow accustomed to a learning process that can be very disorienting at first. The unity and support of the small group enabled the students to acclimate themselves to the academic direction of law school, which, unlike Sonia's undergraduate training, entailed reading more cases than other texts. Legal casework has its own vocabulary, so the skills needed to read and research are entirely different from those

Sotomayor had applied to her history degree at Princeton.

Each small group takes four classes the first semester, three of them larger courses attended by a few combined small groups and one seminar taught by their small-group professor. Sonia's professors were an impressive cross section of the Yale faculty, which consisted of some of the most eminent legal scholars of the day. In the first week, Sonia learned that her small-group professor, Edward Dauer, would also be her group's writing instructor. In addition to a law degree from Yale, Dauer had a master's in public health and health policy management from Harvard and specialized in legal issues surrounding preventive healthcare. Dauer was a proponent of the law and economics school of legal theory, a movement "that says that ultimately much of what the law is about is regulating economic relationships," explained Kougasian. Dauer analyzed law in terms of its economic impact, focusing on the economic relations that undergird decisions and the theory that law should aim toward economic efficiency.

Their small group's torts class was taught by Guido Calabresi, one of the founders of the law and economics movement and an engaging professor whom Kougasian described as charismatic, warm, and funny. Six years earlier Calabresi had published *The Costs of Accidents: A Legal and Economic Analysis,* the first book to present a sophisticated theoretical framework for no-fault insurance.[4] "He gave a very humanistic introduction to the law," said Kougasian, and he treated his students like family, keeping an open invitation for them to visit his Connecticut farm. "Professors like him made a strong effort to keep it a very positive experience for us," Kougasian said. Calabresi would become dean of the law school in 1985 and leave in 1994 when President Bill Clinton appointed him to the U.S. Court of Appeals for the Second Circuit in New York.

The civil procedure class taken by Sonia's small group was taught by legal ethics expert Geoffrey Hazard. For the first half of the semester, Hazard conducted the class in a style reminiscent of the TV show *The Paper Chase,* in which Professor Kingsfield regaled his terror-stricken law students with open-ended questions. "He was a very stern taskmaster, engaging in Socratic dialogue," said Kougasian. The atmosphere of tension in Hazard's classroom was the exception to the rule at Yale, a school that had made its mark in American legal education as the founder of the legal realism movement.

Legal realism emphasized the factors of law "not captured in the rules, ranging from the attitudes of judges and jurors to the nuances of the facts of particular cases," according to Yale historians. That socially conscious emphasis makes Yale graduates "uniquely well prepared to play important roles in the rise of the administrative state, the internationalization following the World Wars, and the domestic civil rights movement."[5]

Robert Klonoff, not in Sonia's small group but another classmate among the 153 or so students that started at Yale with her in the fall of 1976, who is now dean of Lewis & Clark Law School, said that schools like Yale "focus on the ethics of law practice, doing the right thing and examining issues of justice and fairness."[6]

Sonia's fourth small group class was constitutional law with Ralph K. Winter, an expert in antitrust law who, like his colleague Calabresi, would leave Yale when he was appointed to a federal court. President Ronald Reagan selected him for the Second Circuit Court of Appeals in 1981; thirteen years later Calabresi would join him on the same bench. And in 1998, their former student Sonia Sotomayor would be appointed by President Clinton to ascend to the same court.

In spite of the carefully refined spirit of co-operation at Yale and her extraordinary performance at Princeton, Sonia felt as intimidated her first year at Yale as she had during her first semester at Princeton. After all the hard work and activities that had earned her the Pyne Prize, everything about Yale was so imposing that she felt as if she were starting back at square one. "Nothing could prepare a kid from the South Bronx for the extraordinary power and prestige of Yale," she said. "Yale Law school students . . . are a different breed of smart and accomplishment; many of them do not even know they talk, think and live a totally different language and life than the rest of the world."[7]

Not until her second year did she muster up the confidence to make a comment in class:

I never raised my hand in my first-year classes at Yale. I was too embarrassed and too intimidated to ask questions. Only in my second year, in a Trusts and Estates class, did I finally raise my hand and give an answer in class. When Professor Clarke paused and looked at me and said that I had made an observation about the Rule against Perpetuities that he had never considered and that changed the answer to the example he was demonstrating, I felt like a million dollars.[8]

She did not earn an honors-level evaluation in Clarke's class, but his response helped convince her there was a place for her among the "different degrees of smartness, brilliance and accomplishment" at Yale Law.[9]

Sonia found a support system at Yale that allowed her to continue the commitment to recruiting and celebrating minority students that she had developed at Princeton. There were no Latinos on the thirty-person faculty and only one black and two women, and such a small number of minority students that they all banded together under one organization. With Rudolph Aragon, a Mexican-American who was in her small group, she cochaired the club called the Latin, Asian, and Native American Students Association (LANA). In addition to Aragon, her closest friends at the school were a Native American, Puerto Rican, and African American, who were equally interested in advocating for diversity — and enjoying themselves. "We worked hard, we studied hard, we partied very hard," Sotomayor said. She smoked, she drank beer, and she danced at New Haven clubs when it was time to kick back.[10] And she watched the Yankees, including game six in the 1977 World Series, in which Reggie Jackson hit three home runs that won the team their first World Series in fifteen years. "She went berserk" over that game, said Aragon.[11]

Sonia and her LANA friends divided their energies between activities within their own organization and opportunities like the *Law Review* and other campus-wide extracurricular activities: "We segregated and we integrated," said Sotomayor, "we joined the best of all of our worlds."[12] Sonia's focus on her classes and activities never overshadowed her sense of camaraderie with minority students and staff in the largely white school. "She felt an affinity with the African-American janitor, the workers, people in the cafeteria," said Aragon.[13]

With the nickname "S.S. de Noonan" that played on her married name and insinuated the formidability of an ocean vessel, Sonia was well liked at Yale. Her friends are undecided on whether she was aware of her nickname but recall that she fit in with everyone. Her classmate Martha Minow, who is now dean of Harvard Law School, remembers her as warm, funny, and down-to-earth, a person who never forgot where she came from "nor how challenging life can be for people struggling to make it in this country."[14] Just as her mentor Peter Winn had observed at Princeton, Sonia came off as more mature than many of her fellow law students. Being married may have been a factor. And once she regained her confidence, she was "tough, clear [and] very quick on her feet," recalled Minow.[15]

Sonia was awarded scholarships at Yale and also worked a variety of jobs during the school year and on summer breaks. The summer before her first year she worked as a clerk at the Equitable Life Assurance Society of the United States, one block away from St. Patrick's Cathedral, and in the summer between her first and second years worked as a research assistant for Professor Cabranes. Throughout her second year, she was a salesperson at the Graduate-Professional Student Center on campus and after that worked as a summer associate at the firm of Paul, Weiss, Rifkind, Wharton & Garrison in the same Sixth Avenue building that housed Equitable Life. During her third and final year, she worked the counter at the law school's mimeo room.

As minority students, Sonia and her LANA colleagues shared the sense that they had to "be twice as good and work twice as hard," Aragon said. From the outside, they appeared to be fitting in well, excelling in classes and participating in some of the school's most prestigious activities. But an event that played out during Sonia's final year showed the entire Yale community that minority students faced intense pressures and challenges that would probably follow them out into the world.

On October 2, 1978, Sonia attended a recruiting dinner with several other Yale Law students that was held by the large Washington law firm Shaw, Pittman, Potts & Trowbridge. During the dinner, Martin Krall, a partner in the firm, asked her a series of questions that she would discuss with him the next day during her formal interview:

Do law firms do a disservice by hiring minority students who the firms know do not have the necessary credentials and will then fire in three to four years?

Would you have been admitted to the law school if you were not a Puerto Rican?

Were you culturally deprived?

During her interview, Sonia challenged Krall about the discriminatory nature of his questions. He told her that he didn't mean any harm and thought the matter was closed when he invited her for another interview in Washington. But Sonia would not let the issue disappear; instead, she filed a complaint against the firm and urged the school to stop its recruiting privileges.

Word spread about Sonia's situation within hours, and her decision to make a complaint became a divisive issue among faculty and students. Sonia's white friends were amazed that an official representative of the firm would make such remarks and admired her courage in standing up for her integrity, while other students and some faculty thought that making a complaint about such a major firm was going too far.

Sonia's friend Robert Klonoff talked to her about the event and recognizes that her inspirational actions had a long-standing impact on his own career. The questions were "ludicrous to ask someone who was a summa cum laude from Princeton," he said. "Nobody at the law school thought that about her. She was so eminently qualified, so smart."

Klonoff had been considering Shaw, Pittman, Potts & Trowbridge himself but completely wrote off the firm after the episode. To him, Sonia's challenge was incredibly courageous. "Some people might have just buried the incident and not made a big issue out of it," he said. The fact that the faculty was divided over the issue made Sonia's decision seem even more risky. "Some would not have wanted to attract attention, thinking it may make it hard to get a job somewhere else. But she was not intimidated by that at all."

Sonia's complaint went to a student-faculty tribunal, which began to review her charges in light of Yale's antidiscrimination policies. The issue ignited heated debate across the campus, with three groups — LANA, the Black Student Union, and Yale Law Women — supporting Sonia's complaint and other individuals claiming that prohibiting the firm from recruiting at Yale was going too far. In the following weeks, Associate Dean James W. Zirkle would reproach three recent Yale Law graduates working at Shaw Pittman for trying to influence the student-faculty panel.

The panel agreed that the questions were discriminatory and demanded a letter of apology from the firm. Its response to the first letter from Shaw Pittman revealed how seriously the members of the panel took the process. Rejecting the letter, they stated that it would not suffice because "the firm did not seem fully to recognize the consequences of its partner's action." If they did not submit a satisfactory apology, the tribunal warned, they would be barred from recruiting at Yale Law. The firm subsequently wrote a more forthcoming letter, which was accepted by the school, but only after word about the contentious episode had spread to other law schools and shaken the firm's reputation.[16]

Sonia's complaint sensitized Yale students to discrimination. "It was so foreign to me that someone of her caliber and brilliance would be subjected to this sort of treatment," said Klonoff. "Having a classmate like her made me understand how evil racism is. It was one of a handful of signature events from school that I look back on now." Klonoff observed that "my own commitment to diversity at Lewis & Clark Law School can be traced to the events surrounding my classmate, Sonia."

As Sonia's classmate Stephen L. Carter would later write in *Reflections of an Affirmative Action Baby,* those who criticize the qualifications of a person of color project a label on him or her that reads: "WARNING! AFFIRMATIVE ACTION BABY! DO NOT ASSUME THAT THIS INDIVIDUAL IS QUALIFIED!" Speaking for all the minorities at Yale, Carter wrote about what it was like to come of age as a black man in the era of affirmative action, "a time in which every professional who is not white is subjected to that extra degree of scrutiny that attaches to those who are suspected of having benefited, at some point in the development of their careers, from a racial preference."[17]

The Shaw Pittman episode, according to Sonia's professor and eventual colleague on the Second Circuit Court Guido Calabresi, revealed her talent for circumventing confrontation while making a strong point. "The way that Sonia has always stood up for these positions have been in ways powerful, but friendly," he said, "and without that personal edge that says 'I've been hurt, I need revenge,' or something of that sort."[18]

During her final semester, Sonia earned the distinction of membership in the *Yale Law Journal* with the acceptance and publication of her note, "Statehood and the Equal Footing Doctrine: The Case for Puerto Rican Seabed Rights." One of fifty-four students accepted as editors that semester, in addition to the principle editorial staff, she received praise for the thoroughness of her complex argument.[19] When considering Sonia's submission, several members of the editorial board "said admitting her work was one of the easiest decisions they made during their time at the notoriously competitive journal."[20]

Carter served as one of three note editors at the law journal that semester and worked closely with Sonia on the editing process. "I was struck by her diligence in tracking down the most obscure references," he said, "and in trying to steer an original and practical course through thorny issues of constitutional interpretation." Carter, who is currently a professor at Yale Law School and author of best-selling novels and nonfiction, had worked at the same Manhattan law firm with Sonia the previous summer.

In her note, Sonia argues that if Puerto Rico seeks to become a state, it should include in its compact with the federal government a clause that grants it rights to the land beneath the ocean beyond the standard three-nautical-mile limit. The rights to a seabed area that stretches two hundred miles from the coastline could result in essential mineral and oil revenues, she wrote, which would be a political necessity for a new state that suffered from a "dearth of land-based resources and its ongoing economic stagnation and poverty."[21]

Sonia's note provides a detailed history of the often contradicting decisions that address the equal footing doctrine, the law that stipulates that any new state entering the union must be granted the same powers and jurisdiction as the original thirteen states. Sonia states that "the Court has not directly addressed the question whether the equal footing doctrine permits Congress to grant rights to an incoming state that exceed those granted to any existing state at its admission."[22] In other words, try it, Puerto Rico — you never know.

The subject of her note revealed that Sonia's approach to Puerto Rico's political options expanded under the direction of her mentor Cabranes. Her choice to write about a constitutional facet of potential statehood showed an evolution in the pro-independence stance she revealed in the introduction to her senior thesis at Princeton. Researching, writing, and revising her note not only developed her legal writing skills but also gave her the opportunity to delve into Puerto Rican politics with Cabranes, who was as passionate about the topic as she. Cabranes would remain in Sonia's life as a "career adviser," a "good friend," and an "intellect"; he would swear her in as an appeals court judge many years later.

As an editor of the journal, Sonia followed in the footsteps of Supreme Court justices Samuel Alito, Potter Stewart, and Abe Fortas, as well as five U.S. Court of Appeals judges; U.S. senators Raymond E. Baldwin,

Arlen Specter, and Michael F. Bennet; federal cabinet members; college presidents; law school deans; and other leaders in many fields.

Sonia also served as a managing editor of the *Yale Studies in World Public Order,* a secondary journal founded by students in 1974 "for discussing and publishing scholarship in international law, a field then largely ignored by mainstream law journals."[23] Now titled the *Yale Journal of International Law,* members of the journal edit, proofread, and sight-check article submissions. One spring semester, Sonia also took part in the annual Thomas Swan Barristers' Union mock trial competition, advancing to the semifinals.

In addition to publishing her note in the law journal in the spring of 1979, Sonia and a few of her classmates, including Peter Kougasian, began studying together for the bar exam that would be held that July. "The great scamola of legal education is that the real studying begins after you get your degree," Kougasian joked. In his stinging and hilarious essay, "How Not to Succeed in Law School," James D. Gordon III introduces this phase of a legal education as "an initiation rite similar to those of certain college fraternities and sororities. Initiates to those groups get off easy," he writes, "however, since they only have to eat live chickens and stuff goldfish up their noses, whereas you have to go through eight weeks of projectile vomiting called 'Preparing for and Taking the Bar Exam.'"[24]

Most of Sonia's classmates had opted for the BAR/BRI study course, which was designed specifically for the multistate section of the exam, which had been added in 1972. Sonia's group chose the Practicing Law Institute (PLI) "because it was much cheaper," according to Kougasian. Sonia waived her fee for a study course by signing up as Yale Law School's campus representative for the PLI bar review course. She coordinated the eight- to ten-week class for the group, ordering the materials, scheduling study sessions, and setting up the tapes.

The relatively new design of the bar exam included a state-specific section and the multistate part — a six-hour, two-hundred-question, multiple-choice test that covers all the basic legal principles, or black letter law. Making that section separate made the bar exam more portable — if a lawyer moves to another state, he or she needs to take only the state-specific part of the exam. Sonia's group planned to take the New York bar exam, so their review course included New York procedures.

Starting out in the spring while they were still taking their final classes, Sonia, Peter, and about three others continued their review course after graduation. Studying black letter law was all about memorization, and they got together in a room at the school to listen to the reel-to-reel tapes for hours on end every day. "We were miserable," Kougasian said.

But they all passed the bar.

CHAPTER 5
THE TARZAN MURDERER
AND OTHER TALES FROM
THE DA's OFFICE

The times are nightfall, look,
their light grows less;
The times are winter, watch,
a world undone.

— Gerard Manley Hopkins

Through most of his career, New York County District Attorney Robert Morgenthau visited his alma mater, Yale Law School — where he had completed the program in two years instead of three — every year to speak to students about what it was like to work as a prosecutor. When Sonia Sotomayor wandered into the conference room in which he was making his presentation toward the end of her senior year, she had no idea who he was. Only after their casual chat at the wine and cheese table would she realize she was talking to the head of the loftiest district attorney's office in the country and one of the most prominent figures in New York.

Morgenthau became a federal prosecutor in the 1960s when President John F. Kennedy appointed him the U.S. attorney for the Southern District of New York. Unlike most chief prosecutors, Morgenthau played an unusually active role in investigative work and distinguished himself with convictions in racketeering, corruption, and white-collar-crime cases. He continued as U.S. attorney during the Johnson and part of the Nixon administrations, resigning only after the president designated his own appointee. After a failed run as the Democratic candidate for the New York gubernatorial race, he ran for and was elected to the office of Manhattan District Attorney and took office in 1975. The office had been made famous throughout the country by racket-busting prosecutor and later New York governor and presidential nominee Thomas Dewey, who convicted mobsters like "Lucky" Luciano in the 1930s. The Manhattan DA's office was a place of legend and the inspiration for books and films (and in today's generation, TV's *Law & Order*).

By the time Sonia met him, Morgenthau had already distinguished himself as the Manhattan DA, recognized for prosecuting white-collar and organized crime with the same success he had known as a U.S. attorney. He was one of New York's most popular public figures, a power broker whom assistant district attorneys deeply respected for the integrity he brought to the office and to their formative years as lawyers.

Throughout her third year at Yale, Sonia had been interviewing exclusively at big law firms in New York and in cities around the country in which Kevin was applying to graduate schools. The only exception was her application to the Department of State, motivated by her interest in international law. She had worked that summer at one of New York's top firms and, like most of her classmates, expected to enter a similar corner of the metropolis after graduation. She had not given any thought to public service other than the State Department until she crossed paths with Morgenthau. That evening, she had been studying a tax law treatise in the law library when "the insatiable appetite of student life" hit her: "No, it was not the pang of intellectual hunger — it was the hunger pang for food and drink," she said at an awards speech in 1995. Her appetite led her out of the library and onto an entirely new career track:

Down the hall from the library I saw cheese

and wine in the back of the third-floor conference room and that was more than enough to draw my attention. The assembled speakers in the room were public interest lawyers who were discussing the alternatives to private practice. I don't remember the other speakers because Bob Morgenthau — fortunately for me who was only there for the nutrients in the room — was the last speaker being introduced.

After affirming the many benefits of public service which the other speakers had apparently discussed, Bob described his office and its work. He indicated that a position with his office differed from almost all other public and private work because only in his office would you be actually trying a case within your first year and where you would have significant and ultimate responsibility in the development and presentation of your cases. At twenty-four/twenty-five years of age, Bob explained, you would do more in a courtroom than many lawyers did in a lifetime. . . .

He sparked my memory about what I had thought law was about — seeking justice in a courtroom. I stood on the wine and cheese line with Bob and chatted with him — I might have been temporarily distracted from what had drawn me to that room —

food and drink — but I never permanently forget my priorities. I asked Bob questions about his life and where he had been and what he liked about each position. To this day I don't know why he didn't write me off as completely useless, I had no idea who he was or what he had accomplished in life. I did find out fairly quickly.[1]

Morgenthau did not write Sonia off, but instead invited her to interview with him the next day. Before that meeting, he picked up her résumé at the career office and spoke to some of her professors, like José Cabranes, whom he knew well and who had high praise for her. During the interview, Morgenthau asked Sonia about all the activities she had been involved in and persuaded her to visit the office in Manhattan. She showed up two or three weeks later with a classmate, Jessica DeGrazia, to tour the offices and absorb the atmosphere of big-city governance that looms over Foley Square.

Morgenthau offered her a job as an assistant district attorney that day and she agreed — but with a condition. "[I] had the further temerity to explain to Bob that my acceptance depended upon my husband getting into a graduate program he liked in New York City," she said. "My then-husband's graduate plans didn't finalize until the summer, yet Bob kept his offer open and in August 1979 my life in the DA's office began."[2]

Sonia's closest friends at Yale were stunned by her decision to go to the DA's office. The low pay of public service was one thing, but acutely aware of her passionate and committed work on behalf of diversity and raising awareness of minorities' rights, they could not envision her as a prosecutor. "There was a tremendous amount of pressure from my community, from the third-world community, at Yale," she recalled in her fourth year at the DA's office. "They could not understand why I was taking this job. I'm not sure I've ever resolved that problem."[3]

The skyrocketing crime rate in New York and other big cities in the late 1970s was another factor that prevented many law students from giving prosecutorial work serious thought. But as Sonia experienced, Morgenthau brought a dignified and thoughtful perspective to that work, and she was not the only one drawn in. "Morgenthau can be an overwhelmingly charismatic presence," said Sonia's classmate Peter Kougasian, who started at the DA's office with her. Kougasian had also attended Morgenthau's talk at Yale, where one of his colleagues asked Morgenthau how he could enjoy putting people in jail for a living. "And his answer was — I'll never forget it — that the victims of crimes are disproportionately poor, minorities, and disenfranchised," said Kougasian. "He told us to never think a prosecutor was exploiting one class at the expense of another, because it is the only chance many have to lead a meaningful life. He understood the very legitimate concerns that underlay that question." The message had a compelling effect. "I remember thinking, this is it; I have to work for this guy," said Kougasian.

Kougasian had applied to the district attorney's office because he was interested in criminal law and thought he wanted to be a defense attorney. People he admired and from whom he sought advice told him that the best way to develop that career was to learn the system and the nuts and bolts of lawyering by being a prosecutor. Morgenthau's talk put the prosecutor's role in a whole new light. "It was not until I met him that I had any idea of what a calling it would be," he said. Kougasian made a career at the office and is currently a prosecutor in the office of the New York City Special Narcotics Prosecutor. As Morgenthau once put it, the job is full of ironies: "I tell people, half-seriously, half-joking, that there are two main drawbacks to the office. One is that the salaries are not as good as private practice. The other is that they're going to like the job so much they're not going to want to leave."[4]

Most applicants for Morgenthau's office went through a three-tiered process that began with an interview at the law school by an assistant DA, who would then do an evaluation; those whom he or she recommended would meet with a panel of three assistant DAs who would write up their own recommendation to Morgenthau. Morgenthau interviewed everyone on the hiring committee's final list "because he knew that the success of an office of that size depends on the quality of the people you hire," said John W. Fried, chief of the DA's section in which Sonia and Peter Kougasian would work. The DA would then consider their writing samples, law school grades, and activities (such as law review or moot court). He also tried to make the office as diverse as possible, based on the applicant pool that was presented to him. The pool was narrowed to funnel "really the best-quality assistant DAs, all without regard to political parties or affiliations," said Fried. No one cared whether a candidate considered himself or herself a Democrat or a Republican, he said.

Sonia had circumvented the traditional

route. "I remember Morgenthau calling me into his office before Sonia got there to say that he had interviewed and offered a job to this extraordinary law student," said Fried. "He told me a little bit about her background and said that he was going to assign her to my bureau."

While the majority of law school graduates sought work in a firm, there were still many who applied to the Manhattan DA's office every year, which made it a highly competitive search. Each summer Morgenthau hired only about forty new assistant district attorneys out of an initial pool of about two thousand.

The young people who applied to the district attorney's office wanted to do public service and to learn how to try cases. "If you go to a big law firm and you want to get involved in litigation, you're not going to try too many cases," said Fried. But many of Morgenthau's applicants wanted to be trial lawyers and understood that a busy prosecutor's office would give them experience they would not find anywhere else. "If you want to try cases or work in the criminal law area there's no better office in the country than the Manhattan DA's office," said Fried. "We would get excellent candidates." He interviewed some of the top law students from

Stanford, Berkeley, Fordham, and New York University over the years, and while some of them eventually decided that they wanted to make five times as much money working on Wall Street, others came to the office. "We've had some great people," Fried said.

Morgenthau hired assistants who were obviously very bright, successful, and motivated but whom he also sensed were quick studies and able to get along very well with people. In the Manhattan DA's office, "more than in most places where you practice law, you need each other because you learn from each other," said the bureau's Deputy Chief Richard Girgente. Assistants were thrown into criminal court within the first three or four weeks and perhaps asked to cover the calendar for a fellow assistant who suddenly had to interview a witness, and "to get that kind of support, you had to be collegiate," said Girgente. "You had to work well with each other. People got along, they worked hard together and they teamed effectively together, otherwise the weakest link could bring you down." People were hired with that in mind because not only did they need to get along well with their colleagues, they would deal on a daily basis with judges, police officers, and witnesses, who could be very difficult. Morgenthau and Sonia's supervisors recognized this quality in her from the start. "If you can't work well with people," Girgente said, "you're probably in the wrong job. She worked very well with people."

Rookie assistants came in with those traits and honed them in an environment in which they were critically important. With each other's support, they learned how to start making order out of the apparent chaos and not get overwhelmed by the huge caseloads. "You're almost always thrown into the deep end of the pool with cases and matters, and you've got to develop the ability to fly by the seat of your pants," said Girgente. Morgenthau also looked for assistants with the specialized attributes required for trial lawyers. They had to be exceptionally good communicators, able to take complex matters and make them simply understood for people from all backgrounds and socioeconomic levels. This could be challenging for recent graduates of Ivy League schools. "Your jurors are not reflective of that," said Girgente, "they're a cross-section of the melting pot of New York City." Assistants were groomed to speak and write with exacting clarity. "We always used to say that to be effective as a trial lawyer you had to speak effectively to everyone," Girgente said. "You needed all twelve votes, you couldn't miss anyone on the jury. You had to reach the person who was not as intelligent as well as the Ph.D."

Another quality the office looked for in a potentially great trial lawyer was the ability to be strategic. "From the moment you pick up a case, you have to be able to know how it's all going to play through in the courtroom," said Girgente. "How is this witness going to act on the stand? How am I going to talk to the jury about this witness?" As Sonia's supervisor, Girgente observed her strategic thinking and the meticulous approach to each case that would make her stand out among most of her colleagues. "What would clearly distinguish her is preparedness," he said. "There is no great trial lawyer who is not well prepared. She worked so hard; there were not going to be any surprises. That trait, above all others, will carry you — it's the one thing you have control over."

Morgenthau and his deputies instilled their assistants with a set of practical ethical standards that shaped the rest of their careers. The pale gray walls of the offices at One Hogan Place, a wing of the criminal court building that stands at 100 Centre Street, reflect the reasonable, fair-minded atmosphere that pervaded every working day, regardless of how many cases were on an assistant's desk or how swiftly she ran back and forth to court, interviews with witnesses, and investigations with the police. Beneath all the details was a strong awareness of the enormous responsibilities they assumed on behalf of the people of New York and the respect that those responsibilities demanded. "People get the sense of a prosecutor's office being a gritty place — hard reality," said Kougasian. "This was a place of thoughtfulness, idealism. Robert Morgenthau set the tone."

Girgente described the DA's office as a place where people were always asked to be fair and to do the right thing. "Morgenthau's favorite phrase was, 'Handle the matters that come before you without fear or favor,'" Girgente said. "That's your training and that's the tradition of the office." Everyone who goes through the Manhattan DA's office, including Sonia, he said, approaches every matter in exactly that way during those formative years in which they learn the ropes of the criminal justice system. "It's your imprinting," Girgente noted. "That's where you have your first legal experience, and it stays with you."

In the four years that Morgenthau had been on the job by the time Sonia arrived, he had already made a mark on the office with innovative leadership, such as a complete restructuring of the trial division. Instead of different prosecutors handling a felony case at various stages, the horizontal system put a felony into the hands of one prosecutor throughout the case. The traditional vertical system tended to assemble the highest expertise into the homicide bureau, the area to which the most experienced assistants aspired. "The virtue of the horizontal system, which Morgenthau designed and which has proven to be successful, is that it eliminated a lot of the elitism, the concentration of expertise," said Sonia's fellow assistant Hugh H. Mo. "The homicide bureau contained the crème de la crème of the prosecutors in the office at the expense of the felony bureau," Mo said. "You basically had a concentration of talents that didn't serve the office well." Morgenthau created one large trial division divided into six sections, Trial Parts 30 through 80, each of which handled everything from misdemeanors to felonies. Sonia, Peter Kougasian, and Hugh Mo were assigned to Trial Part 50. Morgenthau created additional units for long-term investigations and specialty areas, such as sex crimes and family violence.

Sonia's class of assistants understood how

he gained his reputation for integrity, which he had established as a federal prosecutor, as they trained in and became part of his DA's office during one of the most crime-ridden periods in the city's history. Morgenthau's perception of their duties imbued their work with significance: "At our best, we carry forward the ethical and moral traditions of our civilization," he said in a speech in 1982. "We do so as a profession as much as — perhaps more than — any other. What other profession asks or at least feels that it should ask, with respect to almost every decision, is it just, is it fair, is it right?"[5]

Morgenthau led by example, according to John Fried. "He made it clear to everybody that they had significant responsibilities, significant authorities over the life and liberty of the people with whom they dealt, be they defendants or complainants, and that they had a responsibility to the public to do the right thing, to make judgments on the merits of cases, determine which cases should be prosecuted and which shouldn't be prosecuted."

Sonia and her colleagues entered the DA's office in August 1979, one month after taking the bar exam. The results would not come out until November, at which time those who passed would schedule an interview with the New York State Bar Association's Character and Fitness Committee. After the interview and submission of a long form and documentation about employment and education history, the committee would review all those materials and announce whether the candidate was admitted. That news usually came within the first two or three months of the New Year. In the meantime, rookie associates were legally entitled to practice in the criminal division of the New York court.

In law school, Sonia's coursework on criminal law had been limited to a basic first-year course and the mock trial experience. Traditionally, law school curriculums consider criminal law a specialty, like immigration or environmental law, and after taking the first-year required course, students can take electives on advanced criminal procedure or other aspects of the field. Therefore, all of the new law school graduates going into the DA's office needed training in the broad elements and specifics of the criminal justice system. The office had a long tradition of formal training and ongoing supervision, and for the first two to three weeks on the job, Sonia and the rest of her class were given training seminars that included lectures by more experienced assistants. These classes covered everything from the basics of the city's court jurisdictions and how the various court parts work to the details of writing up complaints and case notes. The rookies watched videotapes of mock trials presented by previous classes while the senior assistants made comments about the opening statements, direct and cross examinations, and summations. They learned by observation, shadowing an assistant DA in the complaint room and during arraignment procedures.

The class also took part in its own mock trial, in which Sonia displayed the focus and earnestness that would mark her career at the office. Marc J. Citrin, the trial part assistant (TPA) assigned to Sonia, recalled that while everyone took the mock trials very seriously, "she treated it like it was a real trial." Citrin manned the video camera during Sonia's mock trial and recalled that she dressed the part by wearing a blue suit and conducted herself with focus and intensity as if she were trying a case in front of a jury. "I knew she took this job very much to heart at the very beginning," Citrin said.

After the brief official training seminar, assistants were plunged into the system, but received supervision from more experienced assistants and their direct boss, the bureau chief. "They are very big on supervision," said Citrin, who was attending law school at night at NYU while working as a TPA. He became an assistant DA at the office three years after Sonia arrived and experienced the office's style of ongoing training and support firsthand. "There's a very organized structure starting with the bureau chief, deputy bureau chief, even senior assistants who took more junior assistants under their wing," he said.

In New York City, misdemeanors are prosecuted in the criminal court and felonies in the supreme court. Rookie assistants begin with misdemeanors and gradually work their way up to felonies. Misdemeanors — like prostitution, shoplifting, petty larceny, criminal trespass, and misdemeanor assaults — came through the system by the hundreds every day.

Crime was on a sharp rise in New York City when Sonia started at the DA's office in 1979, much of it related to the heroin flooding in from the same French connection routes that had smuggled the drug from Iran, Pakistan, Afghanistan, and Turkey into New York in the 1960s and early 1970s. In 1980, Morgenthau said that East Coast cities were "in the early stages of a massive crisis" of heroin addiction — heroin arrests had increased by 85 percent over the previous two years. In 1978, 10.6 kilograms of heroin were smuggled out of southwest Asian countries, and in the first half of 1980 that number rose to 53.3 kilograms. With that dramatic influx came a surge in deaths from overdoses, cases of hepatitis B due to shooting up with dirty needles, and crime. High rates of heroin addiction brought a corresponding increase in burglaries, robberies, and other offenses, Morgenthau said, "because people have to support their one-hundred-dollar-a-day habit."[6]

This was also the era in which the Medellin drug cartel in Colombia escalated its cocaine sales into the United States. By 1983, cocaine had become the primary drug problem in New York in terms of the number of addicts, and although most users were college-educated members of the middle class, the introduction of crack cocaine in 1984 changed the entire landscape. Cocaine was a drug of the affluent, but crack was designed as a cheap and more quickly addictive alternative that would reach a broader market. With the crack epidemic came crack houses and more crime that, mixed with the shooting galleries and related crimes of heroin, pushed the criminal justice system to the limit.

During Sonia's first year at the DA's office, the number of felony crimes in the city increased by nearly 19 percent for a total of over 407,000, and the use of handguns during serious crimes rose by a record-breaking 31.9 percent. Many of those were robberies, crimes against persons by use of force, and burglaries, crimes against property. In the first eight months of 1980, robberies increased by nearly 12 percent and burglaries rose by more than 21 percent. In 1979 the city also saw a record spike in murders, which totaled 2,092 and increased the next year to 2,228.

Comparing the New York crime rates during the years Sonia was an assistant district attorney with those of 2008 paints a stark picture of what ADAs were up against in her day (see page 149).

The heroin crisis and all the crime and social degradation that went along with it came at a time when the police force had been drastically cut back. While Sonia was beginning her senior year at Princeton, New York City underwent a financial crisis that brought about a major decrease in the force that by 1980 resulted in nine thousand fewer police officers.

The rampant violence that the Manhattan DA's office faced in the first half of the

NEW YORK CRIME RATES 1979–1984 AND 2008

Year	Population	Violent	Property	Murder	Forcible Rape	Robbery	Aggr. Assault	Burglary	Larceny Theft	Vehicle Theft
1979	17,649,000	161,906	933,234	2,092	5,394	93,471	60,949	308,302	500,589	124,343
1980	17,506,690	180,235	1,029,749	2,228	5,405	112,273	60,329	360,925	535,783	133,041
1981	17,594,000	188,178	1,026,757	2,166	5,479	120,344	60,189	350,422	539,486	136,849
1982	17,659,000	174,833	967,369	2,013	5,159	107,843	59,818	295,245	534,244	137,880
1983	17,667,000	161,489	881,322	1,958	5,296	94,783	59,452	249,115	504,346	127,861
1984	17,735,000	162,157	826,969	1,786	5,599	89,900	64,872	222,956	488,621	115,392
2008	19,490,297	77,585	388,533	836	2,801	31,778	42,170	65,735	297,684	25,114

1980s was symbolized by the graffiti- and crime-infested subway system in which subway vigilante Bernhard Goetz shot four black teenagers who attempted to mug him. It was the era of John Lennon's assassination outside his apartment on Central Park West, and a time when the most dangerous job in the city was that of the taxi or limousine driver. Targeted for the cash, taxi drivers suffered the highest rate of workplace homicide in the 1980s and the bulletproof windows separating the front and backseats of a yellow cab have been permanent fixtures ever since. It was an ideal environment for young ADAs who wanted to gain the experience of prosecuting the widest range of crimes.

Coming into the office in 1979, Sonia got that experience, and it shaped her life. Law school had developed her skills of critical analysis, but being a prosecutor taught her what the law really is:

> When I say I became a lawyer in his office, it's because in law school — law schools teach you on hypotheticals. They set forth facts for you. They give you a little bit of teaching on how those facts are developed, but not a whole lot, and then they ask you to opine about legal theory and apply legal theory to the facts before you.

Well, when you work in a prosecutor's office, you understand that the law is not legal theory, it's facts. It's what witnesses say and don't say. It's how you develop your position in the record. And then it's taking those facts and making arguments based on the law as it exists.[7]

The system in which she worked with those facts involved a set of procedures that never became routine. A case began in the complaint room, officially called the Early Case Assessment Bureau (ECAB), where Sonia interviewed both the arresting officer and the complaining witness to find out what happened and to make sure the complaining witness was credible. She had to determine, for example, that the crime was actually a robbery "as opposed to two drug dealers getting into a fistfight over a quantity of drugs and the guy who lost the fistfight making a robbery claim against the guy who won the fistfight," John Fried explained. "That sometimes would happen." After establishing whether she had a credible witness, Sonia would then decide what charges were appropriate and draft a complaint, the official document that described the charges and initiated legal action against the defendant.

During that time the defendant, who had been taken to the detention facility known as the "Tombs," which was annexed to the courthouse, was sent to central booking for fingerprints and photographs. His or her prints were faxed to an office in Albany where, in the precomputerized days, a specialist would categorize their characteristics and sort through files to make a comparison. If the defendant's fingerprints were on file, the officers looked for any previous arrests, revised the current arrest report, and faxed it back to the courthouse.

In Morgenthau's new system, each assistant was regularly assigned a day in the complaint room. For the first year or so, assistants handled only misdemeanor cases, so during the first several months at the office Sonia wrote up misdemeanor complaints, while more senior assistants worked with the felony complaints. Once assistants were promoted to felonies, they were responsible for handling each felony case through to its resolution. "We were all starting at the DA's office at twenty-five, twenty-six years old," said Isabelle Kirshner, another of Sonia's fellow ADAs. "We were kids who were invested with an enormous amount of authority and an enormous amount of discretion." The decisions made in the complaint room stayed with them, for better or for worse. "You picked up the case, you were the one who evaluated it, asked the questions, decided what to do with it and what crimes to charge," said Kirshner. "Whatever you do, you're the one who is going to live with the decisions you made the first day."

When the final arrest report and other paperwork came back into the office, the complaint and the fingerprint report would catch up to one another, and the defendant was usually interviewed at the courthouse by a legal aid who would determine what bail he or she would request. The case would then be put on the docket for the arraignment court. In those days, the time span from arrest to arraignment sometimes took twenty-four to thirty-six hours, which "was a whole bone of contention because it was taking too long to get somebody arraigned, which wasn't right," said Fried. But once a misdemeanor case was called up before an arraignment court judge, the process moved along quickly. The defendant received a copy of the complaint and, in the majority of misdemeanor cases, entered a guilty plea and received a fine, probation, or short jail sentence. In cases in which the defendant pled not guilty, the case would move on to a hearing or trial, and felony cases would be prepared for the grand jury.

Sonia's trial part assistant, Marc Citrin, worked longest with her when she was starting out as a misdemeanor assistant, during which time he was assigned to two additional misdemeanor assistants and three felony assistants. "The thing that distinguished Sonia from the other two assistants, all of whom were very good," Citrin said, "was that she didn't really accept the notion that I was going to spend most of my time working for the felony assistants." She approached her misdemeanor cases with the same thoroughness and diligence more experienced assistants paid to their serious felony cases. "In felonies you always had to prepare as if the defendant might testify, if the case went to trial," Citrin said. Felony assistants would investigate the defendant's New York rap sheet, but if they had any reason to suspect the person had lived in another state, they would be particularly thorough and also conduct a multistate search. Sonia went to that length from the start. "Even as a misdemeanor assistant trying a shoplifter from Sears, she would prepare every one of her cases as if A) it was going to trial; and B) it was the Brinks Robbery," Citrin remembered. "She was just that diligent and that thorough." About 99 percent of the DA office's misdemeanor cases pled out because most defendants "were recidivists that committed the same crimes over and over again" and were willing to take plea offers.[8] But in cases that were not immediately pled out she would not only get rap sheets from other states but also ask Citrin to order certificates of conviction. "With those," he explained, "if the defendant actually did testify and said, 'No, I wasn't convicted of burglary in Texas,' you'd have this printed, sealed document to impeach that person's credibility."

Sonia always referred to Citrin as someone who worked *with* her, not *for* her. Citrin also found her to be serious but always upbeat and polite. "The job of a misdemeanor assistant can be very harrying, but no matter how harried she was, [she] never failed to be pleasant and always said 'please' and 'thank you,'" Citrin said. "That was true of virtually all the people I had the privilege of working for, but certainly it was true of her. She always had a smile and was just a very pleasant person to work with."

The office was congenial, but the work was disheartening. Sonia struggled with prosecuting the broad spectrum of misdemeanor cases because the defendants' actions were so closely tied to their miserable circumstances. "I had more problems during my first year in the office with the low-grade crimes — shoplifting, the prostitution, the minor assault cases," she said. "In large measure, in those cases you were dealing with socioeconomic crimes, crimes that could be the product of the environment and of poverty." When she started working with felonies, it became "less hard" to deal with criminals whose brutal actions had such devastating effects on the community.[9]

Traditionally, an entire class would be promoted to felonies at the same time, but John Fried decided to move up Sonia earlier because of the pressing need for more supreme court assistants and the fact that he believed she had gained the experience necessary to do felony work. "She gained it more quickly than some of the other members of her class," Fried said, "and they followed her in very short order — but she was the first to go."

As her bureau chief, Fried observed that Sonia spent a lot of late hours in the office and approached her work in a more decisive way than many of her fellow rookie assistants. Fried's door was always open for young assistants to come in and talk about their cases, from the most humble jostling case committed on the subway (the old "dip and stall" pickpocketing routine) to homicides, and when Sonia came in for advice she had already carefully thought through her issue. Some assistants called on Fried to get a quick answer from the boss, but Sonia presented her case differently. Rather than asking Fried, "What should I do?" she came in with her own scenarios already worked out, asking which of two or more options was best. She asked him if he had experienced a similar problem and, if so, what he had done. "She was more drawing on my experience as opposed to looking for an answer," said Fried. "It was clear to me that she was picking it up and thinking about the problems and seeing the issues."

Sonia had also impressed Fried by the way she functioned in misdemeanor court. "I would go to court and watch how she handled herself in front of judges, with private and legal aid defense attorneys, and there was a certain maturity there that others of course gained, but that she had somehow acquired more quickly," he said. Already performing at the level of junior lawyers in the supreme court, Sonia got the green light to start processing felonies. She eventually moved out of an office with three desks and into her own, Room 626, which had a small window that looked down on Centre Street and tiny but very green Collect Pond Park.

The supreme court was overwhelmed with felony crimes such as assault, burglary, robbery, illegal weapons, rape, drug possession, and murder in the early 1980s. As a felony assistant, Sonia worked closely with the police on more in-depth investigations and spent the bulk of her time preparing plea offers. At that time, only about 13 percent of indicted felony cases went to trial. Felony assistants had office guidelines to follow in determining what kind of plea was acceptable for any particular class of crime, and Sonia spent most days in court arguing for bail amounts and making plea offers before the supreme court judge to which Trial Bureau 50 was assigned. "It was like a triage in those days," said Kirshner. "You had so many cases and there was a big push to get rid of them." Kirshner worked in the Special Narcotics Division of Sonia's trial bureau, where most cases came out of "Alphabet City," the area made up of Avenues A, B, C, and D on Manhattan's Lower East Side. Most of the heroin and cocaine sold in the northeastern United States came through that neighborhood, and most of the murders committed there were drug related. Kirshner saw "hundreds and hundreds of narcotics cases" come out of the area daily. "Those were the years before the Lower East Side was gentrified," she said. "That was when Alphabet City was Alphabet City."

About once a month, Sonia took her turn spending an entire day in the arraignments section where misdemeanors and felony defendants are officially charged. The judge would have fifty to sixty cases on his calendar on any given day, and one prosecutor from the trial bureau was assigned to represent the prosecution in connection with each one of those cases. Assistants who had a case on the calendar that day would put a note in the file that briefly summarized the case, requested a specific bail amount, and stated the terms of the plea offer; he or she then placed the file in a cart that was wheeled into the courtroom.

As each case was called Sonia pulled out the note and explained the case and plea offer to the judge. If the judge wanted more information or disagreed with the plea, Sonia would call up to the DA's office and tell the assistant assigned to the case that the judge wanted him or her in court.

During these proceedings, the defendant would be brought out from the detention cell behind the courthouse, be given a copy of the complaint, and be joined by either his lawyer or a legal aid attorney. Sonia and the defense attorney would make their bail recommendations, and the judge would make the final decision based on the seriousness of the crime and the defendant's background. Felony ADAs would request higher bail for someone with a long criminal record and/or without any apparent connections to the community — somebody "they believed as soon as he hit the street he'd be on the first bus to nowhere," explained John Fried.

After Sonia became a felony assistant, she sometimes had duty day together with Isabelle Kirshner, and the two sat together in the jury box. "She had a lot of serious cases," said Kirshner, "and I had a lot of not-so-serious cases but narcotics cases, and they were always contentious because of the Rockefeller laws and mandatory minimums." The Rockefeller Drug Laws drawn up in 1973 imposed stiff sentences on drug possession and trafficking, including a minimum sentence of fifteen years to life for selling two ounces or possessing four ounces of heroin, cocaine, or other narcotics. "There were always issues with respect to that," Kirshner said.

Sonia's colleague Peter Kougasian recalled reading one of Sonia's file notes during arraignment duty one night. "Because there was oftentimes a heavy docket in night arraignment, it was important to give a very brief summary because it was possible that if the docket was busy, that attorney might not see the file until it's called. As you're walking to the bench you're learning everything you'll know about the case." He stepped up to the bench while reading Sonia's summary and was taken aback by her attention to detail: "There was a theft in a bar. The defendants walk into a bar, ask for change. The bartender came back with two five-dollar bills for a ten-dollar bill."

"That's Sonia," said Kougasian, "details, details. A little too detailed, but I do think it speaks well of her."

The criminal court arraignment part ran all day with a break at dinnertime, then started up again at seven P.M. and went on until about two in the morning. From time to time throughout that long day, Sonia and Isabelle had a chance to lighten things up while waiting for the next case to be called. They caught up on office gossip and "talked about everybody walking in and out of the courtroom, which was fun," Kirshner said. "She had a great sense of humor."

The next step in Sonia's role as a felony assistant was preparing the case for a grand jury, which would either dismiss the case, return it to criminal court as a misdemeanor, send it to family court if it found that a juvenile should not be tried as an adult, or indict. When she won an indictment, the case would move on to the famous supreme court judge to which Trial Part 50 was assigned, Harold Rothwax.

Judge Rothwax, who died in 1997, is a legend in the New York courts as a tough judge whose high expectations for prosecutors and defense lawyers alike earned him the name the "Prince of Darkness." A Brooklyn native, he started out as a legal aid attorney and worked for several years with the New York Civil Liberties Union in support of causes such as defending arrested civil rights and Vietnam War protesters. He was appointed to the New York Supreme Court in 1972 and brought the same aggressive, razor-sharp style he had shown as a legal aid attorney and activist to the bench. Lawyers who were not meticulously prepared came before Rothwax at their own risk.

"Rothwax would hold the DA's feet to the fire and do the same thing for the defense attorneys," said Marc Citrin, who sat in his courtroom many times as Sonia's TPA. He and others recalled that Rothwax could be "intimidating and incredibly sarcastic" when things were not moving along as he would like. One of Rothwax's trademark lines, made to any defense attorney whose client refused to take a plea from an ADA who had an airtight case against him, was, "Your client has a constitutional right to do the maximum time allowable under the law and I'm here to help him protect that right." He also had a favorite expression for ADAs or defense attorneys who were not adequately prepared: "You clearly haven't burdened yourself with the perils of overpreparation." Everyone in the city learned what kind of committed public servant Rothwax was during the high-profile Joel Steinberg murder case in 1988, over which the judge presided. Rothwax lived near Columbia University in the northern part of Manhattan and rode his bicycle down to the courthouse every day. One morning in December a car sideswiped him at Fifth Avenue and Thirty-fourth Street and threw him into the street. He broke both wrists and was taken to a hospital emergency room, after which he went directly to the courthouse and insisted that the trial continue. Sitting at the bench with two white casts on his arms, he turned to the jury and said, "We have good days, we have bad days. This is not one of the good days." He then addressed the ADA and said, "Call your next witness."[10]

Sonia's supervisor, Richard Girgente, described Rothwax as "truly one of the great" figures who stands out, an unforgettable and unique person who left an impression. "Sometimes it was his heel on your neck," he said. John Fried said that Rothwax knew the law backward and forward and had a keen talent for assessing whether cases were provable or not, worth spending court resources on.

Sonia and Isabelle Kirshner spent much quality time before Judge Rothwax. "He was tough on everybody," said Kirshner. "He just didn't like bad lawyering. If he did not like the offer or thought that you were stupid, he'd kill you. He would just kill you. But he was actually very, very fond of Sonia and me."

Kirshner won him over by making sure she never walked into his courtroom unless she was meticulously prepared and had gathered everything he would need to make an intelligent decision about her case. She also teased him a lot. "He gave me a little initiation by fire and I'd give it back to him, and then he became my buddy," she said. "And he liked Sonia very much because she was very prepared."

Just as in the criminal court arraignment part, Rothwax's court operated by a system in which an ADA representing the entire office would spend the day reading the notes and plea offers from a stack of files. The ADA assigned to a particularly complex case would sometimes arrive in court in anticipation of being called up to the bench. Whether speaking on behalf of an ADA or representing herself, Sonia never had a problem with Rothwax. "I remember him having harsh words for other assistants who were not prepared, but I never heard that toward her," said Marc Citrin. "The DA in Trial Part 50 might bear the brunt of getting yelled at for some other assistant's failings, but Sonia never did." If a felony assistant was not completely prepared for any reason, sometimes Rothwax's punishment was to reduce bail or let the defendant out on his or her own recognizance because the judge thought he or she had been in jail long enough. "Frequently it wasn't the DA's fault," explained Citrin. "Cops weren't around or the witness was in the winds — you would tell the judge that straight up, and the judge does what he does. But that was never an issue with Sonia." Judge Rothwax didn't berate Sonia in the rare event that a situation beyond her control slowed down one of her cases because he respected her track record for consistent, efficient preparation.

The street crimes Sonia prosecuted covered the gamut from misdemeanor gun possession and robberies to first-degree murder, and her felony work also included investigations into child abuse, police misconduct, fraud, and child pornography. With up to a hundred cases on her desk on any given day, the sheer volume of crime, suffering, and wasted lives weighed heavily on her mind and attitude. It was the kind of job that made her a chain smoker, a fan of caffeine-laden diet soda, and a driven attorney who worked long hours into the night and contemplated the harsh realities that befell many of her fellow New Yorkers. She was outraged by crimes of violence and the cycle of despair that they caused. "What I am finding, both statistically and emotionally," she said in 1983, "is that the worst victims of crimes are not general society, i.e., white folks, but minorities themselves. The violence, the sorrow are perpetrated by minorities on minorities."[11] She became well acquainted with the sight of a young, promising life spiraling down into the recesses of the criminal justice system instead of developing their potential:

It pains me when I meet particularly bright defendants — and I've met quite a few of them — people who, if they had had the right guidance, the right education, the right breaks, could have been contributing members of our society. When they get convicted, there's a satisfaction, because they're doing things that are dangerous. But there are also nights when I sit back and say, "My God, what a waste!"[12]

By the time most people got arrested the damage had been done, she observed. The DA's office was a place to seek justice for victims, not obliterate the causes of crime. "The one thing I have found," she said, "is that if you come into the criminal justice system on a prosecutorial or defense level thinking that you can change the ills of society, you're going to be sorely disappointed. This is not where those kinds of changes have to be made."[13]

Some days the grim realities were more wearing than others. "After a while, you forget there are decent, law-abiding people in life," she said in her final year.[14] But there were many days, weeks, and months over her five years in the DA's office in which justice was so sweet that she couldn't imagine doing anything else. The days on which juries handed down convictions for murderers and child pornographers made all the rest worthwhile.

Sonia's most prominent child pornography case came on the heels of a U.S. Supreme

Court decision that brought New York's child pornography laws into the national spotlight. In 1981, the New York Court of Appeals reversed the convictions of Paul Ira Ferber, a Manhattan bookstore owner who had sold two pornographic films featuring children to an undercover officer. The court held that the convictions violated the First Amendment, but Morgenthau appealed its decision to the U.S. Supreme Court, which unanimously upheld the original convictions in 1982. In his opinion, U.S. Supreme Court Justice Byron White summarized the legal fight against child pornography, the harm child pornography inflicts on children, and the Supreme Court's response to the New York court's claim that the New York law is "too broad," all of which formed the backdrop of Sonia's 1983 case:

In recent years, the exploitive use of children in the production of pornography has become a serious national problem. The Federal Government and 47 States have sought to combat the problem with statutes specifically directed at the production of child pornography. At least half of such statutes do not require that the materials produced be legally obscene. Thirty-five States and the United States Congress have also passed legislation prohibiting the distribution of such materials; 20 States prohibit the distribution of material depicting children engaged in sexual conduct without requiring that the material be legally obscene. New York is one of the 20. . . .

The distribution of photographs and films depicting sexual activity by juveniles is intrinsically related to the sexual abuse of children in at least two ways. First, the materials produced are a permanent record of the children's participation and the harm to the child is exacerbated by their circulation. Second, the distribution network for child pornography must be closed if the production of material which requires the sexual exploitation of children is to be effectively controlled. . . .

While the reach of the statute is directed at the hard core of child pornography, the Court of Appeals was understandably concerned that some protected expression, ranging from medical textbooks to pictorials in the National Geographic would fall prey to the statute. How often, if ever, it may be necessary to employ children to engage in conduct clearly within the reach of § 263.15 in order to produce educational, medical, or artistic works cannot be known with certainty. Yet we seriously doubt, and it has not been suggested, that these arguably impermissible applications of the statute amount to more than a tiny fraction of the materials within the statute's reach.[15]

Seven months after the U.S. Supreme Court made that decision, Sonia went to trial with the first case in the state to be prosecuted under the upheld child pornography law. The case came to her from New York Police Department (NYPD) detective Chris Montanino who had found child pornography at a Manhattan bookstore. Frustrated over his inability to convince prosecutors that the case was significant, he finally reached Sotomayor. When she answered Montanino's call, he went into a tirade about the city's easy access to child porn and the DA office's unwillingness to do anything about it. Sonia cut him short and told him to be in her office at nine the next morning. "And that is the way it went," Montanino said. "She was no-nonsense."[16]

With assistant DA Karen Greve Milton as co-counsel, Sonia was the lead prosecutor in the case *The People of the State of New York v. Clemente D'Alessio and Scott Hyman,* which went to trial in February and March 1983. New York Supreme Court Justice

Thomas B. Galligan presided over the child pornography case in which forty-year-old D'Alessio, from Farmingville, Long Island, and twenty-six-year-old Scott Hyman, of Queens, were accused of selling pornographic films that used children who were seven to fourteen years old.

Hyman had sold videotapes to an undercover agent, and the prosecutors had circumstantial evidence against D'Alessio. In a summary of the case, Sonia noted that D'Alessio "raised a misidentification defense" and both defendants "filed a plethora of motions before and during trial" that included a request for severance (to try the defendants separately) and motions to suppress statements, evidence, and identification. All those motions were denied, and the defense also attempted to bring in a drug-addiction expert to testify on Hyman's criminal intent and to make the jury hear about the laws on diminished capacity or intoxication when considering Hyman's guilt or innocence.[17]

Sonia used all the narrative skills at her disposal to portray the litany of horrors children suffered in the making of pornographic films and the tragic effects they would experience throughout their lives as a result. "She had the jury crying about what these guys were doing to kids," said her new

Bureau Chief Warren J. Murray. The jury convicted, and the following month Justice Galligan sentenced D'Alessio to three and a half to seven years and Hyman to two to six years in prison. At the sentencing hearing, Sonia and Karen told Justice Galligan that in trading in the child pornography films, the criminals had committed "heinous, reprehensible and vile acts."[18]

Sonia's investigations and other trial preparation for the child pornography case overlapped with her work on the most high-profile trial of her career at the DA's office, *The People of the State of New York v. Richard Maddicks.*

In the winter of 1981, residents of central Harlem were terrorized by a gun-crazed burglar who broke into apartments by swinging from ropes attached to rooftops and crashing through windows. If people were in the apartment, he shot them. Over the course of three months, he murdered three people and seriously wounded seven others in a string of burglaries committed within eleven blocks of each other. A team of detectives from Harlem's 28th Precinct and the Manhattan Detective Task Force investigated the crimes for two months, and on January 28, 1982, they arrested a thirty-seven-year-old suspect, Richard Maddicks, who was carrying a .32-caliber revolver. After detectives found more evidence in Maddicks's girlfriend's apartment that linked him to some of the killings and robberies, he was arraigned on the charge of killing Robert Clark, a seventy-seven-year-old, partially blind retired barber. Clark had been shot at his apartment on Lenox Avenue on December 18 in the middle of the afternoon. During the arraignment, one of the police officers described Maddicks's method with a name that was attached to the case from that point on: "He came through those windows like Tarzan," he said.[19]

Over the next three weeks, two felony assistants at the DA's office worked up the case to bring to the grand jury. The senior assistant, Hugh H. Mo, had come to Trial Part 50 in 1980 after working as a prosecutor in the special narcotics bureau for two years. He and Sonia hit it off as colleagues, partly, Mo believes, because they were unique in the sixth-floor offices. Mo, who was born in China and raised in New York's Chinatown and was the first Asian American at the DA's office. Sonia was one of very few Latinos in the history of the office, a small group that followed in the footsteps of Edwin Torres, the first Puerto Rican assistant DA who was hired in 1959 and is currently a justice on

173

the New York State Supreme Court. Sonia and Mo also had vague notions of each other's humble backgrounds as children raised by widowed mothers in poor sections of the city.

Besides all that, they just liked each other. Mo admired Sonia's work ethic and thorough, focused approach, and she felt comfortable enough with him to ask a personal favor. "She used to come into my office and sit on the raggedy couch and inject herself with insulin," Mo said. "She carried a little pouch with her." During one of those visits, she made her request: "She said to me once, 'Hugh, if I ever really am in distress, I'll need you to do this,' and she showed me how to jab the needle in her arm."

Sonia did not hide her condition, and many of her colleagues saw her inject herself in her office. Her bureau chief John Fried was impressed by the discipline it took to keep the condition so well under control. "When I was with her, she never had an episode where her blood sugar went out of whack and she had to be hospitalized," he said. "She was a very disciplined person and when you have juvenile onset diabetes you have to be. She never used it as some excuse to get out of work and you wouldn't know she had it unless you saw her inject herself."

When it came to doing that a few times a day, she dealt with it, no matter where she was. "When she was in court," said Fried, "she would ask for a recess and go into the bathroom and do it."

When the Maddicks case came up, Sonia had never worked a homicide before, but Mo thought she was ready and he requested that she be his co-counsel.

Working with detectives on the indictment to bring to the grand jury, Sonia and Mo learned that Maddicks's rap sheet went back more than twenty-five years and that the motive for his robberies was a $200-a-day heroin habit. From the age of eleven he had committed assaults, robberies, attempted grand larcenies, and burglaries, and when he was arrested he was on parole after serving time for burglary.

Shortly after Maddicks's arrest, detectives found two .32-caliber handguns that ballistics matched to those used in the crimes and seven of the eleven living victims identified him in lineups. Sonia and Hugh filed a thirty-seven-count indictment on February 19, 1982, charging Maddicks with three murders, three attempted murders, and various armed robberies and burglaries. All of the crimes were organized into eleven incidents, which were named according to the primary victims.

In the Barron Incident, sixty-three-year-old Emory Barron was sleeping in his top-floor apartment "when he heard noise coming from his kitchen," the indictment stated. "Barron went to investigate and was shot in the chest by the defendant. Barron staggered into his living room and died. The kitchen window was smashed and the apartment was ransacked." Investigators believed that Maddicks had used a rope to lower himself from the roof to the window. Among the objects taken from the apartment was a portable shopping cart and packages of frozen meat.

The Robinson Incident involved two brothers who chased after Maddicks after they found him trying to pry open their family's apartment window. When Maddicks saw Michael and Steven Robinson inside the apartment, "he fled to the roof by crawling between the Robinson's building and an adjacent building on his hands and feet. Michael and Steven went up to the roof with a stick. As the defendant was about to scale to the top of the roof, Michael started to hit the defendant with the stick." Maddicks crawled down and slipped into the adjacent abandoned building. The brothers went back inside and spotted Maddicks in the opposite building. Maddicks "fired a shot from a .32-caliber revolver striking Steven in the head and killing him instantly."

The third murder charge went to the Clark Incident, in which Maddicks had entered the elderly man's top-floor apartment by stretching a ladder between the apartment and the building opposite. Six stories above ground, Maddicks crawled along the ladder and broke into the apartment. "While burglarizing said apartment the defendant shot Clark to death with a .32-caliber revolver," the indictment said. Clark's boarder, a man named Isri Persaud, came home to find Maddicks facing him with a pistol in both hands. "The defendant ordered Persaud to kneel down and empty his pockets. To frighten him, the defendant fired two shots from a .32-caliber automatic pistol near Persaud. The defendant then dragged Persaud to the kitchen, bound Persaud with strips of cloth and fired two more shots from the automatic pistol near Persaud." It was Persaud's lucky day, because Maddicks turned away and began grabbing a few items to steal, including Clark's checkbook.

Another victim who got lucky was Louis Simmons, who woke up from an afternoon nap to the sound of footsteps in his apartment. "As Simmons was getting up from his bed he saw the defendant pointing a gun at him." Maddicks shot Simmons in the face with a .32-caliber revolver and fled with some money and personal property. "Simmons survived the gunshot wound after a period of hospitalization." In the second attempted murder charge, Maddicks was accused of breaking into Lucy Brown's apartment by crawling out of an abandoned adjacent building, walking along the ledge to her window, and going in. Checking out the sound of footsteps, Brown came face-to-face with Maddicks and he "fired a shot at Brown when she tried to flee. The defendant took a sum of money from Brown at gunpoint." Maddicks then forced her into the bedroom where her boyfriend was sleeping and robbed him at gunpoint. He left with the money and a few items, including the boyfriend's gloves.

The third attempted murder took place when Maddicks was robbing seventy-year-old Arnold Ernest Johnson at gunpoint in the hallway of Johnson's building. A neighbor, sixty-five-year-old David Wells, came out of his apartment and asked what was going on. Maddicks "turned and shot Wells in the stomach with a .32-caliber automatic pistol." Three weeks later, Maddicks broke into Johnson's apartment, and when the old man tried to flee, Maddicks shot him in the left hand, stole some money, and left.

In the Hall Incident, Maddicks was charged with crashing into the apartment of Martha Hall "by swinging on a rope tied to the roof. Defendant pointed a gun at Hall and removed a sum of money from her." When Hall ran away, Maddicks shot her dog with his .32-caliber automatic. Burglary charges were made in the Gurley Incident, in which Maddicks broke Christine Gurley's window with a flowerpot, jumped into the apartment, and ordered her to leave at gunpoint. In the Bell Incident, Philip Bell came home to his apartment to find a bag containing his camera, radio, and tapes "being pulled out of the window with a rope coming from the roof." Bell slammed the window on the rope and went up to the roof to investigate. Maddicks pulled a knife on him and Bell went back to his apartment, where his bag was gone, pulled out the window and up to the roof.

In the final charge of robbery in the first degree, Maddicks "accosted Ophelia Hudson at gunpoint" on the second-floor landing of her building and demanded money. "When Hudson was slow in complying defendant knocked Hudson to the floor and took her pocketbook."[20]

Sonia and Hugh presented these stories

to the grand jury with the aid of a map that showed the Harlem neighborhood in which the crimes were allegedly committed, marked up with the names of the victims and dates of the attacks, and People's Exhibit #2, a neatly typed flow sheet listing the victims; time, date, and place of the crimes; "Acrobatic Methods" of the defendant; "Pistol Used"; "Victim Shot"; and other categories. They had composite sketches of the attacker drawn from descriptions by the witnesses, which matched up with photos of the defendant and portrayed him as a "male black, five feet seven, 145 pounds, 37 years old, mustache, unshaven, and he had a hood." The team won their indictment and dug further into their investigation with the police.

Sonia and Mo interviewed forty witnesses, taking twenty each, and prepared them for trial. They visited the scenes of the crimes with detectives to try to picture for themselves what the victims had experienced, and Mo recalled the day they went to look at the apartment of one of the murder victims. It was much more grim than anything Sonia had read about in Nancy Drew or seen in the crisp black-and-white of *Perry Mason*:

How could she ever forget going up to Harlem with me to visit the crime scene, the apartment where Robert Clark was murdered? We went with three detectives. We met them at the DA's office and they drove us up. The elevator was not working so we walked up six flights of stairs. It was almost like Starsky and Hutch, here was Sonia with two Irish detectives, Pat Heany and Bill O'Hara, and then Joe Rendine, three veteran detectives on the New York City Police Department. They went into this apartment with their guns drawn to first make a sweep of the apartment, which had been abandoned after the murder.

There was garbage as well as broken furniture in the room and the place reeked of the odor of urine and feces. There were broken hypodermic needles and candles, all evidence that the place [the empty apartment] had been used as a shooting gallery for heroin addicts to mainline. In addition to the rank odor there were no lights, the electricity had obviously been turned off. Daylight was coming through the very dirty windows; the windowpanes were covered with dust and dirt from years and years that hadn't been washed. The detectives pointed out the mattress that Mr. Clarke was sleeping on when he was gunned down. He apparently awoke while Maddicks was in his room and he died on that very dirty mattress. We were examining where the bullets had landed on the door frame.

I think that it should be a prerequisite that trial lawyers, whether prosecutors or defense attorneys, visit the crime scene because you've got to get a feel, you've got to have a sense of the dimension, the visual as well as that visceral feel for the place where the crime took place. You have to get that feel in order to bring it alive in a courtroom through words or through the mouths of the witnesses. So Sonia went through that process and that learning experience.

We had to see the apartment in order to visualize and to feel how Isri Persaud was ordered into the kitchen area and asked to kneel down and then was begging for his life. He was relieved of thirty-nine dollars; he forked over the money he had in his pockets. He thought he was going to be executed then and there. He begged for his life and Maddicks shot at the floor just to frighten him, and then Maddicks ran out of the apartment. We saw the bullet hole right on the floor where Mr. Persaud told us during our interview that he kneeled down and thought he was gone, that that was the end of his life. Then Maddicks for some strange reason decided not to kill him. Who knows what was going through Maddicks' mind? He killed people with impunity.[21]

During preparation for trial, Sonia worked on a motion to consolidate the murder, attempted murder, burglary, and other charges into one trial. Even though this had never been done before, as "most New York courts had limited consolidation to crimes in which an identical modus operandi warranted consolidation," she explained, she successfully argued to Judge Harold Rothwax that there were enough strong common aspects of each event to make a consolidation appropriate.[22] In order for the jury to understand the full extent of Maddicks's actions, the prosecution needed to present all of the incidents in one trial. "There had never been a case quite like that," she said, "where an individual who used different acrobatic feats to gain entry into an apartment was tried with all of his crimes in one indictment." Sonia searched for a basis on which to make that argument:

I researched very carefully the law and found a theory in New York law, called the Molineux theory then, that basically said if you can show a pattern that established a person's identity or assisted in establishing a person's identity — simplifying the argument, by the way — then you can try different cases together. This was not a conspiracy, under law, because Mr. Maddicks acted alone, so I had to find a different theory to bring all his acts together.[23]

Mo described the case as a prosecutor's dream in that it involved so many aspects of a felony case. "You've got murder, you've got robbery, assault, burglary, possession of a weapon," he said, "and it also involved allegations of drug usage, larceny. It involved all the basic fundamentals of investigation." He and Sonia built their case on blood and physical evidence in the era before DNA, ballistics, and the similar ways the defendant gained access and acted toward his victims. "The person did not hide his identity from the victims, did not wear a mask," said Mo. "One of the things we learned very quickly is that the perpetrator had to be very acrobatic, physically fit, and obviously had no fear," possibly because the person was a drug user. The fact that the defendant opened fire on his victims and continued to fire after taking money or property "basically showed the person was calloused and most likely a career criminal," Mo said.

Maddicks's defense attorney, Peter Furst, was granted a motion to have his client undergo a psychiatric examination to determine if he was fit to stand trial, and the two psychiatrists who examined Maddicks reported that he was not incapacitated. Furst then had his own psychiatrist examine Maddicks, but that doctor's findings were inconclusive. On the basis of the second report, as well as Furst's "own inability to communicate with his client," he filed another motion to request a competency hearing. That motion was denied, and the case went to trial.[24]

Tracking down, interviewing, and convincing forty witnesses to remain involved throughout the investigation and trial were often challenging chores. The Tarzan Murderer case, as it was known in the New York press, exposed the deadliest side of the city's drug epidemic through detailed witness testimonies about Maddicks's crimes that left so many tragedies in their wake.

Hugh Mo made the prosecution's opening statement on January 3, 1983, and the trial continued through most of the month. The case was assigned to New York Supreme Court Justice James J. Leff. The final eighteen-count indictment handed down by the grand jury charged Maddicks with three murders, two attempted murders, and various burglary and robbery charges, each of which was presented in detail through visual aids such as charts and maps — including Sonia's eight-column chart that listed the facts of each crime beneath each victim's name — and extensive witness testimony. The witnesses that Hugh and Sonia brought to the stand provided the jury with a lively and emotional narrative of Maddicks's crime spree.

On the murder of Steven Robinson, the murdered man's surviving brother admitted that he initially refused to testify because he wanted to find Maddicks back on the streets. "I was hoping to see this man go free so I could kill him myself," said Richard Robinson, who with several other members of the family saw Steven shot to death in their apartment.[25] On the witness stand, Laurie Robinson told Sonia how she watched as her brother was shot. She answered Sonia's questions about the moment in which her brother Steven stood at the window looking at Maddicks, who was watching the apartment from the abandoned building next door. Laurie, whose daughter was at her side, had just called the police after all the commotion of her two brothers running up to the roof and then returning to the apartment. Then she called her sister:

SOTOMAYOR: Now while you were on the phone with your sister Yvonne, what if anything happened?

LR: Steve came down first, Mike came down behind him. When Steve came down my daughter run into where he was at, in front of the window, and I went to the window where she was at, and we was there for a few minutes. And I heard a shot, and I heard the glass. Then he fell back against the wall, and he just lay down.

SOTOMAYOR: Miss Robinson, when you say he, who was that?

LR: Steve.

SOTOMAYOR: What happened after he fell?

LR: After he fell I stood there for a while, because I didn't know which way to go.

Later, Yvonne's husband Bertram Gay testified about running over to the apartment after his wife got the phone call from Laurie.

SOTOMAYOR: What did you find in the apartment?

BG: When I went into the apartment, needless to say I found my brother-in-

187

law lying there in a pool of blood.[26]

When Sonia described the Robinson murder many years later, she emphasized the devastating impact the crime had on the entire family:

> I saw a family that had been intact, with a mother living with three of her children, some grandchildren. They all worked at various jobs. Some were going to school. . . . The mother stood as she watched one of her children be struck by a bullet that Mr. Maddicks fired and killed him because the bullet struck the middle of his head. That family was destroyed. They scattered to the four winds, and only one brother remained in New York who could testify.[27]

Azilee Solomon, the surviving companion of murder victim Emory Barron, told the jury during Sonia's direct examination that she found Barron's body when she returned from work on January 25, 1982. Maddicks had shot Barron in the chest during his burglary of the apartment earlier that afternoon. Both Solomon and Barron had worked at a Hilton hotel for over twenty years, she as a maid and he as a night-shift cleaner. At about five thirty, Solomon had chatted with a neighbor, Sharon, in the hallway before taking out her key to put in her door:

AS: I didn't have to use it.

SOTOMAYOR: Why didn't you have to use it?

AS: Because the door was opened.

SOTOMAYOR: When you came home during twelve or so years that you lived there with Mr. Barron had you ever found the door open before?

AS: This is my first time.

SOTOMAYOR: What did you do when you found the door open?

AS: I walked back outside, and I asked Sharon, "Where is Barry?" So she said she didn't know.

SOTOMAYOR: What did you do then?

AS: Then we all went in the living room and he was sitting on the — one of the chairs.

SOTOMAYOR: What did you notice about him when he was sitting in the chair?

AS: There wasn't anything to notice, he was just sitting there.

SOTOMAYOR: Did you notice anything about the apartment, Miss Solomon?

AS: It was messed up, everything that was on the floor in the kitchen and where Barry was.

Solomon apologized to the jury for crying as she answered the next question, which made her recall the site of her lifeless companion in the chair.

SOTOMAYOR: What did you do when you found Barry?

AS: When I find him I just fall over. I stay there for awhile, I couldn't move . . . I'm sorry.

In questioning the face-shooting victim, Louis Simmons, Sonia drove home the point that Maddicks had shot at an unarmed man who posed no threat. During her direct examination, the jury learned that Simmons had been awakened from a mid-afternoon nap by the sound of footsteps:

SOTOMAYOR: After you heard the footsteps, what happened then?

LS: I saw a man with a gun in his hand.

SOTOMAYOR: Where was that man standing?

LS: In front of my bedroom.

SOTOMAYOR: Where in front of the bedroom?

LS: In that little hallway. . . .

SOTOMAYOR: Do you remember what he said to you just before he shot you?

LS: "It's a holdup. Don't make a move." A whole bunch — he sounded high, you know, kind of high.

FURST (DEFENSE ATTY): Objection.

THE COURT: Overruled.

SOTOMAYOR: Now, sir, when he said that to you, did you move?

LS: I tried to get up. . . .

SOTOMAYOR: You said you tried to get up, Mr. Simmons, when you got shot, at the moment you got shot, were your feet on the floor or on the bed?

LS: On the bed. . . . my whole body was on the bed. . . .

SOTOMAYOR: Now, sir, what happened? Did you feel anything when you heard the shot?

LS: It like stung me.

SOTOMAYOR: Where did you feel the sting?

LS: In this area.

SOTOMAYOR: The witness is indicating at his right cheek area. . . . What happened after you got shot? What, if anything, did the man who shot you do?

LS: He kept holding the gun at me.

SOTOMAYOR: And then?

LS: He grabbed my pants off my dresser.

SOTOMAYOR: Mr. Simmons, what did you have in your pants that he grabbed?

LS: Ten tokens for the week, some small change, about twenty-three dollars.

SOTOMAYOR: Did you have anything else in the pants?

LS: My keys and a bankbook. . . .

SOTOMAYOR: Mr. Simmons, when the man was taking your pants off the dresser, did you move at all?

LS: No, he had a gun on me. I wouldn't take any chances.

Lucy Brown, whom Maddicks shot at during his ransacking of her apartment, told the jury how she tried to wake up her boyfriend, yelling "Mike! Mike!" and shaking him in the bed before running to another room. She then found herself in front of Maddicks, who had a pistol pointed at her. During Sonia's direct examination, Brown told the jury what she did next:

LB: I then ran from the door, and I pulled the door with me as I was going.

SOTOMAYOR: As you pulled the door towards you, what, if anything, happened?

LB: A shot was fired at me.

SOTOMAYOR: Did you hear that shot?

LB: Yes, I did. . . . And then I stood in the hallway for a few minutes with my hands in my ears, my fingers in my ears.

SOTOMAYOR: Why did — why did you hold your fingers to your ears?

LB: I was holding my fingers to my ears because the sound was so forceful and I thought I had, you know, got hit, so I was standing there waiting to see if I was going to fall.

Brown told the jury that when Maddicks held her at gunpoint again and asked her where her money was, she pointed to the middle of her chest, between her breasts. She gave him the money and he forced her into the bedroom, where he found her boyfriend and her baby. When Brown's boyfriend Michael Davis took the stand, he explained that the gunshot woke him up, and before he knew it he "saw a guy standing at the foot of the bed pointing a gun at me."

SOTOMAYOR: Does he say anything to you?

MD: He says, "Yo, bro. Where is the money?" I said, "You got me, man," like that.

SOTOMAYOR: The witness is indicating that he raised his hands up or extended out to each side of him. And what then, sir?

MD: And I reached down and I took, I took eighty dollars out of my shoe and I handed it to him.

Maddicks told them both to turn around and then left the apartment.

During her direct examination of sixty-three-year-old Martha Hall, Sonia was able to show the jury the terrifying effect Maddicks had on his victims:

MH: A heavy paint can, you know, gallon paint can, old can, heavy with paint, crashed through my window right on through, and this person jumped right through the window. . . . He said, "Give me your money." I said, "Please don't kill me, don't kill me, I'll get the money." So he stood on this floor and

I went in the kitchen, and I got about a hundred some odd dollars. I had it in the stove. . . . It was so cold that night, I had on my sleeping clothes. I ran downstairs. By the time I got on the third floor I hear one shot.

After the police arrived, she went back to her apartment with one of the officers. She was concerned about her dog.

MH: By the time he opened the door I didn't see Curly. So I told the officer, I said, "Well, whole lot of blood down here." I said I didn't see Curly at all. It was a whole puddle of blood by the cabinet and the stove. So the officers went in the living room, he said it's a little dog up here, shot. Said little dog beside the door. He didn't move. I didn't go up because I didn't want to see him.

Sotomayor worked persistently to convince Richard Maddicks's girlfriend, Mabel Ivy, to testify, which allowed the jury to hear details about several of the incidents that in turn incriminated Maddicks. Ivy "botched up on her cover-up for this defendant," according to Mo at trial. Ivy said, for example, that she couldn't remember anything about the meat Maddicks brought home (after the alleged murder of Emory Barron) because she ate it and that she had thrown away one of her three shopping carts, the one in which Maddicks had carried the meat home "What a coincidence," said Mo. "Unfortunately for this defendant, Mabel Ivy threw out the wrong shopping cart." The cart's owner, Emory Barron's friend, had described a broken rung in a specific place on the cart, and a detective found that cart among Ivy's trash.

In the summations given in the final days of the trial, defense attorney Furst argued that there was not enough evidence to prove beyond a reasonable doubt that all the crimes were committed by the same person. Mo, who had the last word in the trial, rebuked that by going through the details of each charge and summarizing the factors that tied all the events to Richard Maddicks. At one point, he addressed the most incriminating evidence in the shootings:

"Mr. Furst says there is nothing unique about the seven crimes. The perpetrator did not leave a scarf or a pair of gloves. He did not do something unusual.

I submit to you he is trying to pull a fast one [on] you. This perpetrator certainly left something behind in each of these seven incidents. He either left behind a bullet in someone's brain or someone's chest or in the body of a little dog. And in the other cases he left them imbedded in walls, doorways, or on the floor."[28]

The jury found Maddicks guilty and he was sentenced to sixty-two and a half years to life.

Convicting New York City's Tarzan Murderer had taken Sonia and Hugh Mo down a dark road, even from the perspective of tough-skinned ADAs. "Crime is always awful and exacts a huge toll on its victims," said Sonia's close friend and fellow ADA Nancy E. Gray, "but this one was a step above. . . . I think she really stared down evil."[29] In spite of all the gruesome crime scene visits and heartbreaking facts borne out at trial, winning the case was an exciting way to start the year in 1983. The Maddicks conviction secured Sonia's reputation as one of the most talented ADAs in Trial Part 50 — she was meticulous about details and every phase of trail preparation, an excellent communicator with everyone from police detectives to witnesses, creative with legal strategies, and a commanding presence in the courtroom. She had natural qualities of leadership and presence that, combined with her other professional attributes made her shine with all the characteristics of a trial lawyer that the office sought when hiring young attorneys. Some of those qualities can be learned, but others cannot. "There are some people who are like victims and some who walk with purpose," said Katharine Law, another ADA. "Trust me, Sonia walked with purpose."[30]

By the end of the year that started out with the Maddicks and D'Alessio trials, Sonia had returned to her maiden name. Her and Kevin's lives had taken equally intense but diverging tracts, and they decided to divorce. Kevin had finished his Ph.D. and was on his way to Chicago to start law school at John Marshall, and although Sonia's fast-moving career was not at the heart of the breakup, the lifestyle it demanded had not been any help. "I cannot attribute that divorce to work," she said, "but certainly the fact that I was leaving my home at seven and getting back at ten o'clock was not of assistance in recognizing the problems developing in my marriage." They were not acrimonious toward each other; rather, they agreed that they had grown apart. "They weren't the same people as when they got married," Sonia's colleague Law recalled. "It was kind of like, 'Let's divide up the milk crates where we stored the books.'"

The divorce went through in October, and Sonia got an apartment in Brooklyn, a short subway ride from downtown Manhattan. She invited her friends over for a party, not to celebrate a broken marriage but simply to mark a major life transition. "She wasn't looking at it as depressing," said Hugh Mo, who attended the gathering with his wife. "She felt that their lives had been gradually drifting apart." When Sonia found Hugh working late before and during the Maddicks trial, she urged him to go home to his wife and their new baby, Elizabeth. "Go home and feed your family!" she would say. "Go home or you're going to lose your wife and child." Her concerns for her friends echoed the compassion her mother showed toward friends, family, and total strangers. Getting divorced did not make her bitter.

Sonia left the DA's office the following spring and moved on to a private law firm. Five years in Morgenthau's office did nothing less than imprint her with the legal skills and approach to the law that would define the rest of her career. The supervision she received from her bureau chiefs John Fried and Warren Murray, as well as Murray's deputy chief Richard

Girgente, made a deep and lasting impression. "John Fried was a very high-minded and idealist leader, a great inspiration," said Sonia's friend and fellow ADA Peter Kougasian. "I know he made a big impact on Sonia. He would meet with us weekly and look at a category of cases we were doing, for example, stolen car cases. He'd say, 'What's fair here? How should we be handling these?' By the time we were done with that lunch meeting we had a sense we were really trying to do a thoughtful job of doing justice."

While the pace of the arraignment courtroom showed that there was a lot of pressure on judges to get through cases, there was nothing rushed about Fried's supervision. He gave every case that his assistants brought to him for discussion the same degree of careful, respectful consideration. "If you brought John a case — from murder to loitering for the purposes of prostitution — he would stop and think and get a look in his eye like he's never seen this kind of case before," said Kougasian. "He would open up a serious discussion with, 'What's the evidence here?'"

Sonia credited her supervisors with giving her a remarkably balanced view of the work they were called to do:

I remember many a session in John Fried's and then Warren Murray's office in which we discussed not the prosecution of cases but their dismissals because we simply had insufficient or unpersuasive evidence. In the office I was a part of, it was never the verdict at the end of the case that mattered but whether we had carefully and fully investigated all avenues of evidence, put forth the best and the most potent arguments in a skilled manner and fairly presented the evidence to the jury for determination.

I also remember many a session with John and Warren when we talked about what was fair and just in the plea offers we extended — fair and just in light of the strength of our case and its impact on both society and the defendant. Although vigorous prosecution was important, so was compassion when the circumstances warranted it.[31]

Years after leaving the office, Sonia still wondered how Morgenthau first recognized her potential as a trial attorney. "I don't know how he saw the chord in me that responded so strongly to trial work," she said. But he was right. The obsession she had as a child for *Perry Mason* hinted at her calling as a prosecutor, commercial lawyer, and judge. Even though she had reasons to move on, she recognized that she came into her own at the DA's office. "I loved litigating," she said. "I loved being a prosecutor. It was wonderful and enormously gratifying work that I enjoyed tremendously. Most of all, however, I loved being in an office surrounded by people whose values I respected and who taught me so many important lessons."

The training, supervision, and years of trial preparation and experience at the DA's office formed the habits that would make her stand out to those with the power to advance her legal career. "I was taught to be thorough in my investigations, careful in my fact finding, meticulous in my legal arguments," she said. "All of this while I juggled hundreds of cases. I was taught to apply facts to law — the cornerstone of lawyering. I was taught to think about the needs of society and to respond to those needs by prosecuting vigorously and with passion. Yet, most of all, I was taught to do justice."[32]

The lessons she learned included an understanding of the unified mission of everyone working in the criminal justice system. She learned to respect the work of defense attorneys as defenders of the Constitution and its "promised rights to individuals and to our society." The DA's office showed her that both sides in the criminal system are equally necessary and equally important to doing justice. "I never saw defense attorneys as enemies," she said, "we were and are soldiers on the same side only with different roles. The goal of the mission is the same: justice."

Sonia described her chance meeting with Morgenthau in a Yale Law School conference room as the most special moment of her life. He gave her the opportunity to live the life that had enticed her since the age of eight. After learning to love crime solving from Nancy Drew books, *Perry Mason* had shown her what law and order was all about — everyone with a title in those final courtroom scenes was a good guy:

> I may have been the only fan of the show who liked the ever-losing prosecutor, Berger. My like for him developed from one episode in which Perry Mason expressed sympathy for the frustration Berger had to be feeling after working so hard on his case and having it dismissed. Berger responded by observing that as a prosecutor his job was to find the truth and that if the truth led to the acquittal of the innocent and the

dismissal of his case, then he had done his job right and justice had been served. His speech stayed with me my entire life and shaped my perception of what prosecutors did.

"Every once in a while, television does a good thing," she said.

The official portrait of United States Supreme Court Associate Justice Sonia Sotomayor, the 111th justice. COLLECTION OF THE SUPREME COURT OF THE UNITED STATES

Isla de Ratones, "Mouse Island," near Cabo Rojo on Puerto Rico's west coast, where Sonia Sotomayor went swimming with her cousins during her summer visits to the island.
ANTONIA FELIX

The Sotomayors moved from the crime-ravaged South Bronx to Co-op City in the North Bronx in 1970 when Sonia was a sophomore in high school. COURTESY OF RIVERBAY CORPORATION

Sonia Sotomayor's class at the New York District Attorney's office, 1983. She is centered in the second row with her supervisor Warren Murray in front at the left and Manhattan District Attorney Robert Morgenthau at the right. FROM THE COLLECTION OF HUGH H. MO

	WINDOW	WINDOW	WINDOW	
⊃ IA GES FT NLING ILDING	FIRE ESCAPE & UNDER WINDOW GATE	LADDER FROM ABANDONED BUILDING ROOF TO OCCUPIED WINDOW APARTMENT IN AIRSHAFT	ABANDONED BUILDING TO OCCUPIED APARTMENT VIA WINDOW LEDGES IN AIRSHAFT	PL/ N B
⊃BINSON ASED)	LOUIS SIMMONS (FACE)	ROBERT CLARK (DECEASED) ISRI PERSUAD (SHOT AT)	LUCY BROWN (SHOT AT)	ARNOLD (H

The handmade chart Sonia Sotomayor produced for the jury when she prosecuted the "Tarzan Murderer" with lead counsel Hugh Mo. ANTONIA FELIX

Newly sworn-in United States District Court Judge Sonia Sotomayor at a party in her honor in 1992 with Richard Mattiaccio (LEFT), her friend and fellow partner at the law firm Pavia & Harcourt, and U.S. Second Circuit Judge Dennis Jacobs (RIGHT). Judge Sotomayor was appointed to this federal bench by President George H. W. Bush and in 1988 would be named to the higher federal court, the Second Circuit Court of Appeals, by President Bill Clinton. RICHARD MATTIACCIO

Courtroom artist Christine Cornell's rendering of the March 31, 1995, Daniel Silverman v. Major League Baseball Player Relations Committee Inc. hearing in the United States District Court for the Southern District of New York, Judge Sonia Sotomayor presiding. Foreground: Daniel Silverman, regional director of the National Labor Relations Board; far left: Francis L. Casey III, representing the owners; seated: Donald Fehr, executive director of the Major League Baseball Players Association (MLBPA), the players' union; and in the background: George H. Cohen, an attorney for the MLPBA. DRAWING BY CHRISTINE CORNELL, COURTESY OF GEORGE H. COHEN

Celina and Sonia Sotomayor on the day of Sonia's formal investiture ceremony to the United States Supreme Court, September 8, 2009. GETTY IMAGES/AFP

President Barack Obama and Justice Sonia Sotomayor talk in the Green Room prior to the start of a reception honoring Sotomayor at the White House, August 12, 2009. OFFICIAL WHITE HOUSE PHOTO BY PETE SOUZA

United States Supreme Court Associate Justice Sonia Soto-mayor in front of the Court after her formal investiture cere-mony, September 8, 2009. ALEX WONG/GETTY IMAGES

New York Yankees' Jorge Posada escorts Justice Soto-mayor onto the field at Yankee Stadium on September 26, 2009, where she threw out the ceremonial first pitch before the game against the Boston Red Sox. JARED WICKERHAM /GETTY IMAGES

Members of the United States Supreme Court photographed on September 29, 2009. FRONT ROW (L-R): *Associate Justice Anthony M. Kennedy, Associate Justice John Paul Stevens, Chief Justice John G. Roberts, Associate Justice Antonin Scalia, and Associate Justice Clarence Thomas.* BACK ROW (L-R): *Associate Justice Samuel Alito Jr., Associate Justice Ruth Bader Ginsburg, Associate Justice Stephen Breyer, and Associate Justice Sonia Sotomayor.* COLLECTION OF THE SUPREME COURT OF THE UNITED STATES

Chapter 6
A Fendi Crush

"Helen! I've found something" she whispered hoarsely. "Better stand back!"
Nancy pressed harder. This time the right side of the cabinet began to move forward. . . . Slowly, very slowly, one end of the cabinet began to move into the parlor, the other into an open space behind it. Helen grabbed Nancy's hand in fright. What were they going to find in the secret passageway?

— From Carolyn Keene [Mildred Benson], *Nancy Drew and the Hidden Staircase*, 1930

Ambition played a role in Sonia Sotomayor's decision to move on from the district attorney's office, but not in the way one would expect. It takes ambition to excel at Princeton and Yale and stand out among your peers in perhaps the most demanding prosecutor's office in the country, but Sotomayor expressed a dynamic of ambition that we don't read much about in the theories of Freud, Maslow, and Adler in Psych 101.

At the farewell party Sotomayor's district attorney's office colleagues threw for her in an Italian restaurant near the office, former Trial Part 50 deputy bureau chief Richard Girgente asked her why she was leaving. Many of the best and brightest who make up each incoming class at the office stay on for years, relishing the opportunity to take on bigger and bigger cases. Girgente, perhaps more than anyone, knew what a great success Sonia had made for herself as a prosecutor, especially in light of her convictions in the Hyman and Maddicks cases. "People make a career out of being in that office," he said. "It's not like some United States Attorney's offices where people are there for three years and move right on to private practice."

Sotomayor gave Girgente a surprising answer. Given the fact that she had childhood diabetes, she told him, she felt that her time was very precious. In case the disease affected her longevity, she wanted to accomplish and give back as much as possible. "She always viewed herself as a role model for Latino women in New York City," Girgente recalled, "and she felt she had opportunities many others did not have and therefore had a higher responsibility to be a role model. There wasn't time to languish in one place."

Sotomayor's response reminded Girgente of the adage that to whom much is given, much is expected. "No one felt that more than she did," he said. "She felt she'd been given much — good family, good education and success in school and at the DA's office. No one expected more of Sonia than Sonia."

The private legal profession was exploding in New York City and everywhere else when Sotomayor made her move to the firm of Pavia & Harcourt in April 1984. In the mergers-and-acquisitions frenzy of the 1980s, the number of lawyers working in every type of private firm across the country increased by 71 percent. For a young lawyer with stellar academic credentials and equally impressive references from Morgenthau's office, the pickings were very good among firms of all sizes.

Pavia & Harcourt, housed about two blocks from Central Park in an office tower at 600 Madison Avenue, worked hard to recruit her. The partners who interviewed her portrayed the firm as the ideal place for a young associate who wanted experience in international law and was keen to start trying cases in the courtroom as soon as possible. Those were real opportunities at Pavia & Harcourt, which employed about thirty lawyers at the time, unlike the scenarios at the mega-firms, which employed hundreds of associates who had to compete for cases and rarely if ever got into the courtroom. "She had other options," said Richard Mattiaccio, who had been working at the firm for one year when Sotomayor arrived. "It was a hands-on practice and a dynamic atmosphere. There was a lot of European investment in the U.S. at the time. She wanted to try cases and argue in court, rather than be a mid-level person on a large legal team."[1]

It was a good fit. Pavia & Harcourt, a boutique firm, or one that worked within a few areas of specialty, promised to train her quickly in civil litigation. Her performance as a criminal litigator at the DA's office left them no doubt she would be a quick study, and her fluency in Spanish would also be an important asset. The firm's specialization in international law dated back to its founding in 1940, when it set up shop specifically to represent Italian companies doing business in the United States. As the firm grew, it continued to bring in bilingual lawyers to work with its European clientele.

Pavia's managing partner, George M.

Pavia, recalled that "we had an opening for a litigator, and her resume was perfect. She's an excellent lawyer, a careful preparer of cases." He attributed her success in winning "victory after victory in court" for the firm to her combination of academic training, work ethic, and self-assured bearing in court. "That's what lawyering used to be all about," he said. "Litigation is a particular side of the law that requires a great number of personal assets. They have to be quick on their feet, they have to be good citizens, they can't go burning flags or dollar bills in the court."[2]

Mattiaccio, who came to Pavia & Harcourt from a large Wall Street firm, was glad to welcome Sotomayor and get her started as a civil litigator. "I remember being so relieved when I heard she was coming," he said, "because we were very busy at the time. We were a small firm and the work was expanding very rapidly because the client base was becoming more involved in the U.S." With more European clients, each investing themselves in the American market, came more problems, more contract disputes, and more litigation, he explained.

His newest colleague faced a steep learning curve to overcome the gulf between criminal and civil law. A big part of her education was weekly meetings with everyone in the firm, including the partners — another advantage of working for a smaller establishment. "Everyone knew what everyone else was doing," said Mattiaccio, "so we would get together and talk about our cases and share our ideas for how to handle them on a regular basis. The youngest associate would be there and get the benefit of being in that discussion; you learn what the considerations are." The exchange was also productive for the more senior members of the firm, as partners would benefit by hearing other perspectives and approaches.

In her eight years at Pavia & Harcourt from 1984 to 1992, Sotomayor worked for European clients such as Ferrari, Pirelli Tire, and Fendi on issues ranging from real estate and customs to product liability and trademarks. She did extensive work with foreign buyers of American grain, conducting arbitration hearings through which they resolved their disputes with sellers out of court. These out-of-court procedures were handled through the American Arbitration Association (AAA), an organization that provides all the administrative resources for resolving disputes. When Sotomayor's grain clients got into a dispute, it was often over quality issues with a very large shipment. "It's a very narrow, specialized area," Mattiaccio said, "but it's a lot like maritime practice because very often you're dealing with a shipload of grain. It's also similar to product liability warranty-type practice because you're usually arguing over whether or not the grain that was delivered was the grain that was ordered, or if it was of inferior quality, and there are usually large stakes involved."

Most of Sotomayor's more than fifteen arbitration hearings involved grain commodity trading, but she also carried out hearings for customers in the banking, tire, fashion, and other industries.

Settling a shipping dispute or defending a luxury auto manufacturer in conflict with one of its franchises in the United States were typical cases for Sotomayor, and the predominantly European client base at Pavia & Harcourt gave her work a lot of international flair. But the work she enjoyed the most was the intellectual property cases, defending the trademarks and copyrights of high-profile designers like Fendi. Fighting the counterfeiting rackets drew most strongly on her experience as a New York prosecutor and literally took her legal battles to the streets.

In her second year at Pavia & Harcourt,

Sotomayor created Fendi's national anti-counterfeiting program with the late Frances Bernstein, a partner at the firm. At that time, the only New York law dealing with fake goods was a little-enforced misdemeanor offense under the Arts and Cultural Affairs Law. Firms like Pavia & Harcourt helped break new ground in the 1980s by vigorously pursuing counterfeiters and bringing the industry into public awareness. Sotomayor was put in charge of the anticounterfeiting program for Fendi when she was made partner at the firm in 1988 until she left in 1992. A significant part of that work involved helping establish and participating in the newly formed New York Anticounterfeiting Task Force, a group of companies and political figures committed to upgrading New York's trademark counterfeiting laws. Veronica Hrdy, the intellectual property attorney at Chanel, Inc., spearheaded the task force, and Sotomayor was one of the first to become involved.

When Sotomayor and Bernstein launched the Fendi program, counterfeiting was organized crime on a global scale and was dramatically expanding its reach into the lucrative knockoff markets in America's big cities. In roughly the span that Sotomayor worked at the firm, the International Trade Commission estimated that losses from counterfeiting and piracy rose from $5.5 to more than $60 billion. New York City was losing about $350 million in tax dollars from sales of illegal products ranging from fake Rolexes and Major League Baseball hats to toys and handbags.

The damage went far beyond overexposing a designer logo and reducing sales of luxury goods, although those were the most direct effects on Sotomayor's clients. The manufacture of fake goods eliminated hundreds of thousands of jobs, such as those in the American auto industry who suffered from trade in counterfeit auto parts, and it continues to exploit child labor in sweatshops in New York and Asia and produces dangerous merchandise such as toys made of toxic and breakable materials. And according to the FBI, U.S. Customs, and Interpol, counterfeiting is also connected to terrorism. In the 1990s, the FBI collected strong evidence that the 1993 bombing of the World Trade Center (WTC) was financed by a store on Broadway that sold fake T-shirts and other textiles. The followers of Sheik Omar Abdel-Rahman, the blind cleric who was convicted of conspiring to blow up New York City landmarks after the terrorist bombing on the WTC in 1993, would later run a large-scale, multimillion-dollar scam involving counterfeit Nike and Olympic T-shirts.

Clamping down on the counterfeiters in New York City was a group effort by a handful of firms who represented targeted designers. The first step in a typical attempt to seize counterfeit merchandise in Chinatown was to hire investigators to purchase some suspected fake products, which would then be inspected by the client. The private investigators went undercover, often posing as tourists and using disguises so as not to be recognized on future assignments. Sotomayor and lawyers at other firms pooled their resources by working with the same investigators who would purchase several fake brands at once, as the counterfeit stores carried an entire range of fake goods such as Fendi, Louis Vuitton, Gucci, Rolex, and Cartier.

Sotomayor would then show the purchased items to her client, often Carla Fendi, one of the five Fendi sisters who owned the Italian company in those days. When Fendi determined they were fakes, Sotomayor would go before a judge to try to get an ex parte seizure order, which allows the representative of a trademark owner to seize counterfeit merchandise without giving advance notice. This type of order was a new tool in the legal trade, the product of a federal trademark protection law passed in 1984. Being a federal law, however, it was out of the jurisdiction of state law enforcement agencies.

Sotomayor went to court to seek a seizure order about once every other month from 1989 to 1992. According to her own summary of those applications, she was required to provide "extensive submission of evidence documenting Fendi's trademark rights, its protection of its marks, the nature of the investigation against the vendors, and Fendi's right to ex parte injunctive relief."[3] That evidence included samples of genuine and counterfeit Fendi items that would be shown to the court to point out their differences. The statute also stipulated that Sotomayor prove that "an immediate and irreparable injury will occur if such seizure is not ordered" and that "the person against whom seizure would be ordered, or persons acting in concert with such person, would destroy, move, hide, or otherwise make such matter inaccessible to the court, if the applicant were to proceed on notice to such person."[4]

Like the multiuse investigator team, the seizure order was a collaborative effort. "Very often it was done in combination with other trademark holders because you'd have half a dozen brands represented at a store with counterfeit product," explained Mattiaccio. "They were called John Doe orders because they were usually not addressed to anyone in particular because you didn't know who was actually doing the selling." With an order in hand, Sotomayor and her anticounterfeiting associates acquired a team of U.S. marshals, the federal law enforcement officers who could enforce the trademark law, or, if they were not available, personnel from private security companies to drive them to the site and guard their safety. The firm also notified the police about the scheduled raids so that if things got out of control, they would be aware of the circumstances.

Sotomayor frequently collaborated with the same private security companies and lawyers in this work. Heather McDonald, one of the lawyers who often accompanied her on raids of counterfeit shops in Chinatown, knew all too well how violent the work could be. On one of her first raids, before teaming up with Sotomayor, she was pulling counterfeit watches out of a display case when someone smashed her hand with a metal pipe. The attack broke all the knuckles in her hand. "It was a wake-up call early on that they weren't messing around," she said.

McDonald and Sotomayor met in early 1987 at a conference of the International

Anticounterfeiting Coalition (IACC), an organization founded in 1979 that offers training, lobbying assistance, and access to experts in the "intellectual property enforcement field" who can help companies protect their patents and trademarks.[5] "We instantly hit it off, talking about our clients and the similar problems we were having," said McDonald. "We joined forces on the enforcement front because it was more cost effective and made a bigger impact."

McDonald, who at the time worked at another firm for clients that included Rolex and Louis Vuitton, is now a partner at Baker Hostetler where she continues to work in anticounterfeiting. Focusing on anticounterfeiting over the past three decades has made her a legend in Chinatown, where she is known as the Dragon Lady. Her photo is taped to the walls and counters of the shops that line Canal Street, including one that contains a red, slashed-out circle imposed over her image as if to say, "Watch Out for this Woman — She Will Take Your Stuff!"

Every store along the north and south sides of Canal Street had countless fake purses, watches, scarves, and other items brazenly on display, as the police did not have the manpower to prioritize enforcing the meager trademark protection in the arts and culture law. "Arts law had a million things wrong with it," said McDonald. "I think if you paid a two-dollar fine you could get your goods back. The counterfeit market was like the Wild, Wild West because the police couldn't do anything about it," she said.

When all the pieces were in place to conduct a raid, Sotomayor and McDonald joined their security team in a van or truck and drove down to the site. Protocol held that the lawyers were to stay in the van until the security team had cleared out any troublemakers, then walk safely into the shop to search for items carrying the label of their clients. Sotomayor and McDonald, however, rarely waited for the all-clear, instead strapping on bulletproof vests and rushing into the mix with the armed security people, many of whom were former NYPD officers. "We didn't take direction that easily," said McDonald. "Before you knew it, we were running down the street chasing these guys down." Although the Chinatown gangs never used guns to try to fend off anticounterfeiting teams, they did use an array of other weapons and street confrontations were routinely dangerous.

All the shop owners paid protection money to the gangs, who tried to protect the shops by attacking the security teams with home-made explosives and knives, smashing up the vans, and slashing their tires. "All of a sudden there would be twenty young men in front of the van when we pulled up," said Andrew Oberfeldt, one of the security men who has worked on raids with McDonald since 1991, when Sotomayor was still working with her. Oberfeldt, a member of the New York Police Department's Emergency Service Unit, or SWAT team, was working off-duty for a private security company when he first teamed up with McDonald, and he now owns his own private security company. Although Oberfeldt did not remember Sotomayor specifically, having worked with countless lawyers on raids over the past thirty years and with only McDonald consistently, his recollections of raids during that time accurately reflect the situations in which Sotomayor repeatedly found herself. "We always hit a few shops at a time and the whole block would react to us," he said. "There'd be a fight, screaming, pushing and shoving, and somebody gets hit with a chair. We'd repel the attack and get everybody out of the way."

The gangs attacked with large (and illegal) M-80 firecrackers, improvised explosives such as a coffee can filled with black powder, knives, box cutters, sharp pieces of metal, baseball bats, and, in one case that Oberfeldt recalled, an oversize steel padlock that hit one of the security men in the head. "They used a lot of explosives," said Oberfeldt. "One guy I brought along got a shrapnel cut the first day and refused to come back."

If anything started getting thrown at the lawyers, the security person assigned to each would perform classic bodyguard technique by covering that person with his body and rushing her back to the van. Oberfeldt recalled grabbing McDonald in a bear hug and running her back to the van on many occasions. Whoever was not assigned a specific person to protect stood and fought. "Heather wanted to fight half the time," said Oberfeldt. "She has a pretty steely resolve."

Protecting the lawyers became standard procedure at the beginning of the raid when they wanted to get into the shop and at the end when they needed to get back in the van. Gang members or store owners sometimes went for the bagged-up goods. "Inside the shops we would be writing the inventory sheets and collecting stuff in bags, out of harm's way," said McDonald. "But at some point you have to come out. They would try to rush us and rip the bags or grab the stuff and run away with it." And they never knew when an M-80 might get lobbed from a dark alleyway.

Crime was at an all-time high in New York City during this period, and Oberfeldt felt more threatened on his runs with McDonald's anticounterfeiting group than in his regular job with the NYPD. "I wasn't afraid to go to work," he said. "I was afraid to go to Chinatown."

After loading everyone back in the vans, the security team would drive away and park two or three blocks away to hit another place. "It wasn't uncommon to raid for seven hours, have lunch and go up to Midtown to raid for another five hours," said Oberfeldt. Those long and grueling yet exciting days built camaraderie. Spending an entire day serving ex parte seizure orders with McDonald and the team, running down counterfeiters and rummaging through dingy back rooms and basements in jeans and a T-shirt took Sotomayor back to her days as a prosecutor, and she thrived on it. Speaking to the International Anti-counterfeiting Coalition a few years later, after she had become a judge, she admitted that she had enjoyed the anticounterfeiting program more than any of her other "diverse and stimulating" work at Pavia & Harcourt and that her "investigative experience with the Manhattan DA's office came in handy" when battling counterfeiters.[6]

Some of her seizures took in enormous hauls of fake product, such as one raid in 1990 that collected twenty-three thousand handbags that would have sold for an average of $45 apiece. The originals, Sotomayor told the *Wall Street Journal* one year later, cost about $350 each.

Finding hidden stashes of counterfeit bags and watches took some creative investigative work in Chinatown. The vendors in Chinatown continually shifted the inventory of their counterfeit goods to try to keep a step ahead of the seizure teams. "It very quickly became obvious that if it was on open display it would be subject to seizure," said McDonald, "so they moved it." First they shuffled items behind the counter, and once investigators began looking there they started hiding goods in the basement. When it became routine to search shop basements, the vendors created elaborately constructed secret compartments and back rooms. McDonald recalled discovering a room hidden behind a door that blended into a back wall and slid open, *Star Trek*–like, with the touch of a remote control device. In another place that appeared to have no basement, they found a ladder hidden beneath a removable piece of flooring inside a row of cabinets.

Fighting the highly organized crime of counterfeiting was serious business, but trips through the back rooms of Chinatown had their humorous moments. "One day we followed a guy who walked into a large closet," said Oberfeldt, "and when we opened the doors it was empty. I leaned on the back wall and it started to move, just like in an old Abbott and Costello movie. It swung open and I fell into a stash of all this stuff."

Sotomayor and McDonald searched for fake goods in every nook and cranny of a vendor's property, sorting through piles in nasty-smelling basements and moldy back rooms. After the secret-room and hidden-door phase, the seizure teams started going after the landlords who rented out the shop space because they could be liable if they had knowledge of illegal activity. When the landlords started to evict people, much of the counterfeit sales moved out of the stores. At first it went into buildings within a six-block radius of the main drag of Canal Street, as McDonald describes it. "Shoppers would come out of the Canal Street subway," she said, "and be met by people who asked, 'You want Gucci?' They'd lead these groups to unmarked doors of buildings and show them all the counterfeit merchandise."

When Sotomayor and McDonald successfully tracked down those locations and put pressure on the landlords, the vendors moved their enterprises into vans. "If you got in a helicopter and took a view from above," said McDonald, "you could watch me come down with a seizure order and probably see anywhere from fifty to eighty vans start driving out of town like in a spiderweb, driving to get away." The rolling shops are still on the streets, parked all over Chinatown, and McDonald has heard stories of shoppers getting locked in and going for an unscheduled ride when a driver flees the scene to prevent getting caught.

Selling fake designer goods wasn't limited to downtown. Steven Skulnik, one of Sotomayor's fellow lawyers at Pavia & Harcourt, recalled going on a raid with Sotomayor to Dapper Dan's Boutique in Harlem in 1988. Renowned for his bootleg designer clothing, which was in high demand among hip-hop artists and other celebrities, Dapper Dan's shop was a famous locale on 125th Street. "He was using the Fendi logo on leather jackets, covers for tires on the back of jeeps, anything that you could do with it," said Skulnik. "They put the Fendi logo on it because that was deemed to be very hot in the hip hop market."

As Nelson George wrote in *Hip Hop Amer-*

ica, "It was at Dan's shop, and in the others that followed his lead, that large swatches of material embossed with designer emblems (Gucci, Louis Vuitton, Fendi, MCM) were cut to fit hubcaps, Jeeps, and furniture, where elite Italian and French brand names were married to hip hop style."[7] On behalf of Fendi, Sotomayor gathered evidence about Dapper Dan's use of trademarked Fendi logos in his own designs and received the seizure order.

When the van arrived at the store, the security team told Skulnik and Sotomayor that they were going to go in and make sure it was all clear, and then they would come back and tell the lawyers to come in. "Sonia wasn't going to wait for any all-clear," said Skulnik. "She went charging right in. I stayed in the van."

Looking back over the development of the anticounterfeiting program at the firm, Skulnik recalled that the Dapper Dan raid was one of the earlier ones in which the security people were carrying guns but the lawyers were not assigned Kevlar vests. "You're coming in to seize somebody's entire business," he said, "and they're a quasi-criminal enterprise, so people do get upset under those circumstances. I had never been to one before, so I didn't know what to expect." When he did go into the store, Skulnik noted that the walls were covered with photographs of famous entertainers and athletes wearing Dapper Dan's fake Fendi apparel. He and the team found a stash of counterfeit inventory in a barely lit "rabbit's warren of warehouse space" situated behind the storefront.

Skulnik described Sotomayor as having a command, take-charge personality and acting like "a kind of cop/prosecutor doing what she needed to do to close up this guy's business." As the case proceeded, Dapper Dan did not show up in court, so the judge issued a default judgment in favor of Fendi. All the merchandise Sotomayor had seized from his store was destroyed.

One raid was enough for Skulnik, and more than enough for another associate at the firm who accompanied Sotomayor on a raid sometime later. "He was very upset," Skulnik recalled. "He didn't realize it was going to be something where people had guns and he was very upset with her. 'I didn't sign up for this,' he said, 'I'm a real estate lawyer; you shouldn't be asking associates to do things like that.'" Skulnik — who has a lot of respect for Sotomayor, enjoyed working with her, and invited her to his wedding — understood the associate's concern.

"I was glad I did it once and didn't have to do it again," he said. "I like to do what I do, commercial litigation."

For a few days in the autumn of 1988, Sotomayor participated in a seizure order related to another counterfeiting niche in the city, professional sports items. Major League Baseball Properties, Inc., which regularly battled manufacturers and sellers of products carrying fake team logos, faced a big challenge when the playoffs came to Shea Stadium that year. They knew that counterfeit vendors would show up in large numbers to catch fans at the exit ramps leading off of Grand Central Parkway and in the parking lots surrounding the stadium, so they engaged a team of investigators and lawyers to assist with seizures.

Tom Ostertag, the attorney with MLB Properties who led the anticounterfeiting program at the time, knew of at least one warehouse in Brooklyn producing fake Major League Baseball products. "They silkscreened team logos onto large quantities of T-shirts, hundreds of thousands of them," he said. The cut-up labels in the shirts indicated that they may have been rejects from a brand-name company, and the cheap silkscreening job made the fakes easy to spot. "When you put it in the wash the first time, the logo was going to wash right off," he said. "That's why we still warn our fans not to buy it — it's not going to be worth the five dollars you paid for it." But many fans did buy T-shirts, sweatshirts, and hats from the vendors who came to their car windows while they were stuck in traffic or sold them out of the back of their station wagons in the parking lot.

The counterfeiters doled out product to a number of vendors from the large quantities they kept in vans around the stadium parking lots so that if a station wagon vendor got served with a seizure, only a fraction of the inventory would get seized. Sotomayor and her investigators targeted the vans to confiscate the larger quantities of goods.

The playoffs between the Los Angeles Dodgers and New York Mets had started in Los Angeles and moved to New York the weekend of October 7. The first game that Friday night was rained out, and the weather wasn't much better the next day. The rain and cold temperatures took a toll on the playing field and on the teams chasing after vendors. "Most of the activity took place with the fans there," said Ostertag, "so they were darting around cars in the parking lot and on the exit ramps. It was a real mess."

Sotomayor spent one of those game days racing after vans full of counterfeit gear with Dempster Leech, a private investigator who was perhaps the most colorful figure working in anticounterfeiting in the 1980s and 1990s. That day, Sotomayor made chase on the back of a motorcycle, zigzagging through traffic and dodging pedestrians in the cold. The experience shook her up enough that she never got on a motorcycle again. She later joked that she "had lost reason in the heat of pursuit by ever getting on the motorcycle as a passenger at all."[8]

Leech was one of the most prominent figures in anticounterfeiting in the city. He had founded his own private investigation company, Harper Associates, and in the course of his career was shot, stabbed, bitten, and hit over the head with a baseball bat. In the late 1980s, his investigations helped lead to the arrest of counterfeiter and Born to Kill (BTK) gang leader David Thai, who cornered the market on fake watches in Chinatown. Thai bragged on TV's *48 Hours* that he made $13 million on watches in 1988 alone.

In his testimony about counterfeiting to a U.S. senate judiciary committee in 1995, Leech described Thai's approach to forcing Chinatown vendors to sell his wares: "With a following of young, disenfranchised and violent boys behind him, David's sales approach to the street vendors didn't have to be subtle. 'Buy my watches or I'll kill you.'"[9]

At another legislative hearing in 1991 Leech described the danger anticounterfeiting teams faced in confronting armed BTK gang members who had committed murder and other "terrible atrocities." The lawyers and investigators "go out in the street and take counterfeit watches and take counterfeit handbags right out of the hands of these guys, and frankly, I have been informed that at least one of the young attorneys here and myself . . . have a ten thousand dollar bounty on our heads."[10] He may have been referring to Sotomayor, because she was at that hearing, but by 2009 Leech had "fallen off the face of the Earth," according to Chanel's Veronica Hrdy, and I was not able to track him down to ask him about the identity of that attorney.

Leech's overview of the high-profit, low-risk business of counterfeiting to one of the legislative committees revealed why Pavia & Harcourt gained so much business from clients like Fendi in the 1980s and 1990s. Counterfeiters had declared war on luxury good companies with profit margins that rivaled those of the narcotics trade:

I can have a low quality quartz watch, similar in outward appearance to a high-priced designer watch, shipped here from Hong Kong (without the trademarks) for $3, my cost to import. I can get a worker to counterfeit the watch — that is, put on the trade names and logos, for fifty cents. Once the counterfeit marks are on this watch, I can sell it to a distributor for $8.00. More than a 200% mark-up. The distributor-retailer will sell the watch for $15 to $25 in New York City. If the distributor ships the watch out of state, he might be able to get $50 to $60 and the retailer could get $100 or more. $100 for a counterfeit watch that cost $3.50 to produce. The profit margins rival the profits from the sale of narcotics. But as one counterfeiter carefully explained to me, the risks aren't nearly the same. And that's what Organized Crime finds so attractive about counterfeiting — high profits, low risks.[11]

Leech made those remarks to the Senate judiciary committee to express his support of a consumer protection law in 1995. Four years earlier, Sotomayor had also supported new legislation, but in an even more effectual way by actually writing it for the state of New York.

Fendi uncovered counterfeit activity in well-known retail stores as well as Chinatown shops and marauding vans. It claimed that one of these chains, Burlington Coat Factory, was knowingly trafficking in counterfeit Fendi bags, perfume, and other merchandise. Sotomayor brought the case to trial in federal court in 1987, and was the sole attorney for Fendi working the trial. The case settled with a monetary award for Fendi as well as a court injunction that prohibited Burlington Coat Factory from buying or selling any Fendi-branded merchandise unless they received permission in writing from Fendi. Even if Burlington were to buy genuine Fendi stock, it was legally obligated to get the manufacturer's permission first so that Fendi could determine whether it was in fact genuine.

In spite of achieving that settlement, Sotomayor's client continued to have a problem with the Burlington stores. In a case still being deliberated in 2009, lawyers representing Fendi have found that the stores continued selling Fendi products without permission, "in willful violation of consent injunction." After receiving the court injunction in 1987, "Burlington did not implement any internal control mechanisms to prevent it from dealing in Fendi-branded merchandise prior to obtaining the necessary consent of Fendi," stated one court record. "In fact, Burlington's in-house counsel . . . admitted that he was not aware of a single piece of writing concerning any steps that the company took to comply with this permanent injunction."[12]

Some of the same players are working the current case, including Richard Mattiaccio, who now represents Fendi at another firm, and New York Southern District Judge Leonard Sand, who tried Sotomayor's case back in 1987 and was assigned the new case nearly two decades later. Mattiaccio, who had slipped into Sotomayor's courtroom a few times during her 1987 trial, said that Burlington Coat Factory has been sued for selling counterfeit Fendi goods and also held in contempt for not adhering to the ruling Sotomayor obtained for Fendi in the settlement.

In late 1986, after nearly two years of amassing Fendi knockoffs during seizure raids, Sotomayor developed an idea for getting rid of the stockpile and drawing attention to her client's legal successes at the same time. Carla Fendi flew in to New York to take part in Sotomayor's publicity event, the

Fendi Crush, set up outside Tavern on the Green, the famous restaurant inside Central Park. The production began at 10:30 A.M. on Wednesday, November 12, with media on hand to watch paint get poured over thousands of counterfeit Fendi handbags, shoes, wallets, and other accessories. Once destroyed in that colorful fashion, the items were crushed in garbage trucks.

At the event, Sotomayor told a *New York Times* reporter that clamping down on counterfeiters was a lot like going after a drug operation:

> We attempt to go after suppliers and secure information that leads back to the manufacturers. We go after U.S. retailers to the degree that we send cease-and-desist orders and request that they voluntarily cooperate and turn over the counterfeits.
>
> We have yet to meet a retail seller who admits "I knew." It is our position that if they had used a standard of diligence and compared them to a genuine Fendi, they would have known.[13]

When looking back at the heyday of Fendi legal proceedings in the 1980s and 1990s, George Pavia called Sotomayor's over-the-top Fendi Crush "the pinnacle of our achievement."[14] But the height of Sotomayor's accomplishments in anticounterfeiting, at least in terms of its lasting effect, was her role in making trademark counterfeiting part of the New York penal code.

In 1990, Sotomayor, McDonald, and Hrdy, the chief intellectual property lawyer at Chanel, worked together to lobby the New York legislature to adopt a state trademark counterfeiting law. Hrdy contacted people who she thought would be interested in lobbying for this change, and Sotomayor was among those who jumped on the bandwagon quickly. Hrdy spearheaded the idea after realizing that the only way companies like Chanel and Fendi were ever going to get law enforcement to take action was to upgrade the law from a slap-on-the-wrist misdemeanor to a felony.

Hrdy developed her first ideas about the general scope of the law out of conversations with someone who had made headway with upgrading copyright law for the recording industry. With that guidance in mind, Sotomayor reasoned that a new statute could be based on existing laws such as those regarding property theft. "Sonia did the initial draft of the new law," Hrdy said, "paralleling it against the larceny statutes in New York." By equating a trademark with a property right, Sotomayor reasoned, prosecutors would "not have to develop new areas of law." The proposed law would refer the courts back to issues already established in the larceny statute.[15]

In August 1991, Sotomayor explained the task force's proposed statute in detail at a legislative hearing arranged by New York Assemblymen Sheldon Silver, Lewis J. Yevoli, and Morton C. Hillman, and Senator D. M. Volker. All four worked on the committees that had drafted anticounterfeiting bills — Assembly Bill 8125 and Senate 5352-A — which Silver described in his introductory remarks as just "one approach." The legislators sponsoring those bills wanted to draw ideas from the task force and others because "there may be other more effective responses" to the counterfeiting challenge, Silver said.[16] The public event, held on a Wednesday morning in the hearing room of a state office building on lower Broadway, drew about thirty people.

The need for tougher state laws arose from the fact that the federal law enacted seven years earlier wasn't having a strong enough impact on trademark counterfeiting in the state. "The Act contains severe penal sanctions and large monetary fines," said Silver, "and was hailed by manufacturers and trademark owners as the long-awaited enforcement tool that would finally curb the epidemic of commercial counterfeiting. It did not."[17]

Sotomayor, one of eleven speakers who testified at the hearing, was joined by Suffolk County District Attorney James Catterson, city of New York Consumer Affairs Commissioner Mark Green, Major League Baseball Properties general counsel Thomas Ostertag, Rolex Watch president Roland Puton, Cartier chairman Ralph Destino, Chanel counsel Veronica Hrdy, private investigator Dempster Leech, task force attorney Bernard J. Ryan, and Fifth Avenue Association president Tom Cusick.

In her remarks, Sotomayor claimed that a trademark deserved to be protected with the same rigor as any other item defined in the larceny statute:

Since trademark counterfeiting is a larceny — it is a theft. It is not just stealing from consumers, it is stealing from the trademark owner. Trademark owners have one valuable piece of property, and that is the prestige of their name. Every time a counterfeiter takes a product and puts it on — and takes that name and puts it on an inferior product, they steal the prestige from the trademark owner.

The value of that theft should be no different than the values and the degree of crimes that are assigned by the larceny statute.[18]

Sotomayor's five years in the Manhattan DA's office gave her the procedural experience to understand what prosecutors were looking for. She also talked to prosecutors around the state about the task force's proposal and summarized their response:

Prosecutors in New York State . . . tell me, "Look, we know that counterfeits are a part of organized crime, we would like to help you, but all we have is a misdemeanor. Give me an Al Capone state statute, like for Texas, on counterfeiting, and I can take the people at the BTK's [Born to Kill] or I can take some of the organized crime figures that are involved in the sale of other products, and put them away, but I can't do it with a misdemeanor. Give me a felony."[19]

Private investigator Leech's testimony affirmed that tougher laws were necessary "weapons" the task force needed. "In order to nail down the problem," he said, "you have to not only cut the head off the dragon, or cut the feet off the dragon, but you have to crush the dragon. We need as many weapons in the arsenal to do this as we can get. We need your help."[20]

Among the examples of counterfeit selling in New York, Brian Brokate, the lawyer for Rolex, described how counterfeit items were sold in well-known retail stores through the use of code words or a special contact. "Out comes the stuff in a very carefully prepared tray," he said, "which is obviously there so they can be put away easily as well. These people are very sophisticated . . . and for somebody to come into court and say, gee, Your Honor, I just had no idea that this was counterfeit, I mean it is almost absurd."[21]

Roland Puton of Rolex told the gathering that the array of fake Rolexes being sold throughout the state threatened hundreds of jobs and the public's trust in the actual product. "Allowing a counterfeiter to sell watches with the Rolex trademarks is allowing him to steal from Rolex," he said.[22]

The hearing in downtown Manhattan gave Sotomayor and some of the major players on the task force the opportunity to clarify the legal reasoning they used in writing their proposal for the law. Preparing testimony for that event was just one assignment for the group enlisted to write up and lobby for the law. Sotomayor, McDonald, and Hrdy worked on the proposal in each other's conference rooms and that of an assemblyman in Albany, with phone meetings and faxing in between. Lobbyists from the IACC shepherded them around the halls of Albany to help them explain to legislatures and their staff why this was important to trademark holders and the industry in general.[23]

McDonald recalled that working with the state legislature was interesting yet frustrating because the nuts and bolts of the process was more complex and full of variables than they had expected. "You go there thinking very idealistically, 'You've got a problem and we've got a solution,'" McDonald said, "but there was so much deal making and back door negotiating to try to get something done."

The three lawyers were particularly surprised to observe the tangle of conflicting views within one politician's office and the morphed version of their draft bill when it finally became law. One staffer they worked with told them behind closed doors that he thought people were overlegislating in the state. He didn't like this particular law, he told them, but because his boss said they were going to do it, at the end of the day they would pass it. Before opening the door to end their secret conversation, he noted that the law that would go on the books was "not exactly what you're looking for."

According to Hrdy, one of the assemblymen did not want to put more felonies on the books because it would result in a higher potential for putting people in jail. When it came to the number of felony counts in the law, "he basically said we could have two, take it or leave it," Hrdy said. "It didn't seem logical at the time, but the more felonies you have . . . the more likely you'll have people get jail time, which was something they didn't want."

Other inconsistencies in the law as it was actually passed included its failure to clarify whether the value of goods in question meant wholesale or retail and whether it referred to the genuine or counterfeit goods. Mattiaccio, who would take over Sotomayor's work on the bill after she was nominated to the federal bench, recalled that "the language was clear as a bell until it finally went into committee behind closed doors and it came out like sausage." Even though the law was clarified in 1993, it was still a compromise and did not contain all the elements of the original proposal. "But it's better than nothing," said Mattiaccio, "it's in the law; it's been very useful since then."

The law Sotomayor and her associates originated — New York Penal Code Statutes 165.70, 165.71, 165.72, and 165.73 — defines three degrees of trademark counterfeiting. The misdemeanor charge involves manufacturing or selling counterfeit items with an aggregate value below $1,000. Making or selling counterfeit goods worth more than $1,000 is trademark counterfeiting in the second degree, a class E felony, and trafficking in goods worth over $100,000 is counterfeiting in the first degree, a class C felony.

When the bill passed in 1991, Sotomayor and McDonald reacted like gung-ho litigators. "I remember," McDonald said, "having a conversation with her in which we said, 'Now we have to get somebody arrested under this law.'" They and Hrdy had accomplished a feat that brought state law enforcement to bear in the war on counterfeiting, dramatically changing the playing field. Although they were too busy to throw a party, they could pat themselves on the back every time they charged someone under the statute.

Hrdy felt gratified about being part of something that had such tangible results. "I felt like it was a real accomplishment, not just mine but of all the people I worked with. You could see the results — it gave law enforcement a way to go after people who are truly committing a crime. The ability to punish them in a more serious manner does matter. Since then a lot of cases have been brought under New York State counterfeit laws and it has been a real help."

After the law passed, members of the task force met individually and as groups with district attorneys and others in law enforcement to familiarize them with the new statutes. "We made efforts to inform them that if people were found to be counterfeiting it was a real crime and worth more of their time," said Hrdy. The upgrade of the law in New York also motivated the IACC to launch a national effort to help anticounterfeiting groups in other states lobby for tougher laws.

Sotomayor fully expected more states to follow suit. "In the next five or ten years," she told the *San Francisco Chronicle* in 1992, "trademark owners will become more concentrated on changing state laws, changing penalties. They will rely more on local police to make arrests. A real threat of jail does have an impact." But because there would always be people willing to run the risk of illegal production and sales, the black market of counterfeit goods would never disappear and "the only thing companies like Fendi can do is contain the problem as much as is humanly possible," she said.[24]

From the formation of the task force to the successful passage of the law, Hrdy appreciated that Sotomayor was easy to work with and brought so much prosecutorial expertise to the project. "I viewed her as a really bright attorney, and she was a team player," Hrdy said. "She was efficient about doing things and it was easy to divvy things up without making a whole production out of it. She had her opinions but she wasn't someone who would be in your face about expressing them."

Brian Brokate, an attorney with Gibney Anthony & Flaherty who also worked closely with Sotomayor on the task force, described her as a great listener who worked for consensus rather than seeking a way to put forward her own agenda. "Of all the committees I've worked on over the years, this was really collaborative," he said.

McDonald's ongoing work in anticounterfeiting has changed as the means of production and sheer quantity of product has grown over the years. The high demand for fake goods and sophisticated new technology for creating them makes it a tough fight for trademark owners. The production of counterfeits is increasing exponentially from decade to decade; from 1993, when Sotomayor was trying intellectual property cases among many others as a district judge, to 2004, for example, the manufacture of all types of counterfeits from sunglasses to pharmaceuticals to DVDs jumped 1,700 percent.

"We can make it expensive for the ones who supply it," said McDonald, "and we can make it as hard as possible to sell it by taking it out of the stores, but at the end of the day it's a money-making proposition, so there will be supply as long as there's a demand."

In 1997, after five years on the federal bench, Sotomayor met up with her former associates as the guest speaker at an IACC luncheon. After reminiscing about rummaging through Chinatown basements with Heather McDonald and racing around Shea Stadium with Dempster Leech, she discussed some intellectual property cases on which she and other federal judges had ruled. She also offered some advice based on her five years of experience in district court, such as a "forewarning" to lawyers to select the jurisdiction of their cases carefully because "circuits and district courts differ widely on the emphasis and tests they apply to many intellectual property issues."[25] Having brought those type of cases to court as a lawyer herself, she knew that the worst case scenario for a lawyer was having a case dismissed because he or she filed it in the wrong court. In situations like the IACC event, she was more than happy to share tips with lawyers.

Working with international clients and drawing a larger salary than she had earned as a government lawyer enabled Sotomayor to do a lot of traveling during those years. She credits her Pavia & Harcourt colleague Alessandro Saracino Fendi and his wife Fe, along with their parents, for introducing her "to the beauty of the international world."[26] She traveled to Israel in 1986 with a group of Hispanic leaders as part of Project Interchange, an educational program of the American Jewish Committee founded by Debbie Berger. She became lifelong friends of Berger and her husband and would travel to Israel with them again. "She liked to travel," recalled Richard Mattiaccio, "and that was one of the things she did when she had some expendable income."

Even though Sotomayor did not speak Italian, she managed to communicate easily with people at Fendi headquarters in Italy on a day-to-day basis. She was not the least bit intimidated by the related yet unfamiliar language. "The dynamic I recall," said

Mattiaccio, "is that the client would say something in Italian and Sonia would reply in Spanish and they would understand each other."

"She got along very well with the Fendi sisters," Steven Skulnik said, "and they didn't speak any English." During Fendi meetings, he would speak "haltingly" with the bit of Italian he knew, while Sotomayor "would just go as if she was speaking Italian but it was really Spanish. Or sometimes she would take a Spanish word and make it sound Italian."

Sotomayor had an intuitive and highly instructive style of working with her clients. She was very patient and thorough in explaining legal details in a way that could be understood to a particular person's level of understanding. "She would get a sense of where that person was in terms of being ready to receive information," said Mattiaccio, "and key what she was saying to that." She had a very New York style of cutting to the chase with people who at times came off as "quite the snob," he added. "She would break that down, get right through that and develop a rapport with the person." Sotomayor did not talk over, under, or down to people, but conveyed to each of her clients that she really cared about him or her and the case. People knew that "she wasn't doing this because someone asked her to do it," Mattiaccio said. "She would very quickly communicate that she really cared about whatever it was she was doing, and clients sensed that."

The focused personality Sotomayor was known for at the district attorney's office was also seen in her corporate work. She would get so wrapped up in what she was doing that she routinely tuned out things going on around her, even blasting alarms. "Someone would have to go into her office and tell her there was a fire drill going on," said Mattiaccio. "That's the way she worked, with that level of intensity." Her friends in the office didn't take it personally if she didn't look up to say hello when they passed by the office, but rather understood that she was simply engrossed in her work. "That's the kind of intelligence she has," said Skulnik, "it's a work ethic, it's a focus, it's ambition and all those things."

That did not mean she was one-dimensional. Her associates saw her ability to leave it all behind when she socialized, whether at one of their weddings or while having lunch at McCann's around the corner for hamburgers and onion rings. Her outgoing nature, which gave her the confidence to speak Spanish to Italians, showed up in her easy transition from work to her personal life, which was rich in close friends. She was a fun person to have around.

Even though Sotomayor's income improved considerably when she started at Pavia & Harcourt, she continued to live fairly modestly in her apartment at Third and Hoyt Streets in Carroll Gardens, Brooklyn. When Mattiaccio and his wife moved to Brooklyn, Sotomayor took them around to her favorite restaurants in her predominantly Italian-American neighborhood and introduced them to the shop owners she knew on a first-name basis.

Over the years, Mattiaccio noticed that she was generous with her money as well as her time. Working at the private firm wasn't making her rich, but she had quite a bit more at her disposal, and she gave it away generously. "Pavia and Harcourt was a very nice firm but it wasn't a firm you went to to make a fortune," he said. "It was a small firm, you went there for other reasons." She spent a lot of money, he recalled, on family and friends. "She was very generous, constantly buying things for people and taking people places. She was very supportive of particular extended family members. She was just very generous. She liked giving things to people." When a friend in Brooklyn mentioned that his small business was going through a rough time, for example, Sotomayor offered to lend him $15,000. She wouldn't hesitate to help out a friend whom she considered as close as family.

Her generosity and commitment to giving back to the community also took the form of an extensive commitment to pro bono work on various boards. She served for twelve years on the board of the Puerto Rican Legal Defense & Education Fund, now known as LatinoJustice PRLDEF, a span that covered her entire legal career before becoming a federal judge. At various times, she took leadership positions on the board, serving as the first vice president and chair of the Litigation and Education Committees.

Coming to the PRLDEF board in 1980, just one year after completing law school, Sotomayor was the handpicked choice of her Yale mentor José Cabranes, who was leaving the board because he had just been named a federal judge. "She was very young at the time," said PRLDEF founder Cesar Perales. "José Cabranes recommended her to the board as someone who would bring young blood and new ideas. He had sensed from her interests that she would like serving on our board."

Founded in 1972 to provide legal support to Puerto Ricans facing challenges in employment, housing, voting, education, and immigration, PRLDEF has a dual mission of advocating for Puerto Rican rights and helping young Latinos enter the legal profession. As chair of the Education Committee, Sotomayor directed the programs that nurtured an interest in the law by arranging student meetings with lawyers and judges and visits to courtrooms and law firms. Students also came to classrooms at the organization's offices on Hudson Street to attend seminars that prepared them for taking the Law School Aptitude Test. The Legal Education and Training Division also made presentations at colleges, gathered data such as the number of minorities passing the bar each year, created internships, sponsored a moot court competition, and offered pre-admissions counseling to prospective law students.

Sotomayor described PRLDEF's mission as promoting "the civil and human rights of disadvantaged Hispanics."[27] This was a common theme of the organizations to which she devoted several hours of her time and energy each week. If she wasn't working at her desk late, one of her colleagues remarked, she was probably at a board meeting somewhere in the city. Lawyers are expected to do pro bono work, which is an ethical responsibility that falls under the American Bar Association's Code of Professional Responsibility, and during some periods she put in as much as eight hours a week on those activities, an extra full day's work.

The ambitions that Sotomayor had discussed with Girgente when leaving the district attorney's office involved more than getting corporate experience. Moving up in her career would require appointments to public jobs that would give her the opportunity to prove herself among those with powerful influence in the city and state. *New York Times* political reporters Michael Powell and Serge F. Kovaleski examined the story of her "maturation as a public figure" during her years at Pavia & Harcourt in a profile published shortly after she was nominated to the U.S. Supreme Court. "She rose with remarkably little help from the traditional arbiters of power," they wrote. "Party bosses recall nothing of her."[28] Instead, her upward moves were guided by a friend at the firm and her former employer, Robert Morgenthau, who used his influence to make the right calls to the right people.

Like Girgente, Morgenthau was aware of

Sotomayor's sense of urgency about doing as much as she could in as much time as she had, whatever that was. Her diabetes "made her think, 'I'm not going to be around forever, I have to keep moving,'" he recalled. When she worked in Morgenthau's office, they had discussed the fact that she spent about an hour each day injecting herself with insulin.[29] Although her condition had not had any negative impact on her performance, it was a fact of life that she felt may affect the number of her working years.

Her first public board membership came in 1987 with an appointment by Governor Mario Cuomo to the State of New York Mortgage Agency (SONYMA). The position arose after a partner at Pavia & Harcourt, David Botwinick, spoke to the governor about her. Botwinick's efforts came at an ideal time, when Cuomo was looking for more diversity in his administration and SONYMA needed an influx of energy and fresh ideas. The state board was a source of low-rate mortgages for low-income families, and Sotomayor worked zealously to provide more funds for needy applicants. According to one state official, "she was the youngest board member but extremely involved in the details."[30]

The following year she was appointed

to a newly created New York City board designed to manage campaign spending. When Mayor Ed Koch's corporation counsel Peter L. Zimroth went looking for another founding member of the Campaign Finance Board, he called Morgenthau, who recommended Sotomayor. After the interview, Zimroth signed her on without talking to any other candidates. Her political status as a registered Independent, combined with the impression she made on Zimroth, landed her the appointment in the nonpartisan, independent city agency. Zimroth believed he had found "a gem" and "a straight shooter, a very serious lawyer who seemed absolutely independent."[31]

Sotomayor's approach to this board was consistent with her style at the state agency: tenacious, demanding, and uncompromising. Throughout cases that scrutinized campaign contributions in the mayoral races of Koch, David Dinkins, and Rudolph Giuliani, she insisted on the highest standards and "emerged as a demanding member." One board member observed that she did not let anything detract from an important meeting; during "a tense interview with a candidate," he recalled, "she would be shooting herself with insulin in the back of the hand."[32]

Sotomayor speaks of her four years on the Campaign Finance Board with pride and credits it with teaching her some very important lessons. "No matter how stringent and detailed your rules might be, those intent on evading them will manage to find a way and those intent on breaking them will."[33]

Other committees, panels, and boards took up her energies during this period as well. Her service on the board of the Maternity Center supported the nonprofit organization's efforts to improve maternity care through research and education. As a member of the Selection Committee for the Stanley D. Heckman Educational Fund, she helped determine college scholarship recipients from a pool of high school students, and her work on Governor Cuomo's Advisory Panel for Inter-Group Relations explored options for conflict resolution.

In between these varied obligations that took up precious hours every week, Sotomayor managed to find time for the cultural delights of the city. Her tastes were typically New York, ranging from a love of Yankees baseball and rock bands to opera, the American Ballet Theatre and Alvin Ailey American Dance Theater, Broadway shows and the New York Philharmonic. Her wide-ranging interests surprised some of her associates who were more accustomed to lawyers who talked shop more than anything else. "We had many discussions about things other than the law, especially music," said Brian Brokate, the lawyer who worked with her on the New York Anticounterfeiting Task Force. "She really liked certain rock bands and loved the symphony as well."

As she established herself as an enormously hardworking attorney in her thirties, Sotomayor experienced some of the best and worst the city had to offer. Spending evenings with her widening circle of friends in great restaurants and concert halls was a world removed from afternoons spent crawling around filthy Chinatown basements searching for designer knockoffs. The next phase of her career would take her to a higher level of the ex parte seizure order process, in which lawyers came to her in hopes of having enough evidence and cause to conduct downtown raids. But she would never be far from the action that had taken up so much of her time in corporate practice.

One afternoon, many years after leaving Pavia & Harcourt and becoming an appeals court judge, she was walking in Chinatown during her lunch hour when she spotted Heather McDonald waving at her from a van with blacked-out windows. The doors flew open and suddenly it was like old times. "She climbed in the back of the van with me," said McDonald, "and we said, 'we've been *here* before.'"

CHAPTER 7
PITCH IT TO THE JUDGE

[With her 1995 ruling on Major League Baseball], Judge Sotomayor joined forever the ranks of Joe DiMaggio, Willie Mays, Jackie Robinson, and Ted Williams.

— *Philadelphia Inquirer*

We were fortunate to get a judge who was going to make up her own mind.

— Daniel Silverman

About two years after Sonia Sotomayor had become a partner at Pavia & Harcourt, the firm's managing litigation partner David Botwinik began urging her to apply for a federal judgeship. New York Senator Patrick Moynihan's Judicial Selection Committee was considering applicants for seven vacancies in Manhattan's federal district court, and Botwinik and his fellow law firm partner David Glasser were adamant that Sonia should submit her name to the search. Botwinik and Glasser were close friends of Judah Gribetz, who chaired Moynihan's judiciary screening committee, and they called him to recommend Sonia. "You know how everybody's talking about how the country's evolving?" they told Gribetz. "Here's a gal that came out of the South Bronx and went to Princeton and Yale, was in Bob Morgenthau's office and is at Pavia & Harcourt, a nice law firm. She has a future."[1] District Attorney Morgenthau also called Gribetz to recommend Sonia for the nomination, which added enormous prestige to her application.

The early 1990s was the perfect time for Sonia's background and experience to converge into a politically appointed judgeship. Blacks, women, and Latinos were beginning to be promoted into positions of power, and even if that recruitment weren't racking up big numbers, it was still being propelled forward. "If you live in the end of the twentieth century, there was nothing incompatible between diversity and excellence," said Gribetz. "Obviously we were looking for people who were representative, and with the right credentials. She fit the bill."[2]

The U.S. District Court for the Southern District of New York tries cases in the state's metropolitan counties of New York (Manhattan) and the Bronx as well as the upstate counties of Westchester, Rockland, Putnam, Orange, Dutchess, and Sullivan. While the majority of criminal cases such as those involving theft, murder, and narcotics and civil cases covering contracts and personal injury are handled in the state courts, the federal court presides over antitrust (protecting trade and commerce from monopolies and price fixing); securities and banking regulation; patent, copyright, and trademark cases; counterfeiting; maritime contracts and other admiralty issues; suits between states; and other federal crimes.

Of the ninety-four district courts across the country, the Southern District Court stands out as the first federal court in the nation, formed in 1789, even before the U.S. Supreme Court. Its first judge, James Duane, was appointed by President George Washington, and it remains the largest federal court in the country. Famous trials such as the Rosenberg spy case, the IBM computer monopoly antitrust megacase, and the Bonanno and Genovese racketeering cases had brought the court international attention since the 1950s.

By 1990, the six vacancies among the forty-three seats on New York's Southern District Court bench contributed to a crushing backlog of cases. Sonia was well aware of the relatively large number of openings in the New York court, but she could not imagine herself getting an appointment to that legendary bench and ignored Botwinik's requests to seriously consider applying. "I had insisted that I had no chance of ever being selected for the most prestigious and respected federal district court in the nation, the mother court," she said.[3] Finally, Botwinik took matters into his own hands, placed the application on Sonia's desk, and cleared her calendar of all other work for a full week. He even allocated the duties of his secretary, Sonia's secretary, and one paralegal at the firm to the work of filling out the detailed application. Confronted with those logistics and Botwinik's unflagging belief in her future as a judge, Sonia spent the week on the application. She completed the lengthy form, outlining the details of her academic and professional life, organized all the attachments, and submitted it to New York Senator Patrick Moynihan's committee.

Federal judges, appointed for lifetime terms, are officially selected by the president of the United States, but traditionally the president allows the senior senator from his party to select nominees from his or her state. During the George H. W. Bush administration that "senatorial courtesy" fell to Alfonse D'Amato in New York, but due to a long-standing agreement D'Amato had made with his Democratic colleague Senator Moynihan, the Democrat was allowed to recommend one out of every four judgeships to the president. In early 1991, it was Moynihan's turn, and the retreat of one nominee opened the door for Sonia to step in.

In February 1991, New York State Supreme Court Justice John Carro formally withdrew his recommendation to the federal bench, which Moynihan had offered to President Bush three years previously. Frustrated at the inaction on his nomination, Justice Carro wrote to Moynihan that he could "only assume" that the president's three-year silence over his nomination "is because he disagrees with the views I have expressed in the opinions I have written in over twenty years on the bench."[4] While the White House would not comment on the matter, an unidentified member of Congress told the *New York Times,* "It's clear the White House simply didn't want him."[5] Justice Carro, a Cuban-American, had been the only Hispanic nominee for a federal judgeship in New York, and his long wait over and ultimate withdrawal from the nomination reignited the debate about the need for Hispanics on the federal bench. One month before Carro's announcement, a judge of the state bench, Justice Frank Torres of the New York Supreme Court in Manhattan, outlined the hard facts in an article in the *New York State Bar Journal*. Remarking that Hispanic judges were underrepresented in the federal courts throughout the nation, he noted that this was "conspicuously so in New York, which is a state with one of the largest Hispanic populations in the nation." Even with a Hispanic population of 1.8 million in New York City and 2,000 Hispanic lawyers practicing across the state, he wrote, there was not one Hispanic judge on any federal bench in New York. "This absence," he said, "is viewed by many Hispanics as a vestige of American unequal opportunity and racial discrimination."

Although Hispanic judges were seated in three parts of the country that had large Hispanic populations — two Hispanic judges served in federal district courts in Florida, three in California, and one in Arizona — Torres's remarks echoed national observations about the disparity between the fast-growing Hispanic population and their representation in the federal courts.

In 1991, that population was approximately twenty-five million, or 10 percent of the nation, and the U.S. Census projected that Hispanics would become "the largest identifiable minority in the nation within the next decade, a fact not lost on George Bush, who actively courted the Hispanic vote in his campaign."[6]

Senator Moynihan was committed to turning the situation around in New York, so when Justice Carro resigned from his nomination, Moynihan was thrilled that his Judicial Selection Committee was already working on its recommendation of another outstanding candidate who happened to be Hispanic. In an enthusiastic introduction that became lore in the committee, the staff reported to Moynihan, "Have we got a judge for you!"[7]

Sonia had been interviewed by at least twelve members of the search committee, which consisted of practicing lawyers, judges, and professors. Part of their review of her career involved determining the range of her experience with different types of law, which was considerable due to her five years of prosecuting criminal cases in the state courts and eight years of arguing a wide range of civil matters in both mediation and in Manhattan's federal court.

Unlike later hearings in her judicial career, which would bring up hypothetical questions, this committee focused on facts about her experience. "Most of the questions were about . . . the degree of my experience in federal court and state court," she said. "It was more about my qualifications in terms of experience in various areas . . . [rather] than asking how I would rule on an issue. At that time people were more sensitive and so no one even came close to that." The nearest the discussions came to a particular issue was when someone asked if she felt okay about the death penalty. "My response," she said, "was no one should feel okay about the death penalty — that is a serious matter — but if you are asking me can I follow the law, that is a different question."[8]

Sonia's background resonated with Senator Moynihan, who grew up in poor New York City neighborhoods, worked menial jobs during school and went on to become a Fulbright Scholar. He was impressed with Sonia on paper and even more certain after interviewing her that she had everything it took to reach the highest bench in the country. "He told me he was absolutely convinced she would end up on the Supreme Court," said one of Moynihan's top aides.[9] Envisioning his actions as the first step in a history-making career for his nominee, Moynihan announced Sonia as New York's nominee for federal district court in March 1991.

Good to his word that he would support Senator Moynihan's recommendation, Senator D'Amato took Moynihan's decision to the Bush administration. "[Moynihan and I] had this agreement," D'Amato said, "and when she came to meet with me and I checked with my committee, they agreed that she was outstanding." Bush's Justice Department did not agree with D'Amato's pick, but he fought for her. "I had a pretty good relationship with them and I said, 'We have this agreement and we were going to honor it.' They didn't like it, but they took it," he said.[10] D'Amato claimed that Sonia's newly aired reputation as a potential nominee for the Supreme Court was partially to blame for the slow process of her first judicial nomination. The Republican opposition to her rise in the federal courts originated in the long months between Moynihan's naming of her as the nominee and the Senate vote that would confirm her to the federal district court in 1992.

The American Bar Association instructed its Standing Committee on Federal Judiciary to review Sonia's career and issue a report, which ultimately stated that she was qualified for the federal appointment. Endorsements flowed in from people like Harry Pachon, director of the National Association of Latino Elected and Appointed Officials (NALEO), who wrote to President Bush about Sonia's "deep-rooted warmth and desire to play a decisive role toward the betterment of her community" and the fact that her nomination would provide Bush's administration with "the opportunity to name the first Hispanic to the federal bench in New York, a state whose Hispanic community has grown three-fold since 1980."[11]

This paved the way for President Bush to announce Sonia as his nominee for the federal bench, but a political setback pushed that announcement back several months. In standard form for another aspect of the federal appointments process, Moynihan had had a "hold" on two federal circuit court judges that the Bush administration sought to confirm and would lift that hold only if his district court nominees were approved. Once that deal was made in November 1991, President Bush made the official announcement about Sonia Sotomayor's nomination and her Senate confirmation hearing was scheduled for June 1992.

Sonia acknowledged Moynihan as the "single most important person" behind her nomination to the federal district court and recognized that, even though he was too modest to admit it himself, he had "expended enormous political capital to ensure my confirmation, despite some very costly political demands."[12] Becoming Moynihan's choice for the third highest court in the land was almost as humbling as assuming the title of judge would be. "There is such a sense of disbelief about being nominated," Sonia said. "One recognizes how few federal judgeship positions there are and how fortunate one is to be nominated."[13]

On the first day of Sonia's U.S. Senate Judiciary Hearing, Committee Chairman Senator Edward Kennedy noted her impressive commitment to pro bono activities and asked her to describe some of that work. She told the committee about her duties on the board of the Puerto Rican Legal Defense and Education Fund, State of New York Mortgage Agency, New York City Campaign Fund, Stanley Heckman Scholarship Committee, and the Maternity Center Association of the State of New York. Addressing Senator Kennedy's question about how she could "convince lawyers of the need to make real commitments to public service," she said:

> I, as an individual, believe that those of us who have opportunities in this life must give them back to those who have less. It is never easy to encourage others to do the same, but I do think it is important for public figures, for legal educators, for the bar to constantly and repeatedly encourage public service.

Senator D'Amato brought up the point that Sonia's nomination, along with that of Loretta Preska, reflected New York's interest in bringing women to the federal bench. "In the eleven years that both Senator Moynihan and I have been making recommendations to the White House," he said, "with the confirmation of Loretta and Sonia, this will bring seven women who will have been appointed to the Federal bench from our State. . . . I think we can be quite proud of that accomplishment."[14]

After similar congenial questions and comments, Sonia's nomination was approved by the Judiciary Committee and the Senate was instructed to vote on her confirmation. Political maneuvering delayed that vote, as well as those of three other women judicial candidates, for several weeks. The specific reason for those delays, which Senator D'Amato described as "unconscionable," were not made clear, but Sonia's vote was finally scheduled for August 11, 1992, at which time the Senate confirmed her by "Unanimous Consent."[15] She received her commission as a judge on the U.S. District Court for the Southern District of New York on August 12, and her induction ceremony was scheduled for October 2, 1992. That swearing-in event, held in the ornate Ceremonial Courtroom 506 in the U.S. Courthouse at 40 Centre Street, was followed by a party thrown by Pavia & Harcourt at Harry's in the Woolworth Building.

After being sworn in, Sonia became the first Hispanic judge on the federal bench in New York.

In spite of all the printed guidebooks on procedures, videos, and seminars carefully prepared and conducted for "baby judges" by the Federal Judicial Center, the prospect of assuming the role was terrifying to Sonia, as it is to most. During her first year on the bench, she would wonder what she was doing there, not out of insecurity but of a sense of the stature of the position, acutely aware that "it is a very powerful position" and that "the responsibility is enormous."[16] Reading up on the development of sentencing guidelines, as she did on the beach for a couple of days during her preparation period, gave her a sense of "how the policies developed" and helped her understand "some of the current open questions under the guidelines," but she soon learned that no one could walk into the job fully prepared. Laws are always in flux, and keeping up with statutes and sentencing guidelines was just one of many ominous factors she faced as a new judge. Once she realized her colleagues were in the same position, she allowed herself to accept that no type of background would make anyone completely ready to assume a federal bench:

There is simply no depth of experience, simply no type of experience that can expose you to everything you'll need as a federal judge. That was the number-one lesson that took me months to realize and months to accept, that I wasn't personally deficient because I didn't know more. And talking to so many of my colleagues that came on board with me, I know that that is a feeling that most of us don't articulate openly at the beginning, that sense of insecurity about not knowing enough. But it's real, it's there and the comfort that I grew to have was with the fact that there is no one who could have enough experience to face all of the topics that a federal judge faces.[17]

As the most junior judge in the district court, Sonia had small chambers and no courtroom of her own when she took the bench in the federal courthouse at 500 Pearl Street. Walking through the brass doorway on that Monday morning in October 1992, she made her way to her sixth-floor suite, which contained an entrance room containing two desks for her secretary, Theresa Bartenope, and court deputy, Susan Scognamillo, with a door to her chambers at the left and another to the office for her two clerks on the right.

The first day was memorable for all of them as they realized that it would take some time to get even the most basic protocols in order. At eight thirty that morning, just after she and Theresa stepped into the office, the phone rang. "I think it's a family member calling to congratulate me again and tell me to have a good day," Sonia said, "and on the phone is a litigant advising my secretary that his case has been reassigned to me and that they want an immediate trial date. My secretary turns to me and says, 'Judge, what do I do?'"[18]

Theresa had been Sonia's secretary at Pavia & Harcourt and would remain with her through her entire judicial career. A good friend whom Sonia described as "the real backbone" of her life, Theresa became the "soul and life" of the judge's chambers, infusing it with integrity, professional skill, efficiency and, as Sonia described, "a very distinctive type of warmth, which makes my chambers an inviting and energetic place to work, where everyone, including myself foremost, looks forward to spending their days."[19]

That first day, Sonia, Theresa, and one of the new clerks spent several hours unpacking the nearly one hundred boxes of books that had been supplied by the government, bound volumes of the U.S. district, appellate, and Supreme Court decisions handed down in the previous fifteen years. Sonia decided where to place the books throughout the three rooms, with many of them allotted to the clerks' room, which was already crowded with tall filing cabinets and two desks. "The judge rolled up her sleeves and helped," said Joseph Evall, one of the two young lawyers who were her first clerks. A magna cum laude graduate of Harvard Law School who had also earned undergraduate and graduate degrees in chemistry from

Harvard, Evall had interviewed with and was selected by Sonia for the clerkship in the summer of 1992 and continued working in a private firm until her confirmation. Sonia's other clerk, Xavier Romeu, a native of Puerto Rico and graduate of Columbia Law School, would join them one week later after finishing up some business in Puerto Rico.

In the midst of shelving books that first day, Evall was stopped in his tracks when a doorbell rang. "We were like, there's a doorbell?" he recalled. He opened the outer door and let in some lawyers who had just filed an emergency request for a temporary restraining order (TRO) and had been told that Judge Sotomayor was assigned to the case. "They asked me how the judge liked presentations for TROs to go, and I listened to them, wide-eyed, like a deer in headlights," he said. He asked them to wait while he spoke to the judge and after he got her response and relayed the information, he couldn't even find a pen or pencil with which to make some notes. But the lawyers had their answers, and the office continued to get set up. "She handled it and we found the pencils and we were able to move on," Evall said.

Evall and Romeu's office was outfitted with a buzzer that Sonia could use to signal them for assistance. She had never used a computer before, and in those first weeks, Evall taught her how to use the word processing program. The DOS-system computer's dark glass monitor was embedded in a computer trolley placed next to her desk, and she buzzed Evall now and then to ask him to remind her how to underline a text or save a document to a floppy disk. Her chambers were decorated with colorful fabrics and patterns on chair pillows, photos of her family, an assortment of gavels she had received as congratulation gifts, and many other mementos, all of which created a cheerful ambiance.

Judge Sotomayor was immediately added to the "wheel," the court clerk's system of randomly assigning judges to new cases, and she also received several cases from each of the other judges. Boxes of files streamed in as the court equalized the docket, and Sonia directed the clerks to go through them case by case to figure out the status of each, write up a memo, and schedule the lawyers in for conferences.

For the entire first month Sonia limited her proceedings to her chambers, where she met with lawyers in conference because she was "a little frightened about taking the bench." Like other new federal judges who often spend the first few weeks observing other judges, if their calendars permit, or holding sessions in their offices, this arrangement allowed Sonia to transition a bit more calmly. "It was a little easier just to do my conferences in chambers and get used to having people call me judge . . . to speaking to the litigants and assuming my new role."

It took a year for her to begin to adjust to the weighty persona that accompanied her new role. The word *judge* signified new dividing lines that took great effort to sort out. "It's very strange to wear the title 'Judge,'" she said after completing her first year on the bench. "Walking to the courthouse and having people call out to me, 'Judge!' or having old friends not know whether to call me Sonia or Judge . . . has seemed strange to me. And defining those lines or drawing new lines or defining how I want my relationships to continue and with whom has been a difficult question during the year."

The enormous caseload and unique jurisdiction of the New York Southern District provided the new judge with a wide range of legal areas to master. As a major port, New York had traditionally brought many admiralty cases to the court, which required a thorough knowledge of the laws dealing with public and private shipping and other aspects of maritime law. New York was also the environment for many Wall Street and other white-collar crime cases, intellectual property issues, and cases involving organized crime, which involved a mastery of the intricacies of the Racketeer Influenced and Corrupt Organizations (RICO) Act. The jurisdiction also gave the judge the opportunity to swear in immigrants as new citizens, a task that carried deep meaning for Sotomayor.

In addition to working her massive caseload, Sotomayor also had to keep up with the decisions being made in the Second Circuit Court of Appeals, the highest federal court in New York. "The first year she was very committed to mastering what was involved," recalled Evall. "She would get the slip opinions from the Second Circuit, the decisions published in little pamphlets, and throw a stack of them in her bag before going home." She brought them in the next day, all marked up and underlined for her clerks. "She would hand some of them to us and say, 'You're working on such-and-such opinion; you should see this,'" said Evall. "She would grill lawyers about what the Second Circuit had just come down with. You did not want to be unprepared in her courtroom."

As a judge for the Southern District of New

York, Sonia was required to live in one of the counties of the district, so she found someone to rent her co-op apartment in Brooklyn and moved back to the Bronx, to an address that was never disclosed. Her salary dropped from the approximately $230,000 she was earning as a partner at Pavia & Harcourt to $129,000, the starting salary for district judges. It was not a difficult transition, however. "I've never wanted to get adjusted to my income because I knew I wanted to go back to public service," she said shortly after becoming a judge. "And in comparison to what my mother earns and how I was raised, it's not modest at all. I have no right to complain."[20]

Even though she was earning about half as much, commuting from the Bronx, settling into a no-frills windowless office far from tony Midtown, and holding trials in whatever courtroom was available instead of her own, Sonia had no reservations about her new judicial career. Her expertly handled political posts and other pro bono work in New York, combined with colleagues at Pavia & Harcourt who had close connections to Moynihan's search committee and a sterling recommendation from Robert Morgenthau, had earned her a seat on the federal bench. At age thirty-eight, Sonia was not only the youngest and only Hispanic federal judge in the city, she had fulfilled the destiny that called to her in childhood. The grade-school girl who wanted to be a lawyer and ultimately a judge achieved her goal in very short order.

During Sonia's tenure on the federal district court from 1992 to 1998, the types of cases to which she was assigned closely followed the breakdown of cases brought before the Southern District. During that period, 20 percent of the cases involved white-collar crimes, 27 percent dealt with illegal drugs, and 52.5 percent addressed other federal crimes such as organized crime, corruption, and immigration and regulatory violations. Judge Sotomayor's caseload reflected that distribution, with 18 percent involving white-collar crime, 29 percent dealing with drugs, and 53 percent other federal offenses.

Aside from her initial fear of presiding over a federal courtroom, Sonia's most difficult moment in her first year on the bench was handing down her first sentence. By comparison, standing before a judge as a prosecutor and arguing that a person should be put in prison for a specific number of years had been relatively easy. "You're in a different position when you're the one signing that judgment of conviction," she said, "and it's your name that's on that line and you're making the choice about how much time that person's life is going to be abbreviated in terms of their liberty."[21] Her first sentence was a five-year prison term given to a convicted drug offender. As she sat alone in her office signing the judgment of conviction, she felt a sense of responsibility that would stay with her throughout her career and recalled the broken lives she had witnessed during her childhood in the South Bronx. "That emotion will never leave me — humility, a deep, deep sense of humility," she said. "And a deep, deep sense of there but for the grace of God could I have gone and many that I have loved."[22]

For as grave as that responsibility appeared to her, a study of Judge Sotomayor's sentences conducted by Syracuse University reveal that she was tougher on criminals in every category of crime:

JUDGE SOTOMAYOR'S SENTENCES ON THE U.S. DISTRICT COURT FOR THE SOUTHERN DISTRICT OF NEW YORK, 1993–1998[23]

Crime	Prison Sentence		Sentence of 6 mos. or more	
	Colleagues	Sotomayor	Colleagues	Sotomayor
White collar	43%	52%	34%	48%
Drugs	81%	86%	79%	86%
Other	53%	60%	46%	56%

Of the approximately 61 cases over which Sotomayor presided in the district court that went to verdict or judgment (some civil and criminal cases go before juries and some just before a judge), 31 percent were criminal.

In addition to sentencing, her other courtroom work included presiding over pretrial motions and plea hearings. One case that made national headlines occurred during President Bill Clinton's Whitewater scandal, when the *Wall Street Journal* sued the Justice Department for the release of the suicide note left by White House counsel Vincent Foster. Sotomayor ruled for the *Journal* in *Dow Jones & Co. v. U.S. Dept. of Justice,* stating in her opinion that the public had "a substantial interest" in viewing the note.[24]

A case that did not make many waves outside New York at the time but that would be highlighted in the judge's future involved a suit brought by homeless advocates who charged that a nonprofit coalition of businesses was not paying homeless people adequate wages in a workforce training program. The coalition, called the Grand Central Partnership, claimed that the homeless trainees were being paid fairly at less than $2.00 an hour instead of minimum wage because they were in a training program that met the exemption requirements of the Fair Labor Standards Act (FLSA). In *Archie v. Grand Central Partnership,* Judge Sotomayor ruled that the program did not in fact meet those exemption requirements as defined in the FLSA. Although the program had significant value, she stated, the work the homeless were doing was legitimate, valuable work that the partnership used to replace labor that would be paid minimum wage. As a judge, it was not her place to create the exemption the program required: "It is not the function of this Court to legislate an exemption," she wrote, "that does not otherwise exist." That, she added, is the job of Congress or the secretary of labor. She was clearly not a judge who believed in "legislating from the bench."[25]

Sotomayor's most prominent case on the district court bench appeared on her calendar in 1995, after the longest baseball strike in history had canceled the 1994 World Series and threatened the start of the new season. The 232-day strike was the longest work stoppage in *all* professional sports history, eliminating 920 games. It was also the first cancellation of a World Series in ninety years.

The players went on strike in response to the owners' call for a salary cap and changes in the free agency system. A year before the collective bargaining agreement between the players and owners had expired in December 1993, the owners voted to reopen negotiations on salaries and free agency. Meetings between the owners and players did not result in any changes, but the owners were making it clear that they wanted to be proactive in solving their most pressing issue: the financial disparity between small- and big-market teams. When the agreement expired at the end of 1993, the owners voted unanimously to come up with a revenue-sharing plan if they could achieve a salary cap. By distributing money from teams in large metropolitan regions to those in smaller areas, they reasoned, teams would become more equally competitive. Small-market teams were simply losing too much money.

After spending a year and a half trying to agree on a formula for revenue sharing, the owners officially presented their proposal on June 14, 1994. They offered a seven-year contract that included clauses to split total revenue fifty-fifty with the players, usher in a salary cap over four years, eliminate salary arbitration, lower the service time for becoming a free agent from six years to four, and raise the minimum salary for players with less than four years of Major League play. Another item stated that players would be required to split their licensing revenue with the owners.

The union rejected the proposal four days later. Playing under a salary cap, sharing their licensing revenue, decreasing the amount of their cut with the owners, losing salary arbitration, and other elements of the owners' plan would cost them $1.5 billion in salary over the term of the contract, according to Donald Fehr, executive director of the Major League Baseball Players Association (MLBPA), the players' union. Fehr took the position that the owners were trying to solve their financial problems by making the players pay for it. He offered a counterproposal, which the owners rejected, and the conflict saturated the media.

The players were outraged that the owners would consider meddling with free agency and salary arbitration, the closely connected systems that defined compensation in Major League Baseball. The free agency system allows a player with six seasons of Major League play to become a free agent, whereby any club can bid for his services. Free agency is closely tied to salary arbitration, the process in which a player's salary dispute is resolved, whereby the arbitrator takes the two figures (last final offer) submitted by the owner and the player and chooses one of the two figures as the player's salary for the next season.

At the end of July, the players announced that they would strike on August 12, but before the strike date, the situation hit another low when the owners announced they would not make a $7.8 million payment to the players' pension fund. To fans and other observers, such a controversial move on the part of the owners made it appear that they were not working with the intent of reaching an agreement, one of the pillars of good-faith bargaining.

When the players went on strike as scheduled on August 12, the prospects of continuing the season any time soon looked bleak. Stopping the season — especially one full of such high expectations — was a big disappointment.

Even with the help of professional mediators, in this case members of the Federal Mediation and Conciliation Service, the meetings in late August went nowhere. And the worst-case scenario played out on September 14 when the owners canceled the rest of the season, including the World Series. "There's an incredible amount of sadness," said acting baseball commissioner Bud Selig at his news conference. "There is a failure of so much. Lest anybody not understand, there can't be any joy on any side."[26]

The strike began winding toward the courts at the end of the year. On December 22, the players' union presented the owners with another proposal that addressed the high-salary issue. After discussing the plan for five hours, the owners rejected the proposal and declared an impasse. At the same time, they announced that they would put a salary cap into effect and eliminate salary arbitration, using their right to make those unilateral changes. Labor law allows an employer to make such changes after contract expiration if negotiations have reached an impasse.

The players' union, however, claimed that an impasse had not occurred because negotiations had been ongoing. By unilaterally imposing the salary cap and other changes outside of an impasse situation, the players accused, the owners had engaged in unfair labor practices. The players' union filed an unfair labor practice complaint with the National Labor Relations Board (NLRB), arguing that the owners had not followed the proper procedures of collective bargaining.

The NLRB was set up in 1935 with the creation of the National Labor Relations Act, the law dealing with relations between unions and employers. Defining the rules of collective bargaining, the act created the ground rules for the negotiating process through which a labor union and an employer define wages, benefits, and other elements of their relationship. The board, which is headquartered in Washington, D.C., consists of five members who are appointed by the president.

On February 3, the Major League Baseball Player Relations Committee (PRC), the organization representing the owners, presented a two-part notice to the players' union. First, the PRC revoked the changes it had made in late December, which prompted the NLRB to drop its complaint. But the PRC also noted that it did not believe it was obligated to adhere to certain parts of the original agreement, primarily salary arbitration, because, in its judgment, it was a "permissible" rather than "mandatory" subject of negotiation; therefore, the union could not insist on it to impasse. Those remarks foreshadowed the PRC's next move, which would head the process to Sotomayor's court.

On February 6, the PRC followed up on its remarks with an announcement that individual clubs could no longer negotiate contracts with players or their agent. Instead, the collective owners' organization, the PRC, would be the sole bargaining representative for the clubs. By prohibiting free agents from signing with clubs, the owners were not only reversing the entire history of salary negotiations with individual clubs but also appeared to be colluding with each other, an offense that had cost them hundreds of millions in fines in the 1980s.

In response, the players' union filed a new charge with the NLRB, arguing that the owners had violated labor law by "eliminating, before an impasse had been reached, competitive bidding for the services of free agents, the anti-collusion provision, and salary arbitration for certain reserved players."[27]

The union's complaint was filed with General Counsel's office in New York City, headed by Regional Director Daniel Silverman. He and his legal team decided that the crux of the case centered around antitrust (antimonopoly), not labor law, and they researched antitrust case law that backed their theory. By centralizing the negotiations with the PRC instead of allowing individual clubs to deal with free agents, Silverman and his team reasoned, the owners were forming a monopoly on the salary negotiation process.

Silverman's office worked on a legal argument to present to the NLRB's General

Counsel Frederick Feinstein, the presidential appointee who was in charge of investigating and prosecuting unfair labor practice cases. They had to convince him that the case deserved to be brought to the board in Washington for a vote on whether to take the case to federal court. The five-member board has the final say on whether an issue will proceed to the courts.

Because of the timeliness of the situation, the NLRB would petition for a 10 (j) proceeding — a request for a preliminary injunction, or order, from a federal judge, to make the owners return to the status quo of the original agreement.

If the baseball union's complaint were to go through regular channels with the board, the process could take two years to resolve. "We thought," said Donald Zavelo, the deputy regional attorney for the NLRB, who worked the case, "that if you allow the owners to continue without free agency and without salary arbitration, and then two years later we win our case, who's going to know how much these players would have gotten paid or where they would be playing?" There were so many variables involved, he explained, that "it would have been impossible to provide a remedy two years later."[28]

In petitioning the federal court for an injunction, the NLRB would need to prove two points: that there was reasonable cause to believe that the owners' violation occurred and that it would be just and proper to preserve the status quo; in other words, to return to all the existing provisions of the last collective bargaining agreement. If a judge ruled that the board made this showing, the owners would be ordered to remove the "new rules" they had enacted and proceed to negotiate toward a new agreement.

As the NLRB worked on the case in early 1994, the U.S. Congress and President Clinton continued their own efforts in Washington. Some members of Congress sought to revise or eliminate baseball's exemption from antitrust laws, which would allow players to sue the owners in federal court for the kind of restrictions the owners were currently trying to put on the free agency system. The new Republican majority was not interested in taking action, however. Speaker of the House Newt Gingrich offered his own recommendation in a press conference on February 11. He advised the players and owners to go on a retreat together at "a nice ski resort" or "someplace in the Caribbean" to watch the movie *Field of Dreams* and reflect on the national pastime.[29]

Clinton had imposed an early February

deadline for the players and owners to come to an agreement, threatening to use government intervention if they did not. When that deadline came and went with no results, Clinton sent a new federal mediator to Congress to meet with Gingrich and Senate Majority Leader Bob Dole to discuss legislation that would create a three-member panel of independent arbitrators that could add some heft to ending the strike. The two congressmen made it clear, however, that they were not about to move quickly to use Congress as a way to end the six-month-old strike.

With no solution in sight from Congress and spring training around the corner, the White House found itself just one more unsuccessful arbitrator of the strike.

On February 16, spring training camps opened in Florida and Arizona with replacement players. "We are committed to playing in the 1995 season," said Bud Selig, "and will do so with the best players willing to play." While spring training limped along, the lawyers at the NLRB continued to research the case law and interview witnesses to prepare the case that would be presented to a federal judge if their board voted to bring the case to court.

The board agreed to meet on Sunday morning, March 26, to conduct their vote.

The impending decision was big news across the country and when the five members arrived at the office on L Street, television cameras were staked out in front of the building. The entire nation was watching to see if the strike was going to go to court.

With a vote of 3 to 2, the board ruled to do just that. That was not the end of the board's involvement, however. In a surprising move, one of the dissenting board members, Charles Cohen, issued a statement declaring that he believed the decision had no merit and the case should be thrown out. "It was the only time in the history of the NLRA that that had been done," said Silverman. "Never before on an injunction case would a member explain why he disagreed. Your regional director is going into court and you're telling the judge the rationale to dismiss the case — that's just not done."

Board member Cohen's actions brought up fears in Silverman's office that the case would go before a judge "who was inclined to take a Republican viewpoint," Silverman recalled. "We were concerned about getting a judge who could make an independent judgment."

When Silverman, Zavelo, and the third NLRB lawyer, Ian Penny, set out for the Federal Building in downtown Manhattan on Monday, they met a crowd of reporters on the sidewalk. "We get a lot of high profile cases," Zavelo said, "but there was nothing like this." They left through the side door of the building, where a cluster of reporters and cameras awaited to walk with them, en masse, across the street to the courthouse at 40 Centre Street. The lawyers docketed the papers at the courthouse and waited for the judge to be selected in the random lot process. Judge Sotomayor's name appeared on the slip drawn by the clerk. "I don't think any of us were familiar with her," said Zavelo. "I know we had never had a case with her before."

Judge Sotomayor received the voluminous paperwork submissions for the case that Monday. During her prehearing conference with all the parties involved (the petitioner, the National Labor Relations Board; the respondent, the PRC; and the Major League Baseball Players Association as amicus, a "friend of the court" that is not party to the lawsuit but participating in it), she admitted that she had not been keeping a close eye on the details of the strike. "I know nothing about this except what a common layperson reads in the *New York Times*," she said.[30]

At Sotomayor's conference, all the lawyers introduced themselves and "each side had an opportunity to tell her what they would do in the hearing," said George H. Cohen, an attorney acting on behalf of the players' union. Sotomayor scheduled the hearing for Friday, but made one last remark, as if speaking for worn-out baseball fans everywhere who would like to see the strike end even earlier: "I think the public would like you to settle this thing without our involvement," she said.[31]

On Thursday, Sotomayor conducted a phone conference to iron out a crucial aspect of the proceedings — whether witnesses would be called at the next day's hearing. She did not think that witnesses would be necessary, she explained to the attorneys through their speakerphones, because the hearing would be "more akin to an oral argument" than a trial requiring witnesses. Working out of new chambers — with a new phone system — that she had acquired in the newly remodeled courthouse, the judge stopped at one point to apologize for the clamor of a ringing telephone that no one knew how to answer yet. When things settled down, she continued the discussion about keeping to an oral argument, and the lawyers agreed because the relevant facts were not in dispute.

Silverman considered that a critical decision because the clock was running out. "If she was prepared to hold a trial and we would all call witnesses, it would go on for months," he said. By that time, however, she knew exactly what kind of proceeding would be necessary. "She had read all the documents," Silverman said. "She was thoroughly familiar with the records and knew everything about the case in quite some detail."

The compressed time frame between filing the papers and conducting the hearing demanded long hours for everyone involved. The owners, or respondents in the case, had two days to respond to the petition, which outlined the NLRB's argument. They submitted that answering brief, as scheduled, on Wednesday. The NLRB, or petitioner, had to respond to that with a reply brief the next day. "They basically had forty-eight hours to reply to our big submission," said Zavelo, "and we had twenty-four hours to reply to their answer. Their answer was huge; we were in here all night."

Among those papers that week was a promise from the players that they would end the strike if the judge ordered an injunction. If the owners were ordered to rescind the changes they had made to the free agency and salary arbitration provisions of the latest agreement, the players would get back on the field and continue bargaining in good faith toward a new agreement. The ball was in Sotomayor's court (excuse the pun), and the emotional stakes over the fate of the national pastime ran high.

On Friday morning, the NLRB team took note of the massive crowds lining Centre Street as they walked over to the courthouse. Reporters and camera crews covered the already cramped Foley Square area that stretched from the Municipal Building to Worth Street. The seven-month strike had finally ground down to this point, an ornate courtroom in downtown Manhattan, where a judge was handed the task of dealing with a dispute that the players and owners, federal mediators, Congressmen, and a president had failed to remedy.

Inside Ceremonial Court Room 101, two sets of tables were set up in front of the judge's bench for the petitioners and respondents. Courtroom artists were seated in the jury box, and the rest of the courtroom was packed with observers. Silverman was surprised to see only one baseball player in attendance, Bernie Williams of the New York Yankees. "They put a microphone in front of him and asked, 'Why are you here?'" Silverman recalled. "He said, 'Why am I here?

I'm the only one this is affecting.' "

The parties at the front tables had no idea if the judge would make her decision that day. She began the hearing with a few words that set a congenial tone:

> Today I can say that after very lengthy sub-
> missions, some of them in pica print with
> no margins, I know a lot more than I did on
> Monday.
>
> The second thing is I hope that none of
> you assumed on Monday that my lack of
> knowledge of any of the intimate details of
> your dispute meant that I was not a baseball
> fan. You can't grow up in the Bronx without
> knowing about baseball, particularly from
> a family where their claim to fame is that
> every member of it has a different team
> that they have rooted for.[32]

After a few other preliminaries, she praised everyone on their work:

> I wish to compliment all of you on excep-
> tionally good papers produced under ex-
> ceptionally tight circumstances. To the ex-
> tent that I required a quick education and
> a thorough one, you have provided me with
> it. I thank those of you who are in this room,
> who I am sure were a large part of that pro-

cess, and those in your back offices who I am sure assisted that process.[33]

The judge asked her first questions of Daniel Silverman, the NLRB regional director, who sat at the front table with Zavelo and Ian M. Penny. When she asked for clarification on the issue of irreparable harm, Silverman responded that only the speedy process of an injunction could prevent the irreparable damages of a prolonged strike. If the issue were to go through lengthy regular court channels, he argued, the owners' original obligations in the latest agreement would become "null and void and permit the employer [owners] to clearly benefit from its unlawful action."

Timeliness was critical, he added: "This is, after all, the reason that there are so many people here, your Honor, a matter of great public interest. We all know that. The nation is watching. The American people, Canadian people, everybody is looking to get baseball back in place."

Judge Sotomayor then asked George Cohen, representing the players' union, to explain why the irreparable harm could not be remedied by monetary means. Cohen's response outlined why the players' compensation process could not be re-created a year or two down the road. The issue was not "exclusively about money damages at all," he said, and proceeded to clarify the workings of free agency.

There are approximately 115 players as of February 10, 1995, who in fact had performed six full years of service and had finally reached what we might call in our profession the nirvana, the moment that they were going to get an opportunity to be free agents and get the benefit of having competitive bids for their services.

Competitive bids, your Honor, does not just mean money. It means an intense variety of personal considerations: Where does a player want to play? Does he want to go back to his home team? Does he want to go back to a team that he thinks is going to be a pennant contender and he hasn't had the opportunity before?

Does he want to go to a team where he believes he will be a regular player, fit into that system and go forward and enhance his professional career?

Each one of these 115, approximately 20 percent of our bargaining unit today, are being deprived of that opportunity, that chance to in fact get the benefit of this system. And without sounding melodramatic, your Honor, time is of the essence because of the unique nature of this particular industry.[34]

Judge Sotomayor then asked Cohen to clarify the salary arbitration component of his argument. By eliminating that piece of the compensation, Cohen responded, "the clubs would have a bargaining chip when they went back into bargaining." This would go against the collective bargaining process. Without an injunction to prevent this scenario, he explained, the owners would be able to return to negotiations with the benefit of their illegal conduct.

The owners argued that they had the right to eliminate salary arbitration because it was a permissible topic of collective bargaining. The owners claimed that salary arbitration wasn't a mandatory topic, but Cohen countered that it was "an integral part, a critical integral part of the whole program," not something that "sits out there all by itself and can be reviewed and evaluated as such."

When the judge took up the salary arbitration issue with Francis L. Casey III, one of the lawyers acting on behalf of the owners, she came right to the point about the owners' act of changing the rules on their own:

"What right do you, as any other employer in this system, have to change wages unilaterally?" In addition, she noted, "What you can't do . . . is change the salary until you reached an impasse in bargaining." The players' lawyers argued that an impasse had not actually occurred, because proposals continued to be exchanged.

After about ninety minutes of listening to both sides, Sotomayor called for a fifteen-minute break, after which time she would tell them what she was planning to do. She had evidently come to the hearing prepared to make a decision after receiving clarification on the key points and was ready to make her ruling. Her comprehensive "Decision and Order" section that followed could not have been written up in fifteen minutes.

After returning from the recess, Sotomayor admitted that she could not help but use some baseball analogies to introduce her decision, and continued:

The often leisurely game of baseball is filled with many small moments which catch a fan's breath. There is, for example, that wonderful second when you see an outfielder backpedaling and jumping up to the wall, and time stops for an instant as he jumps up and you finally figure out whether it is a home run, a double or a single off the wall, or an out.

Unwillingly, I have been drafted onto the deck of this field, with those of you watching out there waiting for one of those small moments to happen. I personally would have liked more time to practice my swing. I would have liked an awful lot more time to prepare and write a more detailed and thorough opinion. I am going to rule here today. . . .

I am ruling today because the issue before me is critical to all the participants who are here and to the public. I also realize that waiting serves no useful purpose. . . . It appears that any delay on my part in rendering a decision would halt the effective continuation of the negotiation process and its ultimate possible resolution.

She kept to the baseball analogy to describe her role as a judge in a case involving the National Labor Relations Act. As a judge, she was not "a player in the collective bargaining process and the terms it ultimately reaches" but rather was assigned to "function as its gatekeeper to ensure that the field upon which the collective bargaining process plays is properly pitched. The moves on the field are then up to the players."

After noting that she had no desire to hold anyone's breath, Sotomayor stated that she had "sided with the Board in its argument that it has reasonable cause to believe that an unfair labor practice has occurred" and that an injunction "is just and proper to avoid irreparable injury to the collective bargaining process."

In her explanation of her ruling, she remarked that the NLRB had not only met their requirements but shown "substantial" reasonable cause that the owners, by changing the free-agency system, had committed an unfair labor practice. She pointed out the weakness in the owners' argument about salary arbitration, noting that they "misconstrue the case law" when trying to prove that it is a permissible rather than mandatory subject of negotiations.

On the issue of an injunction truly being "just and proper," or critical to keeping the collective bargaining process intact, Sotomayor stated that her order was indeed "warranted for several reasons." Looking at the big picture, she emphasized the broad impact the issue had on the overall concept of labor law:

This strike . . . has captivated the public's attention, given the popularity of the sport as well as the protracted nature and well-documented bitterness of the strike. Thus, this strike is about more than just whether the players and owners will resolve their differences. It is also about how the principles embodied by Federal labor law operate in a very real and immediate way. This strike has placed the entire concept of collective bargaining on trial. It is critical, therefore, that the Board assure, and that I protect its assurance, that the spirit and letter of Federal labor law be scrupulously followed.

If the NLRB were not able to do its job, she said, "our national labor laws [would] be permanently and severely undermined."

Timing was another factor in her decision. She made her ruling immediately because without the injunction, the possibility of productive negotiations would be "greatly diminished if this season is lost because of the unfair labor practices committed by the owners." Even if opening day would have to be delayed a bit, she said, the players and owners still had time to bargain in good faith and save the new season.

Her final point involved the issue of irreparable harm to the players, whose lost playing time could not be compensated by monetary damages. The players' "salary and free-agency components cannot be re-created," she said. As "Mr. Cohen was more than eloquent in describing . . . there are personal choices the players make in these systems that money cannot recompense." All players were affected by a disruption of free agency, she explained, as "free agent wages trickle down from top to bottom. They affect the wage of the reserve players today, tomorrow and throughout their entire careers."

After Sotomayor read her decision, there was a rush to the pay phones outside the courtroom. Reporters called in the news that if the players made good on their promise and the owners did not lock them out, the 232-day strike was over.

With just five days to analyze the complex issues and all the corresponding case law, Sotomayor proved she was a quick study. "We practice labor law one hundred percent of the time here," said Zavelo, "and she is responsible for hearing every kind of case that's brought to district court. The fact that she was able to get up to speed in this area of the law on this case so quickly was really impressive because it was a very complicated application of labor law. Dealing with some unusual facts, free agency and salary arbitration, it's not the kind of issue that comes up with the garden-variety labor law case."

Sotomayor's demeanor in the courtroom also struck Zavelo, a trial lawyer who has been with the NLRB for seventeen years. "You run into a lot of kind of imperious types on the bench," he said, "stern judges that are overworked, for one thing, and under a lot of stress. They don't have a lot of time to make people feel comfortable in their courtrooms, or spend a lot of time with people. But she made everyone feel comfortable; I thought she had a great manner for a judge. She had a really human quality that was really striking." He admitted that winning the case could appear to color his perspective, but insisted that that was beside the point. When he watched her Supreme Court confirmation hearings fourteen years later, he was reminded of the impression she made in that courtroom in 1995. "She was clearly a really remarkable person and it wasn't surprising to see where she ended up."

Cohen, who would use Sotomayor's decision in his classes on labor law at Georgetown Law School and elsewhere, believed that everyone involved was struck by Sotomayor's performance:

I think anybody who was in the court that day fully understood that she had amassed terrific awareness of what the relevant facts were and the critical principles of labor that were going to be applied. Just in terms of professional competence, taking account that this was probably the first major labor law she addressed, anyone who reads that opinion would say it was the highest caliber of professional activity by a sitting judge.[35]

National Labor Relations Board Chairman William Gould was equally impressed. "Her opinion and order exceeded our expectations," he wrote. The consequences of her ruling would not only ensure a new season of baseball, he figured, but also allow his agency to ensure that the collective bargaining process would be protected, to everyone's benefit. "The parties were required to return to her court prior to the implementation of any new set of working conditions," he explained. "This was an additional bonus which made our victory complete in that it gave us considerable leverage should the owners attempt to make a new change in working conditions at some point down the road. The Board had been able to demonstrate to the public that the labor law of the nation, however hobbled and deficient, could operate effectively and expeditiously."[36]

The NLRB's concerns about holding the case before a judge that would perhaps be influenced by the dissenting board member's statement were unfounded. "We were fortunate to get a judge who was going to make up her own mind," said Silverman. He was also pleased that Sotomayor took the timing of the process seriously. "If we didn't get a judge like Sonia Sotomayor, but one who was slow to make a decision, it would have had a big impact on the whole case," he said.

Before the hearing, neither Silverman nor any of the other lawyers expected her to make a decision that day. "You expect a judge to say 'I'll take it under advisement; I'll get back to you.' We needed someone who was not only smart but willing to make a decision quickly. I've had an injunction case go on for a year and a half. She was an outstanding jurist, no question."

At the end of Friday's hearing, owners' attorney Casey had immediately asked Sotomayor for a stay of her ruling pending appeal, which she denied. Stating that they had plenty of time to file an appeal, she told Casey that the owners "can go up to the Second Circuit on Monday and ask for an expedited appeal," which they did. She also noted that she would be filing a more in-depth opinion shortly.

The owners' attorneys filed for an appeal of Sotomayor's refusal to grant them an immediate stay, but Judge Roger J. Miner of the Second U.S. Circuit Court of Appeals denied it. They then filed for an appeal of the case, which was scheduled to be argued about two months later.

Sotomayor's injunction ensured that the status quo remained in effect and the owners had no choice but to restore the conditions that existed. The players would resume play and the season would go forward.

Sotomayor's ruling forced the owners to cancel the replacement players' contracts and send them home. The clubs soon announced that April 26 would mark opening day of the 1995 baseball season, allowing for the regular players to get in about three weeks of training. This caused a shortened season of 144 rather than 162 games, but both parties got back to work on an agreement. "We hope to resolve our dispute," said interim Commissioner Bud Selig, "so that we and our fans never have to go through the heartache we've endured for the last eight months."[37] They agreed to a new collective bargaining agreement the following year, but in the meantime the fans showed their frustration over the whole affair with a

20 percent reduction in attendance during the 1995 season.

Magazines and newspapers across the country covered the ruling and the papers had a field day describing Sotomayor's actions in baseball lingo. A *Sports Illustrated* piece quoted replacement pitcher Billy Fultz's colorful summing up: "The owners got a high fastball under the chin, and their knees buckled."[38] By granting the injunction, the *New York Times* wrote:

> U.S. District Judge Sonia Sotomayor in Manhattan did everything but sweep off home plate and bellow, "Play ball!" . . . Sotomayor did not need batting practice. She was like the rare hitter who can "wake up on Christmas Day and pull a curve ball," as the old saying goes. She saw the stitches on the ball and she whacked it into the corner.[39]

The *Boston Globe* dubbed her "the new first lady of Manhattan"[40] and a *Chicago Sun-Times* headline called out that she "delivered a wicked fastball to owners." That article also spotlighted her as "the latest public figure and one of the most inspiring to emerge from baseball's legal wrangling."[41]

In New York's *Daily News* she became "commissioner for a day" in a piece that alluded to the owners' disagreements with Commissioner Fay Vincent that led to his resignation in 1992. "The NLRB took them into court before a 'commissioner' they hadn't counted on: Judge Sotomayor," wrote Bill Madden.[42]

On May 11, 1995, representatives of the players and owners argued the appeals case before the Second Circuit Court of Appeals in New York City. The three-judge panel of Jon O. Newman, chief judge, and circuit judges Ralph K. Winter and J. Daniel Mahoney upheld Sotomayor's decision unanimously. "The fact that she was affirmed by the Second Circuit Court of Appeals," said George Cohen, "affirmed three to nothing by judges who were extremely knowledgeable of labor law cases, was a testimonial to the quality of her work and the opinion she had authored."

The main change in the new collective bargaining agreement that the players and owners ultimately agreed to in November 1996 was a luxury tax on the highest team payrolls and a 2.5 percent tax on player salaries. Those funds, along with some income from TV broadcasts, went into a pool that was distributed to the small-market teams, which addressed the owners' concerns about those teams' ability to compete financially.

With no strikes since Sotomayor's ruling in the spring of 1995, Major League Baseball has had a long run of relative peace and a steady increase in revenue.

Major League pitcher David Cone presented testimony at Sotomayor's Supreme Court confirmation hearings in 2009, speaking "on behalf of all Major League players, both former and current." Having served as a players' union representative for several years during his twenty-two-year career, Cone told the Senate Judiciary Committee that "because of her decision, baseball is in far better shape today than it was fifteen years ago. I believe all of us who love the game — players, owners, and fans — are in her debt."[43]

CHAPTER 8
"ONLY IN THIS COUNTRY"

As it relates to Justice Sotomayor, what can one say but "only in this country." The daughter of a humble working family has risen by way of her legal, scholastic stewardship to the highest trial court in the federal district.

— Senator Alfonse D'Amato, 1997

How disturbing, how petty, and how shameful: Trying to disqualify an outstanding Hispanic woman judge by an anonymous hold. . . . Somehow ethnic and gender biases have crept into the stalling of these nominations. . . . The Senate majority's choices as they stall Hispanic, women and minority nominees is wrong and should end.

— Senator Patrick Leahy on Sonia Sotomayor and other federal court nominees, 1998

Sonia Sotomayor's transition from corporate lawyering to the federal bench was a long-term adjustment, but even after she began to get comfortable being addressed as Judge she still confronted situations no one could have prepared her for. As a woman on the Southern District court bench, she came across a form of gender bias more blatant than any she had confronted earlier in her career. Older male attorneys appearing before her in court often gave her advice, a behavior that she partly attributed to "a paternal attitude." Difficult to imagine occurring before a relatively young male judge on a federal bench, this "lecturing" happened regularly during Sonia's tenure as a district judge. "My experience has been that I do get lectured at frequently, unfortunately," she said in the mid-1990s.[1]

By that point in her career, Sonia's experience revealed that gender bias played a larger role in the workplace for women than racial discrimination. About one year into her work as a corporate lawyer at Pavia & Harcourt, she had reflected on the need to work harder as a woman just to start to compete on an even field. Although not overtly discriminated against as a woman, the staunchly male-dominated legal field gave rise to her perception that she had to be incredibly high-achieving to be taken seriously. "It's not that I feel I've been discriminated against as a woman," she said, "but I've had to devote so much extra time to overcompensating for my gender — time I could have put to use in more productive ways." For a woman raised by a strong, independent, and self-motivated mother, this was a painful cultural fact to absorb:

> I've noticed that if you're a woman you have to work twice as hard, be twice as good. The doors do eventually open, but sometimes it's just so daunting to get them to open. I've had to face that fact that I could probably never be president — not because I'm Puerto Rican, but because I'm a woman. I've come to seriously doubt whether I'll ever see a woman president in my lifetime, and that's very, very disappointing.[2]

Other women in the criminal justice system confronted discrimination to varying degrees. Patricia Gatling, a black lawyer who started out in the Brooklyn District Attorney's office and is now the commissioner and chair of the New York City Commission on Human Rights and a friend of Justice Sotomayor, faced racial, gender, and regional bias. One of four or five black female assistant district attorneys out of about four hundred in Brooklyn, she found that her colleagues were suspect of her because she was black and not from a New York school. She experienced "horrible" discrimination in the office and before the bench. "I would go in the courtroom and the judge would look down and say, 'You know the defendant is not supposed to be on that side, or if you're the mother, you should be on the other side or in the back.' I had a judge say that to me. You had to be tough; you toughened up a lot."

Over the years, Sonia had learned how to avoid one type of discriminatory action by hiding the fact that she could type. "She had always pretended that she didn't know how to type because she didn't want to be relegated to the role of the note taker," said Joe Evall. "It is easy in a lot of work environments to make the woman become the note taker, and she was very savvy about that." Being a woman prosecutor and corporate lawyer in the 1980s and a judge in the 1990s made her a trailblazer, and she was not afraid to take small yet significant steps to show that women belonged in the law, such as wearing a pants suit beneath her judicial robe. Evall recalled the first time she wore that to work, a radical move for a woman in the early 1990s. He told her that he thought it sent a great message to the people who were practicing before her, that a pants suit "is an OK wardrobe for people in a legal work environment." He pointed out to her that it was actually an important statement to make during that transitional time for professional women. "By doing it she was saying, 'This is what I'm wearing, let people get used to it.' If the judge is doing it, it sends a message."

Inside her small suite of offices, Sonia and Theresa maintained a friendly atmosphere that became a second home to the staff. They ordered in from nearby Chinatown restaurants — Sonia liked everything, especially Vietnamese soups, according to Evall — and ate at the conference table while chatting about the latest *Seinfeld* episode and other New York obsessions. "She is a very warm person, very smart, with a lot of interests and a gracious, generous spirit," Evall said. "We were her work family. She was very close with all of her relatives and she has very close friends, so I wouldn't call this a substitute, but she's the kind of person who, when she works with people, forms relationships with them." Every day during that first year brought some new first into their experience and they all got along well. "We worked hard but we enjoyed each other's company very much," said Evall. Like family, the close-knit group was aware of Sotomayor's diabetes and accustomed to seeing her take out her small black pouch when they went out to lunch. From time to time she opened the wallet-size kit, which contained a vial of insulin, hypodermic needle, and blood sugar testing supplies, and quickly gave herself a shot. "She'll be eating Chinese dumplings," said Romeu, "and she'll say, 'Excuse me, sweetie,' and pull out the kit and inject her insulin."[3]

Sonia brought out her natural inclination toward connecting with people that first year in the courthouse. As her first-year clerk, Romeu observed what he called the "real side" of the judge, her "remarkable personal qualities" of "deep caring" that most appropriately described her. Speaking at a court ceremony a few years later, Romeu remarked to Judge Sotomayor:

> It is always in the small things, the details, that you see the beauty of your persona. I remember how when I clerked for you a mere walk through the courthouse would turn into a seemingly endless progression of smiles, gestures and conversations with every member of the extended family that

constitutes this courthouse. Marshals, court reporters, clerks, judges, practitioners and friends would simply come up to talk to you. What never ceases to amaze me, however, is that the conversations always went beyond mere pleasantries, beyond courthouse business, or shallow observations. The conversations were always heartfelt and immediately showed the genuine, deep and caring relationships that existed between you and all that surround you, Judge.[4]

She showed the same consideration in court, as Romeu recalled at the same event:

Although she is a no-nonsense judge in the courtroom, and God have mercy on the hapless soul that shows up unprepared — and that, of course, includes the law clerks — your deep caring is readily apparent even in the midst of trial. I remember many times at trial when you would turn around to the jury and inquire whether everything was all right or you would simply thank the jury for their service. Many a time, I remember, jurors would write letters to chambers thanking you for the unexpectedly wonderful experience they had as jurors with you.[5]

Sotomayor is consistently described as

warm and generous by her friends and colleagues and the emotional support that sustains her has always come from her personal family as well as the work family and friends that surround her. When she became a judge, her brother Juan was married and in his fourth year of private practice as a physician specializing in allergy and immunology. He and his wife, Tracey, had a daughter, Kylie, and adopted twin boys, Conner and Corey, from Korea while Sonia was at the Southern District court. Celina, who had left Prospect Hospital when it closed in 1985, had been working as a nurse at the methadone clinic in the Hunts Point Multi-Services Community Center (HPMSC) in the South Bronx. Founded by Ramon S. Velez, a former teacher in Puerto Rico who migrated to New York and became one of the most prominent community leaders in the Bronx, the HPMSC was designed as a network of health clinics, drug and alcohol treatment services, mental health programs, and Head Start centers that continues to be a vital part of the South Bronx — the corner of New York to which Celina had committed her entire nursing career. While working at the clinic, Celina met Omar Lopez, a man who, in Sonia's words, provided her mother "with the love and companionship that had been missing so long from her life" and whom Celina would eventually marry. In 1992, after working in the clinic for seven years, Celina retired and moved to Florida.

Since her divorce, Sonia had tried to round out her work-intensive lifestyle with international travel and New York culture, and her new career on the bench would pose another challenge to finding time to devote to a rich personal life. "I realized I needed to strike a balance between my ambition and my humanism," she said at age thirty-two while working at Pavia & Harcourt. "I still want to be successful, but I also want to be happy and not sacrifice personal satisfaction for an intellectual one. All of my life I've worked so hard I've never learned to enjoy life. Now I'm learning." She had decided by that time that her personal satisfaction would not include having children, partly because of her diabetes and partly because she felt too driven in her career: "I don't think I could freely devote the kind of attention to a child that a child needs," she said.[6] Instead, she would devote her affections to her niece, nephews, and large extended family, including a large array of godchildren.

After becoming a federal judge, however, she decided she would no longer date lawyers, and she found the missing piece that had eluded her for so many years. The most powerful turn in her personal life came when she fell in love with a New York contractor, Peter White, a man she had known for several years through a mutual friend. President of a company called Commercial and Industrial Construction based in Yonkers, Peter had grown up in the Bronx, like Sonia, but lived in an entirely different professional world. He was tall and distinguished looking with wavy gray hair, a trimmed white beard, and dark Sean Connery–like eyebrows, and Sonia considered him "the best thing that had ever happened" to her. He was a product of the city who preferred the country, a man who ran his own business and was not overawed by Sonia's high-flying career.[7] By 1994 the couple had made a "commitment for life" and planned to marry. For all the success Sonia had earned, all the warm friendships and indestructible family bonds, she had not found "genuine personal happiness" until she met Peter, she said.

In 1998, a year of more transition, Sonia and Peter bought a two-bedroom condominium apartment at 3 Bedford Street in Greenwich Village. The quiet tree-lined street, with its redbrick apartment buildings and storefronts holding bakeries, quaint bars, restaurants, and shops belied the extraordinary possibilities in the air for the Manhattan judge who had moved into a fifth-floor apartment with her fiancé: One year earlier, Sonia had received a call from the White House.

On June 25, 1997, President Bill Clinton called Sonia to offer her his appointment to the Second Circuit Court of Appeals, the highest federal court in New York. The momentous invitation not only opened the door to perhaps the most prestigious court in the country, second only to the U.S. Supreme Court, but intimated Sonia's potential nomination to the nation's highest court. An appointment to a federal appeals court signified the president's consideration of the nominee as a potential justice of the U.S. Supreme Court, and the prospect of that ascension was almost beyond her scope. Peter convinced her to accept and to brace herself for the politicized confirmation process that would surely come.

The initial sense of awe over the responsibility with which she was entrusted on the district court never completely wore off, and her respect for the federal bench helped her become more comfortable with the idea of moving up to the appeals court. As a district court judge, everything about the job kept her intellectually stimulated yet humble:

"Every once in a while I am sitting in the courtroom," she said, "and I feel this kind of inner self looking at myself and saying what are you doing here? How did you get here? I don't think that has anything to do with insecurity or that has nothing to do with anything other than it is a very powerful position. The responsibility is enormous."[8]

The U.S. Courts of Appeals were created in 1891 "to provide intermediate review between the District Courts and the Supreme Court," as described by Chief Judge Ralph K. Winter of the U.S. Court of Appeals for the Second Circuit in New York. The nation is divided into twelve regions, or circuits, that correspond to the circuit courts, and the region covered by the Second Circuit includes the states of New York, Connecticut, and Vermont. "Given the small number of cases that can be heard by the Supreme Court," Winter said, "it is, for most federal litigants in the three states, the final avenue for relief."[9]

Like the federal court for the Southern District of New York on which Sotomayor was serving when she was nominated to the higher court, the Second Circuit Court was the most "important and best-known" of the nation's appeals courts throughout most of its history because its jurisdiction included New York City. "New York was for the greater part of the century easily the leading commercial and financial center of the nation and the world," Winter said. "Litigation in the federal courts arising out of important commercial or financial transactions thus came our way." The fact that New York was an important port made the Second Circuit "responsible for making law in the field of admiralty," and the location was also ("although unfortunately") a center for organized crime and narcotics rings. Several prominent judges have also served on the Second Circuit, including two who became Supreme Court Justices, John Marshall Harlan and Thurgood Marshall.

Serving on an appellate court would cause a significant shift of focus in Sonia's judicial experience. Unlike the trial court on which she had served for five years, the appellate court addresses the legal points of the decision — there is no jury, no retrial, no consideration of evidence. A panel of three appellate judges reviews briefs and hears oral argument to determine whether to uphold the district court's decision. An appeals court decision can be appealed to the U.S. Supreme Court, which has the option of refusing to hear the case. Appeals judges are concerned with questions of law and public policy rather than issues of facts, which are the focus of trials. The opinions written by appeals court judges have the potential to affect many people because their decisions are binding on the district courts within the circuit.

Having won enormous respect for her performance on the district bench, Sonia received immediate support for her confirmation from her previous sponsors, senators Patrick Moynihan and Alfonse D'Amato, as well as hundreds of lawyers and more than ten thousand members of various organizations across the country who sent letters to the U.S. Senate Judiciary Committee to express their support of her confirmation. Her first clerk, Xavier Romeu, organized a group from the Puerto Rican Bar Association to be the first to speak to Judiciary Committee members on her behalf. Romeu, who a few months later became the executive director of the Puerto Rican Federal Affairs Administration in Washington, also secured the endorsement of Puerto Rico Governor Pedro Rosello. The American Bar Association reviewed her record and voted to give her its highest rating of "well qualified."

The divisive political climate in Washington caused long delays in her confirmation process, however, as it did for many federal court nominees awaiting a Senate vote. The Republican-led Congress had slowed the process to a near halt by 1997, a year in which the Senate had confirmed only twenty-two judges to address 115 vacancies. The lack of judges had reached a crisis level: In areas like the Ninth Circuit in the western United States, which was operating without ten judges, more than one third of the court was shut down, and the situation was becoming more critical throughout the country by the day. Chief Justice of the United States Supreme Court William Rehnquist called the rising number of vacancies "the most immediate problem we face in the federal judiciary."[10] Sotomayor's journey to confirmation played out during a period of heated criticism over the highly politicized process.

At the opening of Sotomayor's Senate Judiciary hearings, which took place in September and October 1997, Senator D'Amato emphasized her inspiring story and reiterated his prediction about her future on the nation's highest court:

As it relates to Justice Sotomayor, what can one say but "only in this country." The daughter of a humble working family has risen by way of her legal, scholastic stewardship to the highest trial court in the federal district, and premier district I might add with some prejudice, of the Southern District of New York where she has distinguished herself. And I predicted to this committee, almost five years ago, that Judge Sotomayor would be an exemplary, outstanding justice. She has demonstrated that, repeatedly. She has shown compassion, wisdom, one of the great intellects on the court. Her experience, both as a prosecutor, civil litigator, and federal trial judge, makes her an exceptionally qualified candidate for the Second Circuit.[11]

Questions at the hearings covered issues such as how Sotomayor interprets the Constitution and her opinions on federal sentencing guidelines and the underlying causes of drug use. Strom Thurmond, the Republican senator from South Carolina, asked: "A former Supreme Court justice had expressed his view of Constitutional interpretation as follows, and I quote, 'We look to the history of the time of framing of the Constitution, and the intervening history of interpretation. But the ultimate question must be, what do the words and the text mean in our time?' Do you agree with this statement?"[12]

Sonia replied, "No, sir. Not fully." She explained:

> I agree with the first two parts of it. If you look at the Constitution and what it meant at the time. The last suggests that I would be trying to change its meaning today. And no. I think the first two would inform what the last results should be, which is what does it mean today, and how to apply new facts to that, if the issue is new facts.[13]

Senator Thurmond also asked, based on her experience as a judge, why "many young, poor youth become drug dealers?" She responded that she wished she had the answer, which would solve "one of the worst ravages" on society, but "I simply don't have one reason I can give you. The reasons are myriad and complex."

Thurmond's question about federal sentencing guidelines raised a controversial issue and gave Sotomayor the opportunity to describe how the system called for society to impose its views rather than a judge:

SEN. THURMOND: Some argue that the federal sentencing guidelines do not provide enough flexibility for the sentencing judge. And some even say they should be abolished. What is your view of the federal sentencing guidelines, based on your experience with them?

SOTOMAYOR: Thus far, sir, in the vast majority of cases I have found the guidelines to be very helpful in giving some comfort to me, as a judge, that I am not arbitrarily imposing sentences based on my personal feelings. I believe that congressional sentiment, as reflected in the guidelines, is important, because it permits me, not to impose my personal views, but to let the democracy impose the society's views.

Senator John Ashcroft, the Republican from Missouri, brought up Sotomayor's recent district court case *Holmes v. Artuz*, which involved a gay prison inmate who was refused a job in the mess hall because he had proclaimed his sexual orientation. Sotomayor ruled against the prison, which had claimed that federal law doesn't protect people from discrimination based on sexual orientation. In her opinion, Sotomayor wrote, "The constitutional right not to be discriminated against for any reason, including sexual orientation, without a rational basis is an established proposition of law."[14]

Senator Ashcroft framed his question in terms of whether a new constitutional amendment should be created to grant specific rights: "Do you believe that there's a constitutional right to homosexual conduct, by prisoners?"

SOTOMAYOR: No, sir. There isn't. Case law is very clear about that. The only constitutional right that homosexuals have is the same constitutional right every citizen of the United States has, which is not to have government action taken against them arbitrarily and capriciously. The Supreme Court said that last term, in *Evans v. Romer.* But outside of that, that's a basic constitutional right, not to them in particular, but to the world that constitutes the U.S.

After another round of hearings for several nominees in October, the Senate committee voted 16–2 to approve Sotomayor's nomination. However, instead of moving swiftly to a Senate vote for her confirmation in the midst of the federal courts crisis, her nomination was ignored for months along with many others. Eight months later, in June 1998, Senator Patrick Leahy issued a press release about the "Republican hold against this fine judge" and other disturbing trends in a confirmation process that appeared to be biased against Latinos and women. Speaking specifically to Sonia's nomination, he said:

> In fact, how disturbing, how petty, and how shameful: Trying to disqualify an outstanding Hispanic woman judge by an anonymous hold. I have far more respect for Senators who, for whatever reason, wish to vote against her. Stand up; vote against her. But to have an anonymous hold — an anonymous hold — in the U.S. Senate with 100 Members representing 260 million Americans, which should be the conscience of the Nation, should not be lurking in our cloakrooms anonymously trying to hold up a nominee. If we want to vote against somebody, vote against them. I respect that. State your reasons. I respect that. But don't hold up a qualified judicial nominee.[15]

Senator Leahy also expressed his concerns about the "disturbing pattern" of delays on Hispanic nominees, such as Hilda Tagle, the only Hispanic woman the Senate confirmed in 1998 and whose confirmation to a district court in Texas took thirty-two months; Judge Richard Paez, a district court judge nominated to ascend to the Ninth Circuit, whose twenty-nine-month wait was still in limbo; Anabelle Rodriquez, a nominee for the District Court for Puerto Rico, who had been waiting twenty-nine months for confirmation; and Jorge Rangel, whom Clinton had nominated for the Fifth Circuit in 1997, but who had not yet been given a hearing by the Judiciary Committee.

Rangel, who had represented the Fifth Circuit on the American Bar Association committee that reviewed Sotomayor's record and voted for her "well qualified" rating, would eventually ask the president to remove his name from the list due to the Senate's inactivity. "There was a group of us who were nominated during that period," he said, "and from time to time I would check the website of the Senate to see what kind of activity was occurring. Weeks turned into months, a year and more. Judge Sotomayor got a hearing, which some of us did not."

Concerned about those and other minority and women nominees whose confirmations languished in the Senate, Leahy urged his colleagues to do their "constitutional duty" and take action on the confirmation process. Holding up a large number of confirmations was "preventing the administration of justice," he said, because "Courts cannot try cases, incarcerate the guilty or resolve civil disputes without judges." Leahy's appraisal of the stalling tactics provides a sharp overview of the political milieu in which Sotomayor endured her lengthy route to confirmation:

> For some unexplained reason, judicial nominees who are women or racial or ethnic minorities seem to take the longest in the Senate. Of the 10 judicial nominees whose nominations have been pending the longest before the Senate, eight are women and racial or ethnic minority candidates. A ninth has been delayed in large measure because of opposition to his mother, who already serves as a judge. The tenth is one who blew the lid off the $1.4 million right-wing campaign to "kill" Clinton judicial nominees.
>
> Pending on the Senate calendar, having been passed over again and again, are Judge Sonia Sotomayor, Judge Richard Paez, Susan Oki Mollway and Ronnie White. Held up in committee after two hearings is Clarence Sundram. Still without a hearing are Anabelle Rodriquez, Judge James A. Beaty Jr., and Jorge C. Rangel.

What all these nominees have in common is that they are either women or members of racial or ethnic minorities.

Acting to fill judicial vacancies is a constitutional duty that the Senate — and all of its members — are obligated to fulfill. In its unprecedented slowdown in the handling of nominees in the 104th and 105th Congresses, the Senate is shirking its duty. The Senate majority's choices as they stall Hispanic, women and minority nominees is wrong and should end.

Mr. President, I have served here for nearly 24 years. I know Members of the Senate. I have enormous respect for so many of them, Republicans and Democrats alike. The vast majority of Senators I have served with do not have any bias or ethnic bias against people. They do not have a religious bias. They do not have a gender bias. But somehow ethnic and gender biases have crept into the stalling of these nominations.[16]

An opinion piece in Leahy's home district in Vermont called on the senator to make "a lot of noise over this partisan nonsense" and rebuked criticisms about Sotomayor as an "activist judge" that had circulated in the *Wall Street Journal*. In a May 29, 1998, piece *Wall Street Journal* columnist Paul A. Gigot used Sotomayor's *Archie v. Grand Central Partnership* ruling to portray her as an activist judge, stating: "Her willingness to legislate from the bench was apparent in her recent decision that a private group giving work experience to the homeless must pay the minimum wage."[17] The Vermont editorial pointed out that Sotomayor's ruling revealed just the opposite, and quoted a conservative to make its point:

The *Journal* was upset with Sotomayor's ruling that a coalition of New York businesses promoting a program for the homeless had violated federal law by not paying the minimum wage. This, in the *Journal*'s opinion, constituted "judicial activism."

But a well-known conservative, Gerald Walpin, has rushed to Sotomayor's defense and his message is worth heeding.

"If they had read the case they would see that she said she personally approved of the homeless program but that as a judge she was required to apply the law as it exists," Walpin commented. "She wrote that the law does not permit an exception in this case. That's exactly what conservatives want — a non-activist judge who does not apply her own views but is bound by the law."[18]

In Sotomayor's case, the Senate majority's primary intent was to prevent her ultimate nomination to the U.S. Supreme Court. As reported in the *New York Times,* majority leader Trent Lott of Mississippi prohibited a Senate floor vote on her nomination to disable her ascension to the Supreme Court: "Senate Republican staff aides said Trent Lott . . . has agreed to hold up a vote on the nomination as part of an elaborate political calculus; if she were easily confirmed to the appeals court, they said, that would put her in a position to be named to the Supreme Court." If she were confirmed, the piece stated, and President Clinton nominated her to the Supreme Court, the majority would find themselves in an awkward situation. "Senate Republicans think that they would then have a difficult time opposing a Hispanic woman who had just been confirmed by the full Senate," wrote the *Times.* The reporter quoted a senior Republican staff aide, who requested anonymity, on the Republicans' outlook: "Basically, we think that putting her on the appeals court puts her in the batter's box to be nominated to the Supreme Court."[19]

Sotomayor's supporters worked diligently

to move her confirmation forward and refute claims that she was an activist judge. Senator D'Amato also spoke out against such claims, saying her judicial work was "not a record of some left-wing ideologue — it is a record of individual rights that she stands up for. This is someone of balance."[20]

On October 2, 1998 — fifteen months after Sotomayor's nomination by President Clinton — the Senate voted to confirm her to the Second Circuit Court of Appeals with a tally of 68–28. Responding to the long delay, Sonia set aside concerns that she had been the subject of discrimination and attributed the events to "assumptions" people made based on stereotypes. "I don't think anybody looked at me as a woman or as a Hispanic and said, 'We're not going to appoint her because of those characteristics,'" she said. "Clearly that's not what occurred. But I do believe there are gender and ethnic stereotypes that propel people to assumptions about what they expected me to be." Those assumptions, she added, would not hold up under a close and careful review of her judicial record: "I obviously felt that any balanced view of my work would not support some of the allegations being made."[21]

On November 6, the court held her induction proceedings in the Ceremonial Courtroom of the federal courthouse on Pearl Street. Many of her supporters attended, including Senator Moynihan and Senator-elect Charles Schumer, Robert Morgenthau, U.S. Attorneys Mary Jo White and Zachary Carter, Congressman Jose Serrano, Congresswoman Nydia Velasquez, Bronx Borough President Fernando Ferrer, New York Assemblyman Roberto Ramirez, clerks from her six years at the district court, members of many legal and nonprofit organizations, former colleagues, family members, and friends. Also at the ceremony were the twelve judges from the Second Circuit, which included her former Yale professors Guido Calabresi and José Cabranes.

Before standing across from Sotomayor to administer the oath of office, Judge Cabranes spoke to the audience about how they met and shared highlights of her life and career. Having been her mentor at Yale, he was extraordinarily proud to welcome her to the Second Circuit and opened his remarks with an emphasis on their shared Latino background:

There is in Spanish a nice word for what we all have in mind today — enhorabuena. It is translated into English as merely "congratulations," but the Spanish has a particular, and more nuanced, meaning: The word enhorabuena is a composite of three words that, idiomatically, convey the sense that a landmark event has taken place "at a happy and opportune time."

Sonia Sotomayor's arrival here was (as we all know) delayed, but she is with us at last, "at a happy and opportune time" — a happy and opportune time for her, for our Court, and for our country.[22]

After Sonia took the oath, Peter White helped her slip her new black robe over her red suit, standing behind her to hold open the arms and smooth the top across her shoulders.

Each circuit across the country has its own particular style and reputation, and the Second Circuit is known for its tradition of hearing oral argument. While some circuits may come to decisions based on briefs alone, "the Second Circuit is the last bastion of oral argument of this country," according to a 2006 study of the distinctive practices of the Second Circuit by John G. McCarthy. "Even with a caseload that now exceeds 7,000 filings annually, the court has held firm its conviction that oral argument of an appeal should be the norm, not the exception." Rather than screen appeals to select those deemed worthy to warrant oral argument, the Second Circuit tradition believes "in the importance of giving litigants their day in court and the importance of oral argument to assist occasionally in identifying important issues not readily apparent in the parties' briefs."[23]

Each appeal is heard by a panel of three judges that heard oral argument on about six appeals each day, which required reading about a hundred briefs per week. Sonia's task as an appeals judge was to determine if the law had been applied accurately, and the position demanded a much less social workday than she had become accustomed to on the district court. One of the qualities necessary for an appeals court judge is the "ability to function comfortably in a semi-monastic setting." The solitary hours spent behind closed doors studying cases and writing opinions is a difficult adjustment for "persons not temperamentally suited to a secluded, scholarly existence" such as politicians, practicing lawyers, and trials judges, write two scholars on the federal courts. On many days an appellate judge's only interactions will be with his or her secretary, law clerks, and perhaps other judges.[24]

The isolation of the appellate judge's working life is balanced out, however, during oral argument in the largely vacant courtroom, where judges are free to question and engage in discussion with the lawyers as much as they desire. The Second Circuit is known as a "hot bench," a court in which judges ask a lot of questions, and the style of the court matched Sotomayor's perfectly. H. Raymond Fasano, an immigration lawyer who appeared before her twenty-four times, said "she isn't afraid of running a hot bench" and admired her for it. Fasano, who identified himself as a Republican, explained that "when a judge asks a lot of questions, that means she's read the record, she knows the issues and she has concerns that she wants resolved. And that's the judge's job."[25]

The proceedings of the court took place in the seventeenth-floor courtroom of the Thurgood Marshall United States Courthouse, one of the grand structures of Foley Square. The seven-story base of the grand building, designed as a Corinthian temple with its ten pillars facing Centre Street, holds a twenty-four-story tower topped with a gold pyramid. Designed by Cass Gilbert, who was also the architect of the U.S. Supreme Court Building in Washington, D.C., the courthouse features a pair of courtrooms two stories high, with cathedral-like ceilings.

In an appellate career that would span

eleven years, Judge Sotomayor made three thousand panel decisions and authored about four hundred published opinions on the Second Circuit. Among those she considers the most significant is *Clarett v. National Football League,* in which football player Maurice Clarett, who had left Ohio State, sued the NFL over its rule that a player could not enter the draft until he was three full college football seasons removed from high school. The district court ruled in favor of Clarett, but the NFL appealed, and Sotomayor's panel reversed the ruling based on the rules of collective bargaining. In *United States v. Quattrone,* former bank executive Frank Quattrone had been tried for allegedly obstructing investigations into initial public stock offerings handled by his bank. In the wake of a deadlocked jury and mistrial, a second trial was scheduled, and the district court was ordered that the names of the jurors not be published by the media. Sotomayor's panel, which included Cabranes, struck down the court's order, ruling that it violated the First Amendment.

In another First Amendment case, a district court ruled that a Muslim inmate's First Amendment rights had not been violated because the holiday feast that he was denied was not a mandatory one in Islam. In *Ford v. McGinnis,* Sotomayor's opinion reversed that decision, holding that the inmate's First Amendment rights were violated because the feast was subjectively important to the inmate's practice of Islam. A 2006 Wall Street trading scandal formed the backdrop of *In re NYSE Specialists Securities Litigation,* which involved a class action suit filed by a group of investors. The group alleged that the New York Stock Exchange (NYSE) did not properly regulate trading and misrepresented the market's integrity by helping, and in some cases encouraging, seven investment banks in a multimillion-dollar fraudulent self-trading scheme. When the district court dismissed the claims, the investors appealed, and Sotomayor's panel ruled that the NYSE did have immunity for regulatory failures but the shield of protection did not extend to the allegations that the exchange had misled traders about the market's integrity.

In *Farrell v. Burke,* Christopher J. Farrell challenged his parole officers' ban on his possession of pornography. Farrell had been convicted of sexual crimes involving minors, and when the district court ruled in favor of the parole officers, he appealed. Sotomayor and her two fellow jurists sorted through X-rated materials to determine that Farrell's collection fit a reasonable understanding of the term "pornography" and was thus not unconstitutionally vague, which led to them affirming the district court's judgment.

Shi Liang Lin v. United States Department of Justice was brought to the appeals court by three Chinese men seeking asylum in the United States. Their girlfriends and, in the third case, fiancée, had been forced to undergo abortions or sterilization under China's coercive family planning policies, and the men sought the same refugee status as their partners. The Board of Immigration Appeals (BIA) had denied them asylum, stating that refugee status does not automatically extend to a victim's spouse, boyfriend (girlfriend), or fiancé (fiancée). In a move reserved for extremely significant cases, the court heard the case *en banc,* with all the judges rather than one panel, and upheld the BIA's denial. In the opinion, however, Sotomayor noted that the majority's broad rule ignored the fact that "the state's interference with this fundamental right" affects both spouses, observing that "[t]he termination of a wanted pregnancy under a coercive population control program can only be devastating to any couple, akin, no doubt, to the killing of a child."[26] Sotomayor had observed a striking increase in cases to review asylum denials. "In the last year and a half," she said in 2006, "our total docket has doubled as a result of the filing of those petitions. . . . There are a significant number of claims from China arising from China's family-planning one-child policy and abortion practices of that country." There were also many claims coming from "Albania and other Eastern European countries based on either political or religious persecution," she said.[27]

A ruling written in 2008 that would ignite controversy in the next phase of Sotomayor's career concerned a reverse-discrimination issue among firefighters in New Haven, Connecticut. The city had thrown out the results of an officer-candidate exam because none of the nonwhite candidates had scored high enough to qualify for promotion. In response, twenty white firefighters (including one Hispanic) charged that they had been discriminated against for promotion. In arguing the case, *Ricci v. DeStefano,* the city officials noted a fear of potential lawsuits from the minority firefighters had motivated their act to dismiss the test results. The exam had come under scrutiny as unfair to minorities, and other cities had replaced it with one that assessed skills more fairly. Sotomayor's panel ruled in the city's favor, stating that though "we are not unsympathetic to the plaintiffs' expression of frustration," the New Haven Civil Service Board had "found itself in the unfortunate position of having no good alternatives" and "was simply trying to fulfill its obligations" under the Civil Rights Act "when confronted with test results that had a disproportionate racial impact." The case then went to the Supreme Court, which overturned the appellate court's ruling by a vote of 5–4. The Supreme Court decided a fear of litigation was not a justifiable reason to exclude the test results.[28]

Almost two years after joining the Second Circuit, Sonia threw a party at her and Peter's apartment on Bedford Street to celebrate his fiftieth birthday. During Sonia's confirmation process in 1997 and 1998, they had announced that they would get married after she reached the bench, but that had not yet occurred. They had, however, renovated the apartment, but that did not ultimately reflect a long settling in. Shortly after the party, she and Peter broke up. The *New York Times* reported that "he returned to Westchester County, bought a small boat and married a woman who was an acquaintance of the judge and 14 years her junior."[29]

As Sonia's friend Sandra Guzmán wrote,

"Like the rest of us, she's not been immune to falling in love or getting her heart broken."[30] Her friend and former colleague at Pavia, Steven Skulnik, said that Sonia and Peter had had "a real adult relationship" and the breakup "was very tough" on her.[31] Long hours of work helped her transition to single life, but there was always that silent apartment to walk into every night. Statistics about women in the legal profession reveal that the odds were not great that she would be able to nurture a marriage along with her career, for whatever comfort data can provide during a difficult time. Approximately 33 percent of all women lawyers never marry (compared to 8 percent of male lawyers) and in 2009 nearly 50 percent of women lawyers were unmarried (compared to 15 percent of men), according to the American Bar Association.

There were moments when Sonia was stung by regret over not having children, such as the day she attended the funeral of the mother of one of her best friends, Dawn Cardi. She had met Dawn at the start of her career in the Manhattan District Attorney's Office, when Dawn was working as a legal aid lawyer; Sonia became close friends and Brooklyn neighbors with Dawn and her husband. Like Sonia, Dawn had been very close to her strong, "amazing" mother, and as Sonia listened to her deliver the eulogy at the funeral, she thought to herself that regardless of all the people in her life, no one would ever love her the way Dawn loved her mother. "That's the way it worked out," Dawn said. "If she'd put her mind to it, she could have done it."[32] Many extraordinary things happened to Sonia, and many of them early in her adult life, but becoming the mother of devoted children was not one of them.

Sonia's approach to rejuvenating herself after Peter left included a new focus on her physical well-being. She launched a self-inspired makeover by trading in her large scholastic glasses for contacts, cutting her hair into a fresh, short bob, and working out regularly, which resulted in a forty-pound weight loss. "It seemed to all of her friends that loving herself tenderly became a priority once again," said Guzmán.[33]

She continued to date and accepted the fact that there are more options for love and romance than those handed down by family, tradition, and society. Her evolving views, as she explained to a friend, released the Cinderella fairy tale concept of the perfect relationship and embraced the idea that people are free to make up their own rules to find happiness in love. Changing deeply set beliefs about a woman's role and acknowledging that you can figure out for yourself what makes you happy is not easy, but it is doable, she told her friend. The challenge is finding someone who looks at life and love the same way. She found that person after another few years on the circuit court and described him as "brilliant," a friend who came with no strings attached. They met when it was convenient for them both, and when the romance faded they remained friends.

Judge Sotomayor's social life would take another positive turn in her final months on the Second Circuit Court, according to her fellow judge Rosemary Pooler. "It's hard to find interesting men who are at her level," Pooler said, "but I'm pleased to say she has recently met some. And that's all I'll say about that!"[34]

The love affair that never went stale throughout Judge Sotomayor's eleven years on the Second Circuit was the one she had with New York City. "If you had to describe my sister, you'd say New Yorker — it's her essence," said Juan. "I always joke that her vision does not extend beyond the Hudson River." She continued to go to Broadway shows, including the 2008 Tony Award–winning musical *In the Heights,* which tells the story of a scholarship-winning Latina from Manhattan's Washington Heights neighborhood who struggles over leaving her close-knit community for Stanford. The heroine's story had parallels to her own. When the show's writer Lin-Manual Miranda spotted Sotomayor in a restaurant in 2009, he introduced himself and told her how proud she had made the Latino community. Sotomayor told Miranda that she had seen his musical *twice*.

The atmosphere of her chambers remained friendly from one class of clerks to the next. Kyle Wong, who clerked for her in 2006–2007, told the *New Yorker* how the judge rewarded them for putting in one particularly long, grueling day of interviewing potential clerks for the following year. She told them that as soon as she finished her final interview they would all head to her apartment for burgers. "We went over and she had Scotch and all this wine and beer," Wong said. "We sat down at eight and then she busts out the poker, and we play Texas Hold 'em until two o'clock in the morning." When everyone was ready to leave, she doled out cab fair and yelled after them as they drove off, "I don't have to see you guys before 10 A.M. tomorrow!"[35]

While the rhythm of Sotomayor's casework on the appeals bench kept a steady pace, things were changing in another section of New York that meant a lot to her. Making regular visits to her relatives up in the Bronx year after year showed her the dramatic upswing that had swept through the borough since her childhood. Many of the neighborhoods once devastated by the crime that accompanied the drug epidemic of the 1970s — and forced the Sotomayors north to Co-op City — have been redeveloped through a surge of local, state, and federal programs from the 1980s onward and changed the face of the Bronx. The landscape of burned-out tenements that was imprinted on everyone's mind in the 1970s is history; during the Clinton administration, the borough's sweeping urban renewal earned it the All-America City award from the National Civic League, and development has been steady ever since.

"It's really a fascinating story," said Bronx Borough President Ruben Diaz Jr., whose share of the transformation includes the push for a community center on the site of an abandoned parking lot next to Sotomayors' Bronxdale Houses when he was still a state assemblyman. Today, the once-neglected property is now the home of a $10.4-million, state-of-the-art sports and after-school education complex and the pride of Soundview. Like Sotomayor, Diaz has witnessed firsthand the extraordinary evolution of the Bronx, a phenomenon that mirrors Justice Sotomayor's own trajectory.

Time with family in the Bronx and elsewhere was more about quality than quantity, as Sotomayor committed additional hours every week to teaching. Throughout her long term on the Second Circuit she taught at New York University (NYU) and Columbia Law Schools and lectured at Pepperdine University, the University of Puerto Rico, University of Indiana Law School, and Syracuse University.

At NYU she co-taught a class titled Trial and Appellate Advocacy with Adjunct Professor John Siffert, a class that took third-year law students through each stage of a trial case. Her Appellate Advocacy course at Columbia, co-taught with Professor Gerard Lynch, Lecturer-in-Law Ilene Strauss, and Assistant Dean Ellen P. Chapnick, involved giving classroom lectures on the appellate court system, organizing a student moot court argued before Second Circuit judges, and supervising student externs in her court chambers.

Sotomayor had begun teaching at Columbia during her tenure as a district court judge and surprised Chapnick with a call about six months after being elevated to the Second Circuit. "She called me up and said, 'You know, I really miss your students. Isn't there something we can do about that?'" Chapnick said.[36] The result was Sotomayor and Chapnick's launch of the externship program. Each semester that Sotomayor taught the course, she made room in her heavy schedule to provide three students with real-life experience researching and writing about actual cases pending before the court.

Judge Sotomayor's love of teaching was an extension of her fervor for drawing young people to the law, a quality that also manifested in the significant number of speeches she presented at colleges and law schools throughout the country. She never lost her enthusiasm for inspiring women, Latinos, and other minorities to enter the field, an activity she first took up in her education committee work at the Puerto Rican Legal Defense and Education Fund in the 1980s. She was a prolific speechmaker — among the stacks of materials she submitted with her U.S. Senate questionnaire during her Supreme Court confirmation process were eighty-four speeches.

Sonia credited her own undergraduate experiences for igniting her interest in public service because her activities at Princeton gave her "a sense of having a positive impact," a value that motivated her government career and decades of pro bono work on boards.[37] Her ongoing association with Princeton culminated in her receiving an honorary doctor of law from the university in 2001 for her "wisdom and judgment that cross cultural boundaries" and being named a trustee in 2007. While serving on the Second Circuit Court of Appeals, Sotomayor also received honorary degrees from Brooklyn Law School, Lehman College of the City University of New York, Northeastern University School of Law, and Pace University Law School.

By election season 2008, fifty-four-year-old Sonia Sotomayor had served sixteen years as a federal judge, six in the district court and eleven in the circuit court. When asked if she missed anything about being a lawyer, practicing on the other side of the bench, she said that she valued her years as a prosecutor and private practice attorney and everything they brought to her life but that she didn't feel sorry for moving on. "I am one of those people who has loved every job I have taken," she said. "I have been blessed with working with people that I admire and like, and I have been blessed with working with clients when I was in private practice whom I adored, many of whom are still friends today. . . . And so if I stayed, I think I would have continued to be happy, but I love judging so much that I've never regretted leaving those experiences."[38]

Ever since Senator Patrick Moynihan exclaimed about Sotomayor's gifts and potential during her first confirmation process in 1992, Sotomayor had been on the short list for the U.S. Supreme Court. He had made the prediction earlier than most, convinced that she possessed all the qualities to become one of the nation's top jurists.

Sotomayor had fulfilled her own goal of gaining as much experience in her field as possible to one day serve as a judge and also contribute to her community outside the courtroom, giving back. The life in the law that she had dreamed of with such passionate anticipation as a child had delivered on all its promises. In about ten years she would be eligible for retirement with a full pension, and perhaps she would find a new challenge to engage her at that time.

Or maybe the United States would elect a black president who, early in his term, had an important judicial vacancy to fill.

CHAPTER 9
TWO PROMISES

Walking in the door she would bring more experience on the bench, and more varied experience on the bench, than anyone currently serving on the United States Supreme Court had when they were appointed.

— President Barack Obama

The judge was on her way to the gym before work when the first call came. It was a pleasant spring morning in late April, a Monday that was supposed to get to about seventy-five degrees with no rain — a perfect day in New York. Someone from the president's administration told her that the White House Legal Counsel Office was trying to reach her, and gave her a phone number. She wrote it down while walking to her car, got inside, and made the call on her cell phone.

Sitting in her white Saab, she learned from a staffer that the White House believed there would be a resignation on the Supreme Court and the Legal Counsel Office wanted to include her name on a list of potential candidates to be the next associate justice. The background check would then begin. "Do not tell anyone," the staffer said.[1]

"My heart skipped a beat," the judge said. It had become a truly gorgeous day in New York.

Sonia Sotomayor was one of four candidates on President Barack Obama's final short list for the Supreme Court vacancy, and all of them were women: Diane P. Wood, a judge on the Seventh Circuit Court of Appeals in Chicago; Elena Kagan, the president's solicitor general; and Janet Napolitano, the current homeland security secretary joined Sotomayor on the list. The resigning member of the court was Justice David Souter, who at age sixty-nine was younger than five other justices and was apparently in good health, but it was known he was eager to return to his native New Hampshire. Apparently Souter had waited for the outcome of the election to schedule his retirement under a president who shared the more liberal leanings Souter had brought to his decisions in the past twenty years.

During the presidential campaign, Obama had spoken about what he would look for in a nominee to the Supreme Court, should a vacancy arise. Protecting the individual rights guaranteed in the Constitution required justices who had a connection with "real life" as well as the intellect and experience to handle the responsibilities of the Court, he said. "I will look for those judges who have an outstanding judicial record, who have the intellect, and who hopefully have a sense of what real-world folks are going through."[2]

President Obama, who had taught constitutional law at the University of Chicago Law School for ten years, discussed the "institutionally conservative" nature of the Supreme Court and was critical of some of the more recent conservative decisions, such as *Gonzales v. Carhart,* which upheld the Partial-Birth Abortion Ban Act of 2003. "The decision presumed that the health of women is best protected by the Court — not by doctors and not by the woman herself. That presumption is wrong," he said.[3] He considered a woman's right "to make a decision about how many children she wants to have and when" to be "one of the most fundamental freedoms we have in this country."

He also cited "the blow to equal pay" in

Ledbetter v. Goodyear, a 2007 decision that ruled that workers may not sue their employers over unequal pay as specified by Title VII of the Civil Rights Act if the discrimination occurred more than 180 days before the suit. That decision moved Justice Ruth Bader Ginsburg to make the rare move of reading a dissent from the bench, in which she said, speaking for the three other dissenting judges, "Title VII was meant to govern real-world employment practices, and that world is what the court today ignores. . . . In our view, the court does not comprehend, or is indifferent to, the insidious way in which women can be victims of pay discrimination."[4]

The president also criticized the Supreme Court's 2007 decision that struck down race-conscious admissions plans that sought to integrate school populations in two urban school systems, Louisville and Seattle, in the cases *McFarland v. Jefferson County Public Schools* and *Parents Involved in Community Schools v. Seattle School District No. 1.* He portrayed these recent abortion, pay discrimination, and school integration decisions as reflections of "an approach to the law that favors the powerful over the powerless — that holds up a flawed ideology over the rights of the individual. . . . We're a country founded on the principle of equality and freedom . . . the country that's fought generation after generation to extend that equality to the many, not restrict it to the few."[5]

President Obama sought a nominee who agreed that part of the role of the Court is "to protect people who may be vulnerable in the political process, the outsider, the minority, those who are vulnerable, those who don't have a lot of clout." He would look for a nominee who had life experience and who understood "what it means to be on the outside, what it means to have the system not work for [her]; that's the kind of person I want on the Supreme Court."[6]

When he took office, President Obama was presented with a right-leaning Supreme Court consisting of four conservatives, four liberals, and a "swing" justice who most frequently opted to the right. That position belonged to Justice Anthony Kennedy, seventy-two, who occupied the middle between the conservatives on the Court — Chief Justice John G. Roberts, fifty-three; Antonin Scalia, seventy-two; Samuel Alito, fifty-eight; and Clarence Thomas, sixty — and the liberals, John Paul Stevens, eighty-eight; David Souter, sixty-nine; Ruth Bader Ginsburg, seventy-five; and Stephen G.

Breyer, seventy.

President Obama described three essential qualities for the next justice on the Supreme Court: a rigorous intellect; recognition of the limits of the judicial role as that of interpreter, not maker of law, with a respect for precedent and commitment to impartial justice and applying the laws to the facts at hand; and, finally, experience. In describing that quality he quoted Justice Oliver Wendell Holmes's sentiment that, "The life of the law has not been logic; it has been experience."[7] The life experience Obama looked for was about "being tested by obstacles and barriers, by hardship and misfortune; experience insisting, persisting, and ultimately overcoming those barriers." That kind of background gave someone "an understanding of how the world works and how ordinary people live," he said.[8]

Those were the characteristics the president looked for when he reviewed the records of the four final candidates and sat with each of them in interviews. While he deliberated, Sonia considered the enormous changes the position would require her to make, the lack of privacy that went with being one of the sacred Nine, and the loss of precious time to spend with her mother, brother, and his family. At times, envisioning such a dramatically different life made her question whether it was worth it. She considered withdrawing from consideration, which motivated one of her closest friends to step in. Lee Llambelis, director of Intergovernmental Affairs for New York Attorney General Andrew Cuomo, sat the judge down and drew her the big picture. "This is not about you," she told Sonia. "This is about the little girls and boys, brown and black, who live in the projects and poor communities around our nation, who can dream bigger if you are in the Supreme Court."[9]

Sonia had not had role models for the profession she dreamed of when she was a child other than the white characters on TV courtroom dramas. When she faced college and law school as one of only a handful of women and Hispanics, she had only her fellow Hispanic, black, and Asian classmates to keep her focused on the goal; there were no Hispanic women in the law to pave her way at Princeton or Yale or, later, the Manhattan District Attorney's Office, Pavia & Harcourt, or the federal bench in New York. Would it have been easier if just one woman stood where she wanted to stand, to reside as an image in her mind that it was possible?

She stayed in the running.

Before meeting the president, Sonia underwent a thorough, to the point of intrusive, background investigation that included a visit from the FBI to talk about a parking ticket she had received two years previously. The White House also contacted her physician, Andrew Jay Drexler, for a report on her diabetic condition. He confirmed that she had no signs of complications that are associated with those who do not monitor their condition carefully, such as eye, kidney, or nervous system problems. Instead, her latest cardiac stress test showed that "she was able to exercise at the level of a much younger woman with a completely normal result," he wrote. As an endocrinologist who limited his practice to diabetes treatment, Dr. Drexler was able to provide a detailed assessment:

> During the twenty or more years that I have known Judge Sotomayor she has always had excellent control over her diabetes with consistent blood sugars better than 98% of diabetics. Her hemoglobin A1c levels, the best measure of diabetes control, have consistently been less than 6.5%, the optimal level as defined by all diabetes organizations. . . . Based on my experience and expertise [Sotomayor] is in very good health and with continued good care

should remain so.[10]

Sotomayor's control of type 1 diabetes would be praised by the medical community after it became widely known that she had the condition. Dr. Paul Robertson of the American Diabetes Association stated that Sotomayor's role modeling would "go a long way toward being a major push against the stigma that some people with diabetes feel."[11]

Among the four short-listed candidates, Sotomayor was the only one President Obama did not know personally. On the morning of May 21, the day she was scheduled to meet the president and several of his staff, she packed her usual brown-bag lunch, walked past the crowd of cameras that had become fixtures in front of her building since the news of her making the short list, walked around the corner and into a friend's waiting car.

They drove to Washington and arrived at the White House at one o'clock in the afternoon. Sonia spent the next six hours meeting with Vice President Biden's counsel, Cynthia Hogan; the president's chief of staff, Rahm Emanuel; political strategist David Axelrod; and a few lawyers. Axelrod's job was to determine the strength of her public image. "Part of my interest was how she would present herself to the American people, how she would look in testifying to the Senate," he said.[12] He and the other members of the administration she met with were impressed, and there was just one more interview left.

Sotomayor recalled that she "almost fainted" upon meeting the president. "It was a conversation like none other that I have ever had," she said. One can imagine what they talked about during that one-hour interview, the first black president meeting the potentially first Hispanic Supreme Court justice, two relatively young offspring of the civil rights era who had overcome similar challenges to fulfill their extraordinary potential, who lived out the adage of America as the land of opportunity in ways that rejuvenated the American Dream for women and people of color across the country and the world. The nation's election of Barack Obama proved that the equality at the heart of the Constitution was more than an abstraction, and naming the next Supreme Court justice was his opportunity to prove it again.

Soon after the interview, Sonia was told that the president would make his decision sometime on Monday, May 25, and that she should write a brief speech for the official announcement so that she would be prepared if she was his choice. The president told his top aides that he had made a tentative choice and was going to sleep on it over the weekend at Camp David.

Back in New York the day after the interviews, Friday, May 22, Sonia received a phone call from Vice President Biden and spoke to him for more than an hour. She then told her mother and brother to be prepared to leave for Washington on Monday in case she was chosen. Juan rushed out to buy new suits for his twin boys and Sonia began working on her speech.

On Monday, May 25, Sonia went to her office early and was waiting by the phone by eight A.M. About every hour she got calls from her mother, brother, and other family members asking her what was happening, and through the entire morning she told them the same thing, "I don't know." The White House had made travel arrangements for her family, telling them to follow through with the flights unless they heard otherwise so that they would be in Washington Monday night. At about two P.M. they were getting anxious about whether they should go to the airport, and all Sonia could tell them was, "I don't know."

Three hours later, they were at various

airports and still calling Sonia to ask if they should get on the planes. Juan had arrived in Baltimore and was about to get on a shuttle to Washington, and he called to ask if he should keep going. Sonia told all of them, "I still don't know. If they haven't pulled you back, I guess you should."

At seven in the evening, Sonia was still sitting by the phone in her chambers. Theresa had stayed with her, waiting just as expectantly. Unable to restrain herself any longer, Sonia called the White House and said, "Well, you're getting my family to Washington; have any of you given any thought about how I'm going to get there?" The staffer paused and then said, "Oh, I guess we should figure that out, shouldn't we." Sonia was told that the president had gotten distracted with some important other business and would call her at about eight P.M., but that she should go home and pack to go to Washington. They preferred that she didn't take a plane.

Sonia and Theresa rushed out of the courthouse, got home to the apartment on Bedford Street, and went straight to the bedroom, where Sonia threw a suitcase on top of the bed and they both started packing. Sonia called a friend to ask him to drive her to Washington, and he said he would pick her up shortly.

At 8:10 P.M. her cell phone rang, and the White House operator told her that the president was on the line. Sonia walked over to the balcony doors of her bedroom with the phone in her right hand and her left hand over her chest, trying to calm her beating heart. "And the president got on the phone and said to me, 'Judge, I would like to announce you as my selection to be the next Associate Justice of the United States Supreme Court,'" she said.

"And I said to him — I caught my breath and started to cry and said, 'Thank you, Mr. President.' That was what the moment was like."

The president then made a request.

"He asked me to make him two promises," she said. "The first was to remain the person I was, and the second was to stay connected to my community. And I said to him that those were two easy promises to make, because those two things I could not change. And he then said we would see each other in the morning. Which we obviously did."

During the drive to Washington she revised the draft of her speech. The trip normally takes about four hours, but it rained hard that night, and the car's GPS system stopped working. "We got lost," she said, "and all of a sudden I'm in Virginia and look-ing up because I had been . . . scribbling on the piece of paper and making changes. . . . I look at my friend and say, 'Tom, we're not going into Washington, we're going away from Washington, we'd better stop." They pulled over and she called one of her law clerks who was from Washington, and who stayed on the phone to give them directions all the way into Washington and to their hotel. They arrived in Washington at 2:30 A.M., nearly six hours after leaving New York, but Sonia could not relax until she practiced her speech and nearly committed it to memory. She then slept for three hours, got up and went through her speech without her notes, and when she was satisfied that she had it, she was ready to get dressed and go to the White House.

Chairs and a podium had been set up in the East Room of the White House, the larg-est room in the house and site of press con-ferences, bill signings, receptions, concerts, and other ceremonial events. Presidents Abraham Lincoln and John F. Kennedy were lain in state in the East Room, and President Theodore Roosevelt's daughter Alice was married there. On May 26, a gathering of White House staff, Congress members, and Sonia Sotomayor's friends and family from the mainland and Puerto Rico were seated in the historic room, including Celina and her husband, Omar Lopez, and Juan and Tracey Sotomayor and their children, Kylie, Conner, and Corey. Sonia wore a simple black skirt suit with a bright lime-green blouse and no jewelry.

In his remarks, President Obama said that he had made his choice of Supreme Court justice after "deep reflection and careful deliberation" with members of Congress, constitutional scholars, bar associations, and advocacy associations, and described the selection as one of the most serious and consequential that a president can make. "The members of our highest court are granted life tenure, often serving long after the presidents who appointed them. And they are charged with the vital task of applying principles put to paper more than 20 [sic] centuries ago to some of the most difficult questions of our time." Another aspect of the challenging selection process, Obama said, was meeting "the standard Justice Souter himself has set with his formidable intellect and fair-mindedness and decency." With Vice President Joe Biden behind him to his right and Judge Sotomayor behind him to his left, President Obama proceeded to the official announcement: "After completing this exhaustive process, I have decided to nominate an inspiring woman who I believe will make a great justice: Judge Sonia Sotomayor of the great state of New York."[13]

The president spoke of her Ivy League education, legal career from the Manhattan DA's office to the court of appeals, and family background going back to Celina's childhood in Puerto Rico. He reserved his final statements to expressing his admiration for Sonia's ability to achieve success in the face of humble beginnings and difficult odds, which emphasized his priority in selecting a justice connected with real-world concerns:

> Along the way she's faced down barriers, overcome the odds, lived out the American Dream that brought her parents here so long ago. And even as she has accomplished so much in her life, she has never forgotten where she began, never lost touch with the community that supported her.
>
> What Sonia will bring to the Court, then, is not only the knowledge and experience acquired over a course of a brilliant legal career, but the wisdom accumulated from an inspiring life's journey. Well, Sonia, what

you've shown in your life is that it doesn't matter where you come from, what you look like, or what challenges life throws your way — no dream is beyond reach in the United States of America.[14]

In the announcement of his historic appointment of the third woman and first Hispanic to the Supreme Court, the president acknowledged the broader meaning of Sonia Sotomayor's rise to the court by stating, "When Sonia Sotomayor ascends those marble steps to assume her seat on the highest court of the land, America will have taken another important step towards realizing the ideal that is etched above its entrance: Equal justice under the law."[15]

Sonia was relieved to have memorized her speech because White House aides had shuffled the pages when they put them in the folder that was left for her on the podium.[16] She told the gathering that she stood on the shoulders of countless people, "yet there is one extraordinary person who is my life's inspiration — that person is my mother, Celina Sotomayor." Describing the "daunting feeling" of being the president's nominee, she said that she had been given a private tour of the White House eleven years earlier when she was being confirmed for the Second Circuit, which had been "an overwhelming experience for a kid from the South Bronx. Yet never in my wildest childhood imaginings did I ever envision that . . . I would live this moment." In closing, she said, "Mr. President, I greatly appreciate the honor you are giving me, and I look forward to working with the Senate in the confirmation process. I hope that as the Senate and the American people learn more about me they will see that I am an ordinary person who has been blessed with extraordinary opportunities and experiences. Today is one of those experiences."[17]

Sotomayor's approach to the confirmation process was informed by her two previous Senate Judiciary Committee proceedings, and she set out to speak personally with as many senators as possible beyond the nineteen members of the committee. She thought "the informality of a personal meeting," which gave an opportunity to talk rather than limit themselves to a question-and-answer session, was "important in people's decision-making processes."[18] To that end, she made a flurry of trips between New York and Washington and met with nearly the entire senate.

In her typical New York style, Sotomayor made haste when arriving at airports, and on June 8, escorted by Port Authority officials and U.S. Marshals, she tripped and fell while rushing down a ramp to make a shuttle flight at the US Airways terminal at LaGuardia International Airport. She complained of pain in her right ankle but, determined to make her appointments with six senators at the White House, refused to stop for medical help.

After limping into the White House, she was taken out for a doctor's visit and an X-ray showed that she actually had a small fraction in her ankle. She returned to the White House with a white plaster cast covering her right leg from just below the knee to the front of her foot, leaving her toes — with nails polished bright red — peeking out. The cast was in full view as she, clad in a red and black suit, hobbled on crutches; rather than let the episode slow her down, she invited the senators to sign her cast. The first inscription came from Senator Mary Landrieu, and when she met with Senator David Vitter, he offered a bag of ice for her foot and joked that they could use it later to make a couple of New Orleans's trademark hurricane cocktails. The cast stayed on for three weeks, by which time it was covered in signatures.

One-on-one meetings with senators is a

traditional ritual of the confirmation process, but Sotomayor outdid herself by meeting with eighty-nine of them over the next few weeks. The conversations gave her "an illuminating tour of the fifty states and invaluable insights into the American people," and after the four-day hearing, she met with another three senators. That gave her an introduction to all but eight members of the U.S. Senate, the body that would ultimately vote on her confirmation. Meeting ninety-two senators was a new record.

The Supreme Court justice confirmation process includes rigorous behind-the-scenes preparation in which the nominee undergoes mock hearings — which are conducted in eight- to ten-hour sessions that reflect the actual time frame nominees would experience during the days of the hearing — and receives advice on every detail of what to expect while sitting in front of the panel. Vice President Biden played a major role in these activities, and his chief counsel, Cynthia Hogan, led the White House team in charge of Sotomayor's preparation. Having served on the Judiciary Committee for more than ten years, New York Senator Charles Schumer, one of Sonia's longtime supporters, knew the ropes of the hearings process inside out and was thus also selected to play a large role in the process.

Those hours-long, unrelenting, and mentally exhausting practice sessions, known in Washington as "murder boards," include the participation of experts in constitutional law who pose as senators and grill the nominee with questions. The justice-to-be becomes highly sensitized to questions that try to evoke a discussion about how he or she would vote on a specific point of constitutional law. While dry responses such as "The ABA rule says no judge should make comments on the merits of any pending or impending case" may not reveal anything about a nominee's judicial philosophy or make good television, it prevents potential justices from boxing themselves into a corner once they're on the bench.

Nominees do not speculate on how they will decide an issue because, they affirm, "judicial independence forbids it," according to Sotomayor's Yale Law colleague Stephen L. Carter in *The Confirmation Mess.* Carter wrote that nominees could recall "the estimable Justice Felix Frankfurter" to support their view, "who declined an invitation to testify before the Judiciary Committee on the ground that anything he would say might compromise his ability to serve as a fair-minded jurist."[19] As Carter explained, the controversial issue over what kind of questions should come up at a hearing is formed by two powerful and opposed feelings toward the Supreme Court: "There is a deep tension between our understanding of the Court's power, which makes us wonder how potential Justices might vote," he explained, "and our respect for judicial independence, which means that we dare not ask what we really want to know. That tension leaves nominees the space to pick and choose their issues, giving a little to both sides."[20]

The White House prep team also advised Sotomayor to wear a neutral shade of nail polish and to show them a few of her suits so that they could select what she would wear each day. Tom Korologos, a former U.S. ambassador to Belgium who had assisted more than three hundred presidential nominees to various departments over forty-five years, published some practical advice for nominees in a *Washington Post* piece just before Obama took office in January 2009. "Hearings can be judged by the 80–20 rule," he wrote. "If the senators are speaking 80 percent of the time, you're doing fine. If it's 60–40, you are arguing with them. If it's 50–50, you've blown it." He also advised nominees to go with their instincts and offered the very practical tip of pouring oneself a glass of water if asked a contentious question. "It will give you an additional 10 seconds to think of a good answer," he said.[21]

With two federal confirmation journeys behind her, Judge Sotomayor was aware of the likelihood that she would be a target for the Obama administration's opponents, so it came as no surprise that the first line of attack came immediately after the president announced her nomination. A widely discussed article by Jeffrey Rosen titled "The Case against Sotomayor" in the *New Republic* quoted some of Sotomayor's former law clerks and clerks for other judges who appeared skeptical of her abilities. Quoting these sources anonymously, Rosen wrote that "the most consistent concern was that Sotomayor, although an able lawyer, was 'not that smart and kind of a bully on the bench,' as one former Second Circuit clerk for another judge put it."[22]

In the wake of that piece, conservative opponents of Sotomayor's nomination quoted from it extensively while expressing their own wariness about her intellect. President George W. Bush's former senior adviser Karl Rove, for example, went on FoxNews to say that he was "not really certain how intellectually strong she would be."[23] In an interview on Washington, D.C., talk radio station

WTOP, Curt Levey, executive director of the Committee for Justice, said Sotomayor "is someone who clearly was picked because she's a woman and Hispanic, not because she was the best qualified."[24]

This line of criticism, implying that Sotomayor's entire career was a product of affirmative action rather than her abilities, would be expanded on in the weeks ahead as she prepared for the Senate hearings.

The hearings took place on July 13–16, 2009, in Room 216 of the Hart Senate Office Building. Sotomayor entered the room in a walking cast and took her place between New York Democratic Senators Chuck Schumer and Kirsten Gillibrand at the cloth-covered table that held a microphone and two plastic glasses filled with water. After being introduced by the senators, she remained alone at the table to face the panel of sixteen committee members.

President Obama had repeatedly stated that he had found in Sotomayor the judicial excellence, intellect, and connection with the real world he sought on the Supreme Court. If her moderate record did not reflect the left-leaning behavior of Warren and other justices he admittedly admired, her long-term commitment to organizations that supported minority rights such as the

Puerto Rican Legal Defense and Education Fund and personal background as a child of migrants growing up in the Bronx left no question that she was well acquainted with "the minority" and "those who don't have a lot of clout." That left-leaning portrayal, although not reflected in her extensive and consistently moderate judicial record, drew criticisms from the right that were expressed in the press by some members of the Judiciary Committee during the hearings.

The two most hotly debated aspects of her career during the seven weeks leading up to the hearings were her vote to uphold the New Haven city official's decision to toss out firefighters' promotional exam results in *Ricci v. DeStefano* and remarks she made about "a wise Latina" woman's perspective in a speech at Berkeley in 2001 and later published in Berkeley's *La Raza Law Journal*. Sotomayor's critics used the Ricci case as a basis to label her a judicial activist who sought to impose a liberal bias in her decisions. Immediately after President Obama announced Sotomayor's nomination, the Judicial Confirmation Network, a conservative group formed by Gary Marx, the former head of the Virginia Christian Coalition, claimed that Sotomayor's agreement with two other judges to dismiss the Ricci case was a racist move. The group's legal counsel, Wendy Long, described Sotomayor as a "liberal judicial activist of the first order" and stated that Ricci showed that she "reads racial preferences and quotas into the Constitution, even to the point of dishonoring those who preserve our public safety."[25]

Former House Speaker Newt Gingrich swiftly released remarks about Sotomayor's Berkeley speech. In the speech to law students, Sotomayor discussed a famous quote from Supreme Court Justice Sandra Day O'Connor, which stated that "a wise old man and wise old woman will reach the same conclusion in deciding cases." Sotomayor said that she was not sure she agreed with that statement because "there can never be a universal definition of wise" and second, "I would hope that a wise Latina woman with the richness of her experiences would more often than not reach a better conclusion than a white male who hasn't lived that life." As examples, she said that "wise men" like Oliver Wendell Holmes and Justice Cardozo "voted on cases which upheld both sex and race discrimination in our society." Those remarks fed an uproar of criticism leading up to the hearings and beyond, even while there was little disagreement that President Obama's nominee would be confirmed.

Another prominent issue brought up after her nomination was President Obama's remark about "empathy" as an important quality in a Supreme Court justice. During a surprise appearance at the White House press secretary's daily press briefing on May 1, 2009, the president announced Justice David Souter's retirement and discussed what he was looking for in his replacement. "I will seek someone who understands that justice isn't about some abstract legal theory or footnote in a case book," he said, "it is also about how our laws affect the daily realities of people's lives. . . . I view that quality of empathy, of understanding and identifying with people's hopes and struggles as an essential ingredient for arriving at just decisions and outcomes."[26] Conservatives assessed his remarks as a signal that a future nominee would use his or her personal biases to made decisions on the bench.

On the first day of Sotomayor's hearings, July 13, the appointee told the story of her parents' separate moves to the mainland, her mother's sacrifices to raise her two children alone, her educational opportunities and legal career. At one point early in her statement she turned to Celina, who was sitting in the front row behind her, and said, "Mom, I love that we are sharing this together."

Sotomayor brought up her judicial philosophy, about which many senators had asked during her many rounds of visits. "It is simple: fidelity to the law," she said. "The task of a judge is not to make the law — it is to apply the law. And it is clear, I believe, that my record in two courts reflects my rigorous commitment to interpreting the Constitution according to its terms." She also addressed the empathy that the president had referred to several weeks earlier and the experience that he highlighted in his nomination speech, putting it in the context of her judging: "My personal and professional experiences help me listen and understand, with the law always commanding the result in every case," she said.

The opening remarks by her supporters on the committee praised her achievements and outstanding reputation on the federal bench while those of her critics expressed concerns over her ability to be fair and impartial. This was the first hearing in which Senator Edward Kennedy was not present, due to his battle with brain cancer. He had served on the committee since 1963, longer than any other senator in history. Ninety-one-year-old Senator Robert Byrd was also absent due to illness, but he would make his way to the

Senate to vote for Sotomayor the following month.

Committee Chairman Senator Patrick Leahy opened the hearing by putting Sotomayor's nomination in a historical context:

Those who break barriers often face the added burden of overcoming prejudice. That has been true on the Supreme Court. Thurgood Marshall graduated first in his law school class, was the lead counsel for the NAACP Legal Defense Fund, sat on the United States Court of Appeals for the Second Circuit, and served as the Nation's top lawyer, the Solicitor General of the United States. He won a remarkable 29 out of 32 cases before the Supreme Court. Despite his qualifications and achievements, at his confirmation hearing, he was asked questions designed to embarrass him, questions such as 'Are you prejudiced against the white people of the South?' . . .

I trust that all Members of this Committee here today will reject the efforts of partisans and outside pressure groups that have sought to create a caricature of Judge Sotomayor while belittling her record, her achievements and her intelligence. Let no one demean this extraordinary woman, her success, or her understanding of the

constitutional duties she has faithfully performed for the last 17 years.[27]

The ranking minority member on the
committee, Senator Jeff Sessions, discussed
his misgivings about several of Sotomayor's
statements made in speeches over the past
fifteen years and the "empathy standard"
that he described as "another step down the
road to a liberal activist, results-oriented,
and relativistic world." Halfway through his
statement, he made a firm point about his
serious problem with the issue. "Call it empathy, call it prejudice, call it sympathy —
whatever it is, it is not law," he said. "I want
to be clear: I will not vote for and no senator
should vote for an individual nominated by
any president who is not fully committed to
fairness and impartiality toward every person who appears before them."[28]

Senator Dianne Feinstein highlighted Sotomayor's broad experience, which would
bring to the Court "more federal judicial
experience than any Justice in the past hundred years" and the virtues of Sotomayor
"having seen the law truly from all sides"
as a prosecutor, lawyer in private practice,
and federal district and circuit court judge.
Feinstein believed that those experiences
would "do only one thing — and that is to

strengthen this high institution of our great country."[29]

Senator Lindsey Graham opened his remarks by lamenting that the committee never had a chance to conduct a federal circuit court confirmation hearing on Miguel Estrada, a conservative Hispanic candidate who graduated from Columbia and Harvard Law School and had a "stellar background like yours," Graham told Sotomayor. Estrada, who was appointed by President George W. Bush to the D.C. Court of Appeals although he did not have any experience on a municipal, county, state, or federal bench, had been given a hearing and his nomination approved by Senate Judiciary vote on January 30, 2003. The controversy to which Graham had evidently been alluding was the Democratic filibuster that prevented Estrada from getting a floor vote in the Senate.

Senator Graham's most memorable remark during his opening statement was his candid statement to Sotomayor that "unless you have a complete meltdown, you are going to get confirmed."[30]

Senator Russ Feingold stated that Sotomayor "is living proof that this country is moving in the right direction on the issue of race, that doors of opportunity are finally starting to open to all of our citizens." He emphasized the unfairness of the widespread attacks over her "wise Latina" comment, declaring that the "shocking" charge that she would be biased against some litigants because of her racial and ethnic heritage "is not based on anything in her judicial record because there is absolutely nothing in the hundreds of opinions she has written to support it."[31]

Senator Charles E. Schumer also made several points about the unsupported claims of Sotomayor's racism by discussing how her record "bespeaks judicial modesty — something that our friends on the right have been clamoring for — in a way that no recent nominee's has." Sotomayor's record, Schumer said, showed that she was in the mainstream because she had agreed with "your Republican colleagues" 95 percent of the time, ruled for the government in 83 percent of immigration cases, ruled for the government in 92 percent of criminal cases, denied race claims in 83 percent of cases, and split evenly in a variety of employment cases. She also, Schumer insisted, showed no inclination toward putting a personal agenda into her decisions. "In case after case after case," he said, "Judge Sotomayor rolls up her sleeves, learns the facts, applies the law to the facts, and comes to a decision irrespective of her inclinations or her personal experience."[32]

Senator Amy Klobuchar included remarks about the importance of bringing a woman before the Senate Judiciary Committee and pointed out that she was one of only two women members of the panel. She recalled the gender bias that Supreme Court Justices Ginsburg and O'Connor faced in their careers: "I think it's worth remembering that when Justice O'Connor graduated from law school, the only offers she got from law firms were for legal secretary positions," she said. "Justice O'Connor — who graduated third in her class at Stanford Law School — saw her accomplishments reduced to one question: 'Can she type?'" In spite of those obstacles, Klobuchar said, both of them persevered and prevailed. She said that she was impressed that Sotomayor's record showed "a keen understanding of the real-world implications" because she was often concerned that "those pragmatic experiences are missing in judicial decision-making." Another quality she found in Sotomayor that she looked for in a Supreme Court Justice was humility. "I'm looking for a Justice who appreciates the awesome responsibility that she will be given, if confirmed," she said.

After analyzing Sotomayor's judicial record and background, Klobuchar was convinced that she possessed that quality. "With excellent judgment and a sense of humility, I believe you can be a Justice 'for all of us,'" she said.[33]

The junior Democratic senator from Minnesota, Al Franken, who had battled for eight months over his contested election, had been sworn in only the week before. The Harvard-educated former *Saturday Night Live* writer and cast member, author, and liberal radio talk-show host had decided to run for the Senate while on a USO tour in Iraq, and his win gave the Democrats a filibuster-proof sixty-vote majority. In his opening statement, Franken said that he was "concerned that Americans are facing new barriers to defending their individual rights," which made his work on the Judiciary Committee especially significant. "The Supreme Court is the last court in the land where an individual is promised a level playing field and can seek to right a wrong," he said, mentioning discrimination, unfair business competition, voting and securities fraud, and threats to a woman's reproductive rights as some of those wrongs.[34]

On day two, Senator Leahy opened the discussion with a request for Sotomayor to explain her "wise Latina" remark, inviting her to "tell us what's going on here, Judge." Sotomayor began by saying with a laugh that no words she had ever spoken or written had received so much attention, which won a laugh from the room. She said that she had given that speech to groups of women and young Latino students and lawyers to "inspire them to believe that their life experiences would enrich the legal system, because different life experiences and backgrounds always do." She then explained the context of her words in some detail:

I was also trying to inspire them to believe that they could become anything they wanted to become, just as I had. The context of the words that I spoke have created a misunderstanding . . . and to give everyone assurances, I want to state up front, unequivocally and without doubt, I do not believe that any ethnic, racial or gender group has an advantage in sound judging. I do believe that every person has an equal opportunity to be a good and wise judge, regardless of their background or life experiences. . . . The words that I used, I used agreeing with the sentiment that Justice Sandra Day O'Connor was attempting to convey.

I understood that sentiment to be what I just spoke about, which is that both men and women were equally capable of being wise and fair judges. . . . I believe my 17-year record on the two courts would show that in every case that I render, I first decide what the law requires under the facts before me, and that what I do is explain to litigants why the law requires a result, and whether their position is sympathetic or not, I explain why the result is commanded by law.[35]

In spite of that attempt at clarification, many subsequent questions from Republican members of the committee continued to focus on her alleged gender and ethnic bias. When Senator Sessions asked her about the "wise Latina" remarks, her response included the statement that "We're not robots who listen to evidence and don't have feelings. We have to recognize those feelings, and put them aside. That's what my speech was saying."[36]

Senator John Kyl began a ten-minute monologue stating that he characterized her speeches as containing evidence that she believed that "gender and ethnicity are an appropriate way for judges to make decisions in cases." After a lengthy back-and-forth on the same issue, Senator Leahy reiterated a point already brought up that Justice Samuel Alito, during his confirmation hearings three years earlier, had referred to the role that his background played on the bench. One of the Court's conservative justices, Alito had told the committee, "When I get a case about discrimination, I have to think about people in my own family who suffered discrimination because of their ethnic background or because of religion or because of gender and I do take that into account."[37]

Later that day, Senator Graham questioned Sotomayor about *Roe v. Wade* and abortion but, in nearly every instance, interrupted her response before she had made her point. For example:

JUDGE SOTOMAYOR: *Roe versus Wade* looked at the Constitution and decided that the Constitution as applied to a claimed right applied.

SEN. GRAHAM: Is there anything in the Constitution that says a state legislator or the Congress cannot regulate abortion or the definition of life in the first trimester?

JUDGE SOTOMAYOR: The holding of the court, as —

SEN. GRAHAM: I'm asking the Constitution. Does the Constitution as written prohibit a legislative body at the state or federal level from defining life or regulating the rights of the unborn or protecting the rights of the unborn in the first trimester?

JUDGE SOTOMAYOR: The Constitution in the 14th Amendment has a —

SEN. GRAHAM: I — I'm talking — is there anything in the document written about abortion?

JUDGE SOTOMAYOR: There — the word "abortion" is not used in the Constitution, but the Constitution does have a broad provision concerning a liberty provision under the due-process —

SEN. GRAHAM: And that gets us to the speeches.[38]

By showing little interest in the nominee's responses — even though he had initially told Sotomayor that he liked her and may vote for her — Senator Graham appeared to be intent on presenting his concerns about abortion rights in the highly publicized forum of the public hearing. The senator then quoted from the *Almanac of the Federal Judiciary,* which contained anonymously submitted critiques of Judge Sotomayor that portrayed her as "temperamental," "a terror on the bench" and a judge that "can be a bit of a bully." Graham read through the phrases and then said, "You stand out like a sore thumb in terms of your temperament. What is your answer to these criticisms?"[39]

Sotomayor said that she did ask tough questions at oral arguments and explained the unique style of the Second Circuit Court, which follows a vigorous oral-argument process that is "different than in most other circuits across the country." The entire court, she said, is described as a "hot bench," and lawyers who "are unfamiliar with the process in the Second Circuit find that tough bench difficult and challenging."[40]

The relentless comments and questioning about Sotomayor's ethnic and gender statements sent a chill as cold as the gray marble wall behind the Senate panel into some observers. Senator Feinstein admitted during her turn at questioning that Senator Graham's speech about Sotomayor's temperament made her adrenaline start moving. "And you have just sat there," she said to Sotomayor, "very quietly, and responded to questions that in their very nature are quite provocative."[41] Through every lengthy day of the three-day hearings, Sotomayor scribbled notes on a legal pad and gave measured, dispassionate responses, regardless how repetitious or provocative the questioning became.

On day three, the "wise Latina" comment came up within four minutes of the gavel sounding as Senator John Cornyn asked Sotomayor to explain herself once again.

Senator Arlen Specter tried to quell the divisiveness of some of the questioning by offering a broader perspective on the issues of bias and judicial activism. "There has been a lot of talk about a wise Latino woman," he said. "And I think that this proceeding has tended to make a mountain out of a molehill. We have had a consistent line of people who are nominees who make references to their own backgrounds. We all have our perspective." He offered Justices O'Connor, Alito, and Scalia as examples.[42]

Senator Specter added that "A lot has been made of the issue of empathy, but that characteristic is not exactly out of place in judicial determinations."[43]

Questions on *Roe v. Wade* came up repeatedly on day three, and Sotomayor avoided much of the discussion. Her limited confrontation with the issue on the bench had resulted in little evidence of how she would approach the issue at the high court. She had written an opinion in the 2002 case *Center for Reproductive Law & Policy v. Bush,* which addressed the Global Gag Rule or "Mexico City Policy" that prohibited overseas organizations that received U.S. funds from providing abortions. The plaintiffs argued that denying them funds for services vital to women violated the group's First Amendment, due process, and equal protection rights. Relying on Second Circuit and U.S. Supreme Court precedent, Sotomayor's panel rejected the plaintiff's claims. The opinion did not offer a view on international abortion reform efforts or the Global Gag Rule but focused on applying to legal precedent. In spite of the ruling against a pro-choice group, the Center for Reproductive Rights supported Sotomayor's nomination, stating her "strong understanding of the real life experiences of women" gave her a perspective that is "sorely needed today as women's reproductive rights remain under attack."[44]

But Senator Specter pressed Sotomayor on abortion questions, including whether the large number of cases already brought before the Supreme Court regarding *Roe v. Wade,* none of which had succeeded in overturning the law, was a sign that *Roe* was invulnerable. "The history of a particular holding of the court and how the court has dealt with it in subsequent cases would be among one of the factors among many a court would likely consider," Sotomayor said. "The court has considered in other cases the number of times the issue has arisen and what actions the court has or has not taken with respect to that."[45]

On day four, Sotomayor faced more questions on abortion, the Ricci case, the "wise Latina" remark, her role on the board of the Puerto Rican Legal Defense and Education Fund, and gun rights. After repeated questions on gun laws related to the Second Amendment by Senator Tom Coburn, Sotomayor made a firm statement about the inadvisability of answering such questions:

Senator, would you want a judge or a nominee who came in here and said, "I agree with you, this is unconstitutional" before I had a case before me, before I had both sides discussing the issue with me, before I spent the time that the Supreme Court spent on the Heller decision?

And that decision was mighty long; went through two years of history, did a very thorough analysis and discussion back and forth on the prior opinions of the court. I don't know that that's a justice that I can be.[46]

After the final round of questions, the rest of the day was devoted to witness testimony by: Arkansas Attorney General Dustin McDaniel; New York City Mayor Michael Bloomberg; Manhattan District Attorney Robert Morgenthau; civil rights leaders Wade Henderson, Peter Kirsnow, and Linda Chavez; and New Haven firefighters Frank Ricci and Ben Vargas.

Sotomayor's first boss, Robert Morgenthau, testified about her work in almost every level of the judicial system, including prosecutor, private litigator, trial court judge, and an appellate court judge "in what I think is the second most important court in the world." He joked that her experience on New York City's criminal court may have "helped her prepare for these hearings" and described her as "highly qualified for any position in which a first-rate intellect, common sense, collegiality and good character would be assets."[47]

New Haven firefighter Frank Ricci spoke about studying for the promotion exam and receiving the court of appeals disposal of his case in "an unsigned, unpublished summary order that consisted of a single paragraph."[48] As *Washington Post* columnist Dana Milbank wrote, Ricci was the Republicans' secret weapon in the hearings: "Frank Ricci was to be Sotomayor's Anita Hill." In reality, he turned out to be "a false alarm."[49] When Senator Leahy gave him an opportunity to speak more about his view of Sotomayor's decision — "Do you have any reason to think that Judge Sotomayor acted in anything other than good faith?" — Ricci replied, "That's beyond my legal expertise. I simply welcome an invitation by the United States Senate to come here today."[50]

Three weeks after the hearings, on August 6, the Senate voted 68–31 to confirm Sonia Sotomayor's nomination. Sotomayor gave herself credit for how well her time had been spent shuffling around the Senate Office Building on crutches to visit nearly every senator in the 111th Congress. Those visits changed a few minds, she said, resulting in "six unexpected votes."[51] All Senate Democrats, Independents Bernie Sanders and Joe Lieberman, and nine Republicans voted for her, including Senate Judiciary member Lindsey Graham. Republicans joining Graham were Lamar Alexander, Christopher Bond, Susan Collins, Olympia Snowe, Richard Lugar, Mel Martinez, Judd Gregg, and George Voinovich.

Senator Leahy framed the official vote

tally and presented it to Sotomayor as a gift. The journey from President Obama's announcement in the East Room of the White House — the moment in which her heart was "bursting with gratitude" over receiving "the most humbling honor" of her life — to final confirmation as an associate justice on the Supreme Court was complete.

After the vote, President Obama said that he was "pleased and deeply gratified," by her confirmation. "This is a wonderful day for Judge Sotomayor and her family, but I also think it's a wonderful day for America," he said. The American ideals of justice, equality, and opportunity, which he said had made her journey possible, were upheld by the Senate, "breaking yet another barrier and moving us yet another step closer to a more perfect union."[52]

On August 8, Sotomayor's private and public swearing-in ceremonies took place at the Supreme Court Building at 1 First Street NE in Washington, D.C. The place, the person, and the media presence made it a day of three firsts. President Obama broke with tradition and emphasized the independence of the three branches of government by ordering the swearing-in ceremony to take place at the Supreme Court instead of the White House. This change eliminated the close association between the president and the new justice that could be made in White House swearing-in ceremonies, which had taken place over the past seventy years. Supreme Court justices had expressed discomfort with the White House tradition. "They figure if the picture that goes out is of them being sworn in at the White House it somehow conveys the idea that they're beholden to the president, they owe him a favor and that they are some kind of political trophy," said Tony Mauro, the Supreme Court correspondent for *National Law Journal*.[53]

"The president as somebody who has studied the Supreme Court believes that it's simply best for independence to have the new justice sworn in where she'll do her work independent of any interference from the executive or legislative branch," said White House Press Secretary Robert Gibbs.

The first oath took place at about noon in a private ceremony in the Supreme Court conference room, in which Chief Justice John Roberts administered the Constitutional oath required for federal judges. The public ceremony, in which Sonia was given the judicial oath, took place minutes later across the hall in the gilded east conference room. Cameras were allowed at this swearing-in ceremony for the first time in history, and President Obama further drove home the "independence" message by not attending the event. Sotomayor, wearing a cream-colored suit, stood facing black-robed Chief Justice Roberts beneath a portrait of Justice Thurgood Marshall. The suit was Sotomayor's symbolic gesture, a Tahari bought off the rack. Two weeks earlier, Venezuelan designer Carolina Herrera had offered to create a couture outfit for the occasion, but Sotomayor politely declined, explaining that she did not want to make other women think that she was becoming someone else, removed from them. She had always worn and loved Tahari suits that can be bought at any department store, and she didn't want to change that.

Celina stood between them, holding the Bible upon which Sonia placed her left hand. Her brother Juan stood to her left as she took the oath:

I, Sonia Sotomayor, do solemnly swear that I will administer justice without respect to persons, and do equal right to the poor and to the rich, and that I will faithfully and impartially discharge and perform all the duties incumbent upon me as Associate

Justice of the Supreme Court of the United States under the Constitution and laws of the United States. So help me God.[54]

At fifty-five years old, Sonia Sotomayor became the 111th associate justice of the U.S. Supreme Court, the third woman to serve in the Court's 220-year history, and the first Hispanic.

CHAPTER 10
HER HONOR

*I feel great that I don't have to be
the lone woman around this place.*

— Supreme Court Justice Ruth Bader Ginsburg

The new associate justice of the Supreme
Court had not even begun her term and she
was already a month behind. The court,
which normally goes into session on the first
Monday of October, had scheduled a rare
special session in September to hear more
oral arguments on *Citizens United v. Federal
Election Commission,* a case on campaign finance law that arose from a 2008 campaign
film critical of Hillary Rodham Clinton and
that the Court first heard in March. Taking
the oaths on August 8 allowed Justice Sotomayor to begin working, even though her
formal investiture would not take place until
September 8. She had one month to study
the case, which had expanded to approxi-

mately two thousand pages of arguments, as well as other cases scheduled for early in the Court's term. In the midst of that pressing work, she had to move to Washington and hire her four law clerks.

The new justice turned to a close colleague on the circuit court to help her select her first clerks, each of whom would serve a one-year term. She had received many applications since her nomination, but not wanting "to jinx the process by becoming involved in thinking about picking clerks" she asked her colleague to review the applications and come up with a short list of those whom she should interview. This friend and colleague, whom she described as "like a brother" to her on the circuit court, may have been Judge Robert Katzmann, as he was the only judicial colleague she invited to the small, invitation-only private swearing-in ceremony at the Supreme Court on August 8. Sotomayor gave him two criteria, stating that she wanted "smart people . . . who are good people, too," she said. "They have to be kind and caring and really smart."[1]

Because about ten thousand petitions of certiorari ("cert petitions") are submitted by the losing parties in federal appeals court cases to the Supreme Court each year, the clerks' job of determining which are worthy of the justices' discussion gives them enormous responsibility. The clerks are tasked with narrowing that list down to about a thousand. Edward Lazarus who clerked for Supreme Court Justice Harry Blackmun from 1988 to 1989, explained the clerks' important role in the process and the considerable weight their recommendation carried. "Rather than each Justice considering every case independently," Lazarus wrote, "a clerk for one Justice in the 'cert pool' circulates an advisory memo to all the Justices in the pool."[2] This memo assesses whether the cert is certworthy, raising an issue that has drawn differing decisions on the lower courts and/or is of considerable national importance. The thousand petitions are further narrowed down by the justices to a "discuss list" that affirms which cases will be voted on at discussion sessions. A cert must receive a vote of at least four to become a writ of certiorari, or decision to hear the appeal. By the end of the process, about 1 percent, or eighty to a hundred cases, are accepted by the Court each year.

Sotomayor interviewed the candidates shortly after the hearings and was "absolutely delighted with" her ultimate choice of two men and two women: Lindsey Powell and Robert Yablon, veteran Supreme Court clerks who had just finished clerking for Justices Ruth Bader Ginsburg and John Paul Stevens; Jeremy Marwell, who had served in the prestigious Office of Legal Counsel at the Department of Justice (the department that drafts legal opinions for the White House) and had clerked for D.C. Circuit Judge Stephen Williams; and Eloise Pasachoff, who had clerked for Judge Robert Katzmann.

Sonia made time in August to attend a handful of events that celebrated her confirmation, including a lavish dinner party thrown for her by fellow Nuyorican Jennifer Lopez and her husband, Marc Anthony, at their Long Island mansion. Guests included U.S. Representative and chair of the Congressional Hispanic Caucus Nydia Velasquez, one of Sotomayor's major supporters who was born in Puerto Rico and elected to the New York City Council before running for Congress. Other high-profile attendees included New York Police Department Commissioner Ray Kelley and Puerto Rican pop star Ricky Martin. Sotomayor insisted on meeting all of the cooks and staff who had prepared the meal to thank them and express her appreciation, and then lined up with the entire group of twenty for a photo. The head chef of the event, Ricardo Cardona, who frequently prepares formal dinners for celebrities and dignitaries, had never seen anything like it. "She showed us — all these Latino immigrants who were in the kitchen working to make the meal special — that she is one of us," he said.[3]

President Obama sponsored a White House reception for the newly sworn-in justice on August 12, which was held in the East Room. Among the guests were her new colleagues Justices John Paul Stevens and Ruth Bader Ginsburg; First Lady Michelle Obama; Senators Patrick Leahy, Robert Menendez, and Benjamin Cardin; Representative Velasquez and six other members of Congress; six U.S. Court of Appeals judges; New York Governor David Paterson; former FBI Director Louis Freeh; Sonia's high school classmate and former NAACP President Ted Shaw; Secretary of Labor Hilda Solis; White House Counsel Gregory Craig; Environmental Protection Agency Administrator Lisa Jackson; many others from the political, academic, and civil rights community; and Sonia's family.

Justice Ginsburg had been vocal about her hopes for Sotomayor to be confirmed to the Court. An associate justice since 1993, she had been the only woman on the bench since Justice Sandra Day O'Connor retired in January 2006. She told the press that she cheered when Sotomayor was nominated and believed that Sotomayor would bring "a wealth of experience in the law and in life" to the bench. "Women belong in all places where decisions are being made," she said. "I don't say [the split] should be 50-50. It could be 60 percent men, 40 percent women, or the other way around. It shouldn't be that women are the exception."[4]

In September, Sotomayor was invited to the National Hispanic Foundation for the Arts' celebrity-filled annual gala held at the Corcoran Gallery of Art, where she danced a well-rehearsed mambo with Esai Morales, star of the 1987 movie *La Bamba*. A video of Justice Sotomayor, decked out in a glittering black outfit with black spike heels, made the national news the next day. They danced to "Sotomayor Mambó," a tune written for the justice and performed by fellow Bronx-born percussionist and composer Bobby Sanabria, just one of the Latin music greats who wrote a piece in her honor. Commissioned by the Bronx Museum of the Arts and Symphony Space, Grammy award–winning pianist-composer Arturo O'Farrill wrote "Wise Latina Woman" for Sotomayor and debuted it with his Afro-Latin Jazz Orchestra at New York City's Symphony Space in November 2009. O'Farrill said that Sotomayor's rise to the Supreme Court gave him "a lot of hope."[5]

On September 7, the day before her formal investiture ceremony at the Supreme Court, Sonia and a group of family and friends celebrated in Washington, D.C., and finished up the night at the Irish Channel Pub, a small bar in the city's Chinatown district. The group of about forty danced in the cramped quarters, and at one point Sonia and a few of her relatives took the karaoke stage with microphones to sing the Sister Sledge song "We Are Family." Dancing in a hole-in-the-wall bar in the nation's capital was a first for members of the Supreme Court, as were many things about the new associate justice. As Justice Sotomayor had told President Obama at her White House reception the previous month, when she showed him her fire-engine red fingernails and hoop earrings, "Mr. President, you have no idea what you've unleashed."[6] The president laughed and said he had been briefed about her nails and earrings and was well aware that he had made her a lifetime appointment and could not take it back.

The Supreme Court called a special session on September 8 to grant the new justice her official commission in a formal induction ceremony. Conducted in the Supreme Court Chamber, the room draped in burgundy velvet with stately marble columns where the nine justices hear oral argument, the ceremony gave Sotomayor her first opportunity to join her fellow justices in the historic room. Her black robe, a gift from some of her former law clerks, was accented by a white lace collar, or jabot, that Justice Ginsberg had given to her. Sotomayor was seated in Justice Thurgood Marshall's chair while the clerk read her commission, a symbolic act that affected her deeply. Justice Marshall, who as a forty-six-year-old African American lawyer had successfully argued the *Brown v. Board of Education* case, served as an associate justice of the Supreme Court from 1967 to 1991.

Supreme Court Clerk William Suter read President Obama's commission that officially brought her into the Court, written in the more than two-hundred-year-old language of the ritual: "Know ye that reposing special trust and confidence in the Wisdom, Uprightness and Learning of Sonia Sotomayor of New York, I have nominated and by and with the advice and consent of the Senate do appoint her an Associate Justice of the Supreme Court of the United States." She was then escorted to the raised, curved mahogany bench, where she stood with her fellow justices as Chief Justice John G. Roberts administered the judicial oath.

The Bible on which she placed her left hand was handed down from Associate Justice John Marshall Harlan, who served from 1877 to 1911 and made his mark in Court history as a visionary proponent of civil rights with his impassioned dissents over segregation-supporting decisions such as *Plessy v. Ferguson*. The Bible had been signed by every Justice who has served since then. "The most symbolically meaningful moment for me . . . was sitting in Justice Marshall's chair and taking the oath with my hand on Justice Harlan's Bible," Sotomayor said. "It was like history coursing through me." She admitted that the powerful message contained in that chair and Bible had an imposing effect. "I don't think any person can be assured that they're up to the task," she said. "I don't know that. And so those moments are at one point incredibly meaningful and in a different way, incredibly frightening. It's hard to convey the coursing of emotions that goes through one at a moment like that."[7]

The short and dignified ceremony was attended by President Obama, Vice President Biden, Attorney General Eric Holder, Solicitor General Elena Kagan, White House staff members who had worked for her confirmation, senators who had voted for her, family, and friends — including Ricky Martin — and her predecessor, retired Justice David H. Souter. After the four-minute event, Chief Justice Roberts wished her a warm welcome and said, "We wish for you a long and happy career in our common calling." He and Justice Sotomayor then left the chamber, took off their black robes and went outside to make the traditional walk down the Court's steps, where a crowd of reporters and camerapeople was waiting for them.

President Obama's Democratic convictions may be a powerful indicator of how Sotomayor will vote on the Court. Traditionally, Supreme Court justices tend to make decisions that align with the party of the president who appointed them. William Landes and Richard Posner confirmed this in 2008 in their detailed statistical analysis of judicial behavior, which revealed "a strong correlation between the political party of the appointing President and the voting behavior of the Justices appointed by a President of that party." The widest discrepancy in voting comes in the areas of civil rights, due process and unions, the categories in which justices appointed by a Republican "are more than 50 percent more likely than those appointed by a Democratic President to vote conservatively," the study found.[8]

There are exceptions to the party correlation, of course. The appointee of a Republican president will not always cast a conservative vote, just as an appointee of a Democrat will not always cast a liberal one. The most vivid example of a justice who did not conform to traditional expectations was Earl Warren, the Republican California governor appointed by President Dwight D. Eisenhower who served as chief justice of the Supreme Court from 1953 to 1969. Warren's label as a "liberal Republican" sounds like an oxymoron in 2009, but he spearheaded a liberal leaning in the court that began with *Brown v. Board of Education,* which prohibited segregation in the public schools, and proceeded in many other areas of public policy. "On freedom of speech, on the rights of criminal suspects, on the emerging field of privacy, the Warren Court transformed American law," wrote Jeffrey Toobin in *The Nine.*[9]

The Landes and Posner study brings up another significant factor in considering how Sotomayor would affect the balance of the Court. According to their findings, a justice like Sotomayor who came from the federal appeals court bench would be more likely to be a left-leaning justice. Their statistical analysis discovered that Supreme Court justices who ascended from the federal courts of appeals vote more liberally because, they suspected, "these Justices have been socialized by their lower-court experience to be respectful of precedent, and the most controversial Supreme Court precedents are those created in the liberal Warren Court era."[10] Sotomayor's record shows her as a judge with a meticulous standard for adhering to precedent, so it will be fascinating to observe how the study's findings bear out in her case.

It is interesting that the study also found that when there are more Republican-appointed justices on the bench than Democratic-appointed ones, the latter "become more liberal as they become more outnumbered." While conservative justices tend to be "ideologically more committed — their views are less affected by the views of liberal Justices," the Democratic-appointed justices "are not roused to assert their full liberalism until pushed into a corner by a growing conservative bloc."[11]

As an associate justice of the Supreme Court, Sotomayor began earning a salary of $213,000 a year, about $29,000 more than she had been making as a circuit court judge. She had never earned the big money that came with a career at a major law firm — when she left Pavia & Harcourt, she walked away with about $25,000 for her partnership interest in the firm. Sotomayor's financial disclosures submitted to the Senate Judiciary Committee showed that she lived comfortably but had a lot of debt, like the majority of Americans. Even though she had been earning nearly $200,000 in combined salaries from the Second Circuit Court and teaching, she had only $32,000 in savings, owed $16,000 in credit card debt, and had $15,000 in dental bills. She owned one third of the Florida condo in which Celina and Omar lived, which was worth $20,000, and a Saab convertible and other personal property that added up to about $108,000. Her Greenwich Village condo was worth about $1 million, but she was still paying a $382,000 mortgage on it, so her net worth was listed at about $740,000. She did not sell her condo when she moved to Washington, but decided to wait out the recession, stating that "like many Americans, it would not be wise for me to sell my home in New York because the market is so low."[12]

Filling out the financials on her lengthy Senate questionnaire in 2009 had been a breeze. "When you don't have money, it's easy," she said. "There isn't anything there to report."[13] Her lack of substantial savings after seventeen years on the federal bench did not reflect a lack of concern for her retirement because judges retire with a generous pension. Rather than tucking money away, she spent it on her family and friends, such as the lavish Christmas party she had thrown for many years at the federal courthouse, which included gifts she bought for more than sixty colleagues and the entire custodial and lunchroom staff.

Photographs of Justice Sotomayor standing alone on the sprawling granite terrace in front of the steps of the Supreme Court building after her investiture ceremony are my favorite representations of the significance of her ascension to the Supreme Court. The forty-four steps leading up to the four-columned portico were architect Cass Gilbert's way of conveying to visitors "the magnitude and importance of the judicial process taking place within the Court's walls," Toobin wrote. Completed in 1935 and situated between the Capitol and Library of Congress, the Supreme Court was deliberately set farther back so that the stairs would dominate the visitor's experience. "The walk up the stairs would be the central symbolic experience of the Supreme Court," Toobin wrote, "a physical manifestation of the American march to justice. The stairs separated the Court from the everyday world — and especially from the earthly concerns of the politicians in the Capitol — and announced that the justices would operate, literally, on a higher plane."[14]

Sotomayor's lone figure in front of the white marble steps that sweep up at a gentle angle to Cass's temple of justice represents how singly she met her challenges as either the only woman Hispanic or one of very few at each stage of her university and professional careers. Her image recalls her mother's solitary trip to the United States as a seventeen-year-old enlistee in the Women's Army Corps and Sonia's confirmation as the first Hispanic on the federal bench in New York and the U.S. Supreme Court. The seated figures that flank those steps, "The Contemplation of Justice" on the left and "The Authority of Law" on the right, are stern guardians that demand her respect as she turns and walks up to the portico, which brings to mind the humility she has brought to each bench and sense of awe for her life's journey. The words inscribed above the entrance, *Equal Justice under Law,* summarize her achievement and the heart of a nation in which, President Obama said at the White

House ceremony, "the doors of opportunity must be open for all."

As one of three independent branches of the federal government, the Supreme Court has the authority to nullify laws written by the legislative branch and cancel actions made by the executive branch. With this power of "judicial review," the Court is responsible for protecting individual rights and ensuring that the broad provisions of the Constitution are applied to the complex and varied issues of the times. The workload of the Court is performed within routines steeped in formality and tradition. With rare exceptions — including the revised schedule under which Justice Sotomayor began — the Supreme Court term runs from the first Monday in October until late June or early July. Two weeks of the sitting court, in which arguments are heard, alternate with two-week periods of recess, in which the justices study cases and write opinions. During a Court session, each side — the appellant, who lost the lower court case, and appellee, who won and tries to persuade the Supreme Court to agree with the lower court's decision — is allowed up to thirty minutes for oral argument. The justices are free to question them, just as in the lower appellate courts. With four hours of oral argument conducted on Monday, Tuesday, and Wednesday, a two-week sitting can involve up to twenty-four cases.

Oral argument sessions are the only parts of the Supreme Court open to the public, and visitors can wait in one of two lines in the morning to make a brief trip into the courtroom or stay for a longer period. For cases argued on Mondays, the justices meet in conference on Wednesday, and for cases argued on Tuesdays and Wednesdays, they hold conference on Friday. Following long-standing tradition, the justices shake hands with each other before sitting down to conference or assembling to go to the bench, a practice that reflects the Court's standard for keeping harmony in all its proceedings, regardless of differences of opinion.

On each Monday that the Court sits, a public report called an Order List is released that states the actions taken by the Court. The document released on December 14, 2009, for example, listed the orders in 15 pending cases, 3 cases to which certiorari was granted and 151 to which certiorari was denied. Opinions are usually released on Tuesday and Wednesday mornings.

In May and June, the Court sits without hearing argument and only announces orders and opinions. After recessing in late

June, the justices study new petitions that they will vote to hear or dismiss when the new term begins and prepare for scheduled cases they will hear in the fall.

Justice Sotomayor shook hands with her fellow justices before entering the chamber to hear oral argument for the first time on September 9, 2009. As she walked through the opening of the draperies and took the junior justice's seat at the far left of the Chief Justice at ten A.M., the gavel sounded, everyone in the room stood, and the marshal shouted out the traditional call to order:

The Honorable, the Chief Justice and the Associate Justices of the Supreme Court of the United States. Oyez! Oyez! Oyez! [Hear ye!] All persons having business before the Honorable, the Supreme Court of the United States, are admonished to draw near and give their attention, for the Court is now sitting. God save the United States and this Honorable Court!

Justice Sotomayor saw the white quill pens placed on the attorneys' tables in front of the bench, another tradition that dated back to the earliest sessions of the Court. She had done her homework on the case that had brought them into session early, *Citizens*

United v. Federal Election Commission, and was ready to face the parties and the audience.

Justice Sotomayor's first case dealt with an issue of great national interest — the regulation of corporate donations to federal election campaigns. The case involved a scathing ninety-minute documentary titled *Hillary: The Movie* by the conservative nonprofit group Citizens United, an organization that receives corporate funding, and commercials produced to publicize the film.[15] The Federal Election Commission (FEC) blocked the group from airing the movie through cable television pay-per-view services, arguing that it was a lengthy campaign (attack) ad and therefore needed to adhere to campaign ad regulations as stipulated in the Bipartisan Campaign Reform Act (BCRA). Those rules prohibited ads that expressed support or opposition to a candidate from running thirty days before a primary election and sixty days before a general election, and Citizens United wanted to make *Hillary: The Movie* available on cable in the weeks leading up to the primary. Citizens United sued the FEC, claiming that its First Amendment rights were violated, and the three-judge panel of the U.S. District Court for the District of Columbia found for the FEC. The court concluded that the film could not appear on cable because its sole purpose was "to inform the electorate that Senator Clinton is unfit for office, that the United States would be a dangerous place in a President Hillary Clinton world and that viewers should vote against her." Appeals from the district court go directly to the Supreme Court.

After hearing arguments in March, the Court decided that it wanted to hear the lawyers address the constitutionality of limiting corporate funding of federal elections. Specifically, the justices ordered the parties to focus on whether the Court should overrule either or both of its previous rulings that had upheld the restrictions — *Austin v. Michigan Chamber of Commerce* and part of *McConnell v. Federal Election Commission*. A decision to overrule those decisions would be an affirmation that the Constitution grants corporations the same First and Fourteenth Amendment rights of people, thus vastly expanding corporations' rights to spend money on federal campaigns. The case, which had begun as a narrow argument about "electioneering communications," turned into one about the much wider issue of corporate personhood.

Standing before the bench at oral argument

for the first time, Solicitor General Elena Kagan, representing the FEC, argued that the lower court's decision to restrict Citizens United was proper, and that Congress has the authority to restrain corporate spending on communications that are plainly oriented toward supporting or advocating against a particular political candidate. Campaign finance laws, the government stated, had been instituted to protect the election process from the enormous sway that wealthy corporations would hold if allowed to freely spend on supporting or opposing candidates.

Former solicitor general Theodore Olson, representing Citizens United, argued that corporate and union funds are equivalent to speech and should not be regulated: "Robust debate about candidates for elective office is the most fundamental value protected by the First Amendment's guarantee of free speech" he said. "Yet that is precisely the dialogue that the government has prohibited if practiced by unions or corporations, any union or any corporation."[16]

Corporate identity was the main issue of argument on September 9. Justice Sotomayor had gone into the session prepared with several questions, most of which were asked by the other justices, so the questions she eventually asked "were a product of the flow of the conversation."[17]

Justice Ginsburg got to the core of the issue when she asked one of the attorneys about corporate identity: "A corporation, after all, is not endowed by its creator with inalienable rights," she said. "So is there any distinction that Congress could draw between corporations and natural human beings for purposes of campaign finance?"[18]

Shortly afterward, Justice Sotomayor followed up that point with a reflection on the origins of the issue, stating that courts "created corporations as persons, gave birth to corporations as persons. There could be an argument made that that was the court's error to start with . . . the fact that the court imbued a creature of State law with human characteristics."

Justice Sotomayor's willingness to jump in during her first day of hearing oral argument revealed that she was not only comfortable with the appeals court question-and-answer environment, in which she had worked for the past eleven years, but that she was ready to participate in the high court's process from day one. Asking questions of the attorneys came naturally, as it always had. "Something most people will learn about me," she said as she reflected on that first day, "[is that] I get so intensely engaged in argument that it's never fake. Every question I ask has a purpose, it has some importance to something that is troubling me or that I'm curious about."[19] Her questioning in *Citizens United v. Federal Election Commission* fulfilled her first promise to President Obama to remain the person she was — a justice who engaged vigorously on the bench.

It was widely expected that Justice Sotomayor would vote to uphold the regulations limiting corporate spending on federal elections on the same lines that her predecessor Justice Souter would likely have followed. Her tough stance on campaign finance rules offenders during her tenure on the New York Campaign Finance Board made a strong case for that. But observers believed that the September 9 argument showed that a conservative decision would come from the Court on at least some of the elements of the two campaign finance laws involved in the case. If a five-justice majority ruled to overturn all or part of the old laws, the decision would have an effect on the upcoming midterm elections of November 2010.

The Supreme Court announced its decision on *Citizens United v. Federal Election Commission* in early January 2010, with a 5–4 ruling that the government cannot ban corporate spending on federal elections. The five conservative justices voted to overrule two precedents about the First Amendment rights of corporations, and Justice Sotomayor, as expected, voted to dissent with Justices Stevens, Ginsburg, and Breyer. Justice Stevens called the ruling "a rejection of the common sense of the American people, who have recognized a need to prevent corporations from undermining self-government since the founding, and who have fought against the distinctive corrupting potential of corporate electioneering since the days of Theodore Roosevelt."

The decision on this case, the first one Justice Sotomayor began to review after her confirmation, also provoked heated responses outside the Court's bronze doors. The ruling gave "voice to the powerful interests that already drown out the voices of everyday Americans," said President Obama.[20] Sotomayor's longtime supporter Senator Chuck Schumer said that the Court had predetermined the winners of the upcoming midterm elections: "It won't be Republicans. It won't be Democrats. It will be corporate America."[21] If the same degree of passion was expressed in the justices' closed-door conferences on *Citizens United,* Justice Sotomayor's opening months on the Court were anything but dull.

Taking her end-of-the-row seat at the bench for the first time on September 9, 2009, Justice Sotomayor felt a sweep of history, especially the course of her own legal career. Her many years on the federal bench, both in practice and during the confirmation process, had brought her into contact with all the attorneys now facing her and with most of the interested parties sitting in the public area behind them. She perceived the tensions in the opposing views of the important issue at hand, something that can easily be lost in the abstract when dealing with arguments on paper:

The moment that I sat down and was able to look out and see all of the people in the audience, that's probably the moment I will most intensely remember because there were lawyers who I've known for years sitting at the table in front of us ready to argue, but then watching the intensity of everyone's face [. . .] I'd forgotten how much people believe — believe and know that they're affected by the Court's decisions. And you see the anticipation and I can't actually say that it's pleasurable. You note in people's faces their concerns and clearly I knew the sides some parties in the audience were in because some of the actual parties were there, and I forget how important it is to people sometimes. Because when you're in your office reading the briefs you understand the voices that they're giving you, but when you see their faces it just reinforces that importance in a way nothing else can.[22]

The other emotion she experienced that day was absolute fear. "You don't know what it's like to sit with eight other colleagues," Sotomayor said. "I've sat en banc when I was on the circuit court, but to sit on the Supreme Court and listen to the questions of your colleagues is somewhat humbling. Somewhat completely humbling."[23]

At the closed-door Friday conference after Wednesday's Court session, Sotomayor was seated in her designated tall-back leather chair closest to the door in the wood-paneled conference room with chandeliers and floor-to-ceiling draped windows that is connected to Chief Justice Roberts's chambers. Seniority rules in these proceedings, with Chief Justice Roberts speaking first, then Justice Stevens and down the line of seniority, with Sotomayor speaking last. As the junior justice, the position she inherited from Justice Alito, she was also the note taker and doorkeeper and was to deliver any messages or notes delivered to or from the other justices. At the vote on the petitions of certiorari they discussed, the seniority worked in the opposite direction, with Justice Sotomayor voting first, Alito second, and so on up the line to Chief Justice Roberts. Sotomayor said that the tone and approach taken during her first private conference met her expectations. "The justices are actually very thoughtful about what they're doing and each one was very thoughtful about giving their reasons for their vote," she said. "I didn't expect any less, but I was very pleased that my expectation was confirmed." [24]

Justice Sotomayor brought a New York touch to the end of her first conference by bringing in cookies from an Italian bakery in Brooklyn. Some court personnel helped deliver the coffee, and when the justices were finished and started heading for the door, one of those staffers stepped over to open it. Opening the door was the junior justice's job, so Sotomayor told him, "No, you can't take my job, I just got here!" and jumped ahead of him to open the door.

The new justice appreciated stepping into the traditions that had helped establish the Court's identity for more than two centuries and perceived them as significant elements that measured the nation's history:

> I think because those traditions anchor us in a process that's greater than ourselves, they remind us that the role that we're playing is not a personal role and not a role that should have a personal agenda, but one that has an institutional importance and that that institutional importance is bigger than us. . . . I think that that is an important role for tradition, to underscore that for us. And so yes, where you sit, what order you sit in, how you vote, all of those traditions, all of those practices remind us of our institutional importance, not our individual importance.[25]

In the first few weeks of her term, Justice Sotomayor came upon areas of the law that she was surprised to have never encountered before in the busy New York courts. The demands of the Supreme Court bench would include studying these areas of controversy that she readily admitted she did not know existed. "I, as a circuit court judge, thought that I had [addressed] and knew about whatever — what all of the areas of legal contention were," she said. "That's not true. There are so many new areas of law that I will have to become involved in, new processes that the Court's involved in that I'll have to become aware of. . . . I have no reason to doubt it will take years to feel some degree of comfort in this process."[26]

Justice Sotomayor also figured that it would take time to become accustomed to the process of carefully analyzing all the cases in her workload. "I'm finding that most people outside the Court have very little understanding of the burdens of the Court," she said. "Reviewing cert petitions of which the numbers have been growing exponentially each year is an extraordinarily time consuming process." The thousands of pages involved in preparing for *Citizens United v. Federal Election Commission* were a glimpse of the relentless and time-consuming work to come. It was no wonder that one of her closest friends feared the worst when she learned of Sotomayor's nomination to the Court: "My first reaction was, 'Oh boy, I'm never going to see my friend again,'" said Nancy Gray, who had known Sonia since their days together at the Manhattan DA's office.[27]

The consistent media focus on Justice Sotomayor allowed men, women, and children of all backgrounds who had heard and been inspired by Sotomayor's story during her nomination to keep an eye on her first term in Court. Two and a half weeks after hearing her first case, Sotomayor's home team gave her an opportunity to show her stuff in front of her fans in New York. Yankees management invited her to throw out the ceremonial first pitch at the Saturday, September 26, game against the Boston Red Sox at the new Yankee Stadium in the Bronx. The crowd broke into cheers when she came onto the field wearing a Yankees pinstripes jersey, black slacks, and tennis shoes, escorted by Yankees catcher Jorge Posada. Sotomayor's joy was unmistakable as she waved at the fifty thousand baseball fans with a baseball clutched in her fist. Standing a few yards from home plate, she paused, raised her shoulders with a big breath and tossed the ball to catcher Jose Molina.[28] With that pitch, the judge who had saved baseball in 1995 claimed her own place in the big leagues and proved that her heart had never left the Bronx.

During President Obama's speech at the White House reception for Justice Sotomayor on August 12, 2009, the crowd was moved from time to time to applaud his words about the impact of her ascension to the Court. He told them that the historic moment was not just about her. "It's about every child who will grow up thinking to him or herself, if

Sonia Sotomayor can make it, then maybe I can, too," he said. "It's about every mother or father who looks at the sacrifices Justice Sotomayor's mother made, and the successes she and her brother have had, and thinks, I may not have much in my own life, but if I work hard enough, maybe my kids can have more." Finally, he said, "It's about everyone in this nation facing challenges and struggles in their lives, who hear Justice Sotomayor's story and thinks to themselves, if she could overcome so much and go so far, then why can't I?"

Justice Sotomayor had already seen proof of those words. Ever since the president's announcement of her nomination in May 2009 she had been receiving letters from people all over the country. "Many tell a unique story of hope in spite of struggles," she said. "Each letter has deeply touched me. Each reflects a belief in the dream that led my parents to come to New York all those years ago. It is our Constitution that makes that dream possible, and I now seek the honor of upholding the Constitution as a Justice on the Supreme Court."[29]

Oyez! Oyez! Oyez! God save the United States and this Honorable Court!

NOTES

Chapter 1

1. Debra Cassens Weiss, "Obama Announces Nomination of Sonia Sotomayor," *ABA Journal,* May 26, 2009.
2. Sonia Sotomayor, "Remarks Prepared for Delivery at the Lehman College Commencement, June 3, 1999."
3. Victor S. Clark, *Porto Rico and Its Problems* (Washington, D.C.: Brookings Institution, 1930), 612.
4. César Ayala, "The Decline of the Plantation Economy and the Puerto Rican Migration of the 1950s," *Latino Studies Journal* 7, no. 1 (winter 1996): 65.
5. Earl Parker Hanson, *Transformation: The Story of Modern Puerto Rico* (New York: Simon & Schuster, 1955), 38.
6. "Induction Proceedings for Judge Sonia Sotomayor," November 6, 1998, United States Court House, 500 Pearl Street, New York, NY.

7. Ibid.

8. Quoted in Judd Polk, "The Plight of Puerto Rico," *Political Science Quarterly* 57, no. 4 (December 1942): 484.

9. Judith Bellafaire, "Puerto Rican Servicewomen in Defense of the Nation," Women in Military Service for America Memorial Foundation. Available at www.womensmemorial.org/Education/PRHistory.html; accessed February 2010.

10. Mattie E. Treadwell, *The Women's Army Corps* (Washington, D.C.: United States Army Center of Military History, 1991). Available at http://www.history.army.mil/books/wwii/Wac/ch30.htm#b1; accessed August 2009.

11. *WAC Handbook, 1944*, Women Veterans Historical Collection, University of North Carolina-Greensboro. Available at http://library.uncg.edu/dp/wv/results28.aspx?i=4708&s=2; accessed February 2010.

12. "Concepcion Alvarado Escobedo," U.S. Latino & Latina World War II Oral History Project, University of Texas at Austin. Available at http://lib.utexas.edu/ww2latinos; August 2009.

13. "Induction Proceedings for Judge Sonia Sotomayor."

14. "Vera E. McCraney," Flagler County

Families. Available at www.flaglercounty families.com/mil-mccraneyvera.html; accessed February 2010.

15. Treadwell, available at http://www .history.army.mil/books/wwii/Wac/ch18 .htm#b6; accessed August 2009.

16. Ibid.

17. Ibid.

18. "Induction Proceedings for Judge Sonia Sotomayor."

19. Ibid.

20. Julia de Burgos, "To Julia de Burgos," transl. by Roberto Márquez in *Puerto Rican Poets: A Selection from Aboriginal to Contemporary Times*, ed. Roberto Márquez (Amherst: University of Massachusetts Press, 2007), 222.

Chapter 2

1. Virginia Sanchez Korrol, *From Colonia to Community: The History of Puerto Ricans in New York City* (Berkeley: University of California Press, 1983), 36.

2. Sonia Sotomayor, "Remarks Prepared for Delivery at the Lehman College Commencement, June 3, 1999."

3. *A Biographical Sketch of Sonia Sotomayor* [video], producer unknown, YouTube. Available at www.youtube.com/ watch?v=yYjuS-d8PL8; accessed Febru-

ary 2010.

4. Ibid.

5. Mark Naison, "Sonia Sotomayor's Appointment Highlights a Time When Public Housing Was a Place of Hope and Possibility for Working Class Families in the Bronx," History News Network, May 30, 2009. Available at http://hnn.us/roundup/entries/88 690.html; accessed March 2010.

6. Sotomayor, "Remarks Prepared for Delivery at the Lehman College Commencement."

7. *A Biographical Sketch of Sonia Sotomayor.*

8. Robin Shulman, "Supreme Change," *Washington Post,* June 16, 2009, C1.

9. Neal Kumar Katyal, "Architecture as Crime Control," *Yale Law Journal* 11, no. 5 (March 2002): 1053.

10. "Supreme Change."

11. "Induction Proceedings for Judge Sonia Sotomayor," November 6, 1998, United States Court House, 500 Pearl Street, New York, NY.

12. Sonia Sotomayor, "A Latina Judge's Voice" [Judge Mario G. Olmos Memorial Lecture, University of California, Berkeley, School of Law, 2001]. Reprinted, *New York Times,* May 15, 2009.

13. Shulman, "Supreme Change."

14. Ibid.

15. Ibid.

16. Ibid.

17. Meghan O'Rourke, "Nancy Drew's Father," *New Yorker,* November 8, 2004, 120.

18. Greg B. Smith, "Judge's Journey to Top," *New York Daily News,* October 24, 1998, 17.

19. James Hillman, *The Soul's Code: In Search of Character and Calling* (New York: Random House, 1996), 6.

20. Smith, "Judge's Journey to Top," 17.

21. Jan Hoffman, "A Breakthrough Judge: What She Always Wanted," *New York Times,* September 25, 1992, B16.

22. Jennifer Ludden and Linton Weeks, "Sotomayor: 'Always Looking Over My Shoulder,'" National Public Radio, May 27, 2009. Available at http://www.npr.org/templates/story/story.php?storyId=104538436; accessed September 2009.

23. Joe Beck, "Sonia Sotomayor Reflects on Her Success," *Hispanic Outlook in Higher Education* Vol. 13, no. 3 (November 4, 2002): 25.

24. Hoffman, "A Breakthrough Judge."

25. Tom Furnari, "Sotomayor's Speeches Detail Life, Uncertainties," Associated Press, June 5, 2009.

26. Sonia Sotomayor, "A Latina Judge's

Voice," Speech delivered October 26, 2001, at University of California at Berkeley. Available at http://berkeley.edu/news/media/releases/2009/05/26_sotomayor.shtml; accessed March 2010.

27. Hoffman, "A Breakthrough Judge."

28. Nancy Carson, *Believing in Ourselves: A Celebration of Women* (Kansas City: Andrews McMell, 2002), 24.

29. Scott Shane and Manny Fernandez, "A Judge's Own Story Highlights Her Mother's," *New York Times,* May 28, 2009, A16.

30. Sotomayor, "Remarks Prepared for Delivery at the Lehman College Commencement."

31. Ibid.

32. Amy Goldstein, "A Steady Rise, Punctuated by Doubts," *Washington Post,* July 12, 2009, A1.

33. Mallory Simon, "Sotomayor Was Schoolgirl with Focus, Determination, Friends Say," CNN, July 14, 2009. Available at www.cnn.com/2009/US/07/14/sotomayor.childhood/index.html; accessed September 2009.

34. Jason Carroll, "Growing Up Sotomayor," CNN video, July 13, 2009. Available at http://www.cnn.com/video/#/video/politics/2009/07/13/carroll.sotomayor.cnn?

iref=allsearch; accessed September 2009.

35. Sandra Sobieraj Westfall, "Sonia Sotomayor: From the Bronx to the Bench," *People,* August 17, 2009, 75.

36. Nina Totenberg, "Sotomayor: Tough Kid Turns Unintimidated Judge," National Public Radio, July 9, 2009. Available at http://www.npr.org/templates/story/story.php?storyId=106415875; accessed September 2009.

37. Robin Roberts and Claire Shipman, "Sotomayor's Brother Calls Critics 'Derogatory and Insulting,'" *Good Morning America,* June 10, 2009; ABC News Transcript accessed on LexisNexis Academic September 2009.

38. Paul LaRosa, "Here Is New York," July 19, 2009. Available at http://www.paullarosa.com/blog/?s=Sotomayor; accessed September 2009.

39. Hoffman, "A Breakthrough Judge."

40. Shulman, "Supreme Change."

41. William Grimes, "A City Gripped by Crisis and Enraptured by the Yankees," *New York Times,* March 30, 2005, E8.

42. "It's a Young Family's World," Posted on The Unofficial Co-op City Page. Available at: http://home.comcast.net/~coopcity/advertising.html; accessed September 2009.

43. Shane, "A Judge's Own Story Highlights Her Mother's."
44. Ibid.
45. "Induction Proceedings for Judge Sonia Sotomayor."
46. Ibid.
47. Ibid.
48. Ibid.
49. Ibid.
50. "Testimony of Theodore Shaw," U.S. Senate Committee on the Judiciary, July 16, 2009.
51. Goldstein, "A Steady Rise."
52. Mike Pesca, "Housing Project Part of 'Inspiring Life's Journey,'" National Public Radio, May 27, 2009.
53. "Induction Proceedings for Judge Sonia Sotomayor."
54. Shane, "A Judge's Own Story Highlights Her Mother's."

Chapter 3

1. Sonia Sotomayor, "Reflections of a Latina Princetonian," talk presented to the Princeton Club, February 26, 2002.
2. Sheryl Gay Stolberg, "Sotomayor, A Trailblazer and a Dreamer," *New York Times,* May 27, 2009, A1.
3. Jerome Karabel, *The Chosen: The Hidden History of Admission and Exclusion at*

Harvard, Yale, and Princeton (New York: Houghton Mifflin, 2005), 398, 437.

4. Jay Mathews, "The Bias Question," *The Atlantic,* November 2003. Available at http://www.theatlantic.com/past/issues/2003/11/mathews.htm; accessed September 2009.

5. Sonia Sotomayor, "Facing the Nineties As a Woman Lawyer in Corporate and Litigation Practices," remarks at a program of the Practicing Law Institute, n.d. Available at http://video.nytimes.com/video/2009/06/10/us/politics/1194840834851/practising-law-institute-panelist.html; accessed September 2009.

6. William G. Bowen and Derek Bok, *The Shape of the River: Long-Term Consequences of Considering Race in College and University Admissions* (Princeton, NJ: Princeton University Press, 1998), 278.

7. Sotomayor, "Reflections of a Latina Princetonian."

8. Ibid.

9. Ibid.

10. Ibid.

11. Ibid.

12. "Recalling Sotomayor '76 at Princeton," *Princeton Alumni Weekly,* July 15, 2009. Available at http://paw.princeton.edu/issues/2009/07/15/pages/9033; accessed February 2010.

13. Ibid.

14. Peter Winn, "The Education of Sonia Sotomayor," *The Washington Post,* July 12, 2009, B1.

15. Ibid.

16. Ruth Stevens, "Princeton Alumna, Trustee Confirmed as Supreme Court's First Latina Justice," *News at Princeton,* August 6, 2009. Available at http://www.prince ton.edu/main/news/archive/S24/95/61C10/ index.xml?section=topstories; accessed September 2009.

17. Winn, "The Education of Sonia Sotomayor."

18. "Sotomayor, A Trailblazer and a Dreamer."

19. Gabriel Debenedetti, "At Princeton, Sotomayor '76 Excelled at Academics, Extracurriculars," *Daily Princetonian,*" May 13, 2009. Available at www.dailyprincetonian. com/2009/05/13/23695; accessed February 2010.

20. Sotomayor, "Reflections of a Latina Princetonian."

21. Alexander Leitch, *A Princeton Companion* (Princeton, NJ: Princeton University Press, 1978). Available at http://etcweb.prince ton.edu/CampusWWW/Companion/ third_world_center.html; accessed February 2010.

22. "Recalling Sotomayor '76 at Princeton."

23. David Liemer, "Latin Student Groups Assail University Hiring Performance," *The Daily Princetonian,* April 22, 1974. Available at http://www.dailyprinceton ian.com/2009/05/27/23730/; accessed September 2010.

24. "Puerto Ricans Find Bias at Princeton," *New York Times,* April 23, 1974, 87.

25. Sonia Sotomayor, "Letter to the Editor: Anti-Latino Discrimination at Princeton," *The Daily Princetonian*, May 10, 1974. Available at http://www.dailyprince tonian.com/2009/05/15/23731/; accessed September 2009.

26. Ibid.

27. Avi Zenilman, "School Days," *New Yorker,* June 8, 2009. Available at http:// www.newyorker.com/online/blogs/news desk/2009/06/school-days.html; accessed September 2009.

28. Ibid.

29. "Recalling Sotomayor '76 at Princeton."

30. Winn, "The Education of Sonia Sotomayor."

31. Ibid.

32. Dori Jones, "Students Complain about Selection of 'Minority Dean,'"

The Daily Princetonian, September 12, 1974. Available at http://www.dailyprince tonian.com/2009/05/27/23728/; accessed September 2009.

33. Ibid.

34. Peter Nicholas and James Oliphant, "Two Sides to Sonia Sotomayor," *Los Angeles Times,* May 31, 2009. Available at http://articles.latimes.com/ 2009/may/31/nation/na-sotomayor -profile31; accessed September 2009.

35. Nancy Carson, *Believing in Ourselves: A Celebration of Women* (Kansas City: Andrews McMell, 2002), 26.

36. Sonia Sotomayor, "Remarks Prepared for Delivery at the Lehman College Commencement, June 3, 1999."

37. Evan Perez, "In College Thesis, Sotomayor Appeared to Support Puerto Rican Independence," *Wall Street Journal,* May 26, 2009. Available at http://blogs.wsj. com/washwire/2009/05/26/in-college-the sis-sotomayor-appeared-to-support-puerto -rican-independence/tab/article/; accessed September 2009.

38. Ibid.

39. Winn, "The Education of Sonia Sotomayor."

40. Zenilman, "School Days."

41. Sotomayor, "Reflections of a Latina

Princetonian."

42. Winn, "The Education of Sonia Sotomayor."

43. Jennifer Ludden and Linton Weeks, "Sotomayor: 'Always Looking Over My Shoulder,'" National Public Radio, May 27, 2009. Available at http://www.npr.org/templates/story/story.php?storyId=10453 8436&ft=1&f=1003; accessed September 2009.

Chapter 4

1. David D. Kirkpatrick, "Judge's Mentor: Part Guide, Part Foil," *New York Times,* June 21, 2009, A1.

2. José A. Cabranes, "Citizenship and the American Empire: Notes on the Legislative History of the United States Citizenship of Puerto Ricans," *University of Pennsylvania Law Review,* Vol. 127, no. 2 (Dec. 1978): 391–492.

3. José A. Cabranes, *Citizenship and the American Empire: Notes on the Legislative History of the United States Citizenship of Puerto Ricans* (New Haven: Yale University Press, 1979).

4. Guido Calabresi, *The Costs of Accidents: A Legal and Economic Analysis (New Haven: Yale University Press, 1970).*

5. "History of YLS," Yale Law School.

Available at http://www.law.yale.edu/about/ historyofyls.htm; accessed September 2009.

6. Interview with Robert Klonoff.

7. Sonia Sotomayor, "The Genesis and Needs of an Ethnic Identity," talk presented to the Latino Law Students Association at Columbia Law School, October 3, 2006.

8. Ibid.

9. Ibid.

10. Sheryl Gay Stolberg, "Sotomayor, A Trailblazer and a Dreamer," *New York Times,* May 27, 2009, A1.

11. Sandra Sobieraj Westfall, "Sonia Sotomayor: From the Bronx to the Bench," *People,* August 17, 2009, 75.

12. Sotomayor, "The Genesis and Needs of an Ethnic Identity."

13. Stolberg, "Sotomayor, a Trailblazer and a Dreamer."

14. Elizabeth Landau, "Sotomayor 'Always Willing to Speak Up' At Yale Law," CNN. com, May 26, 2009. Available at http://www .cnn.com/2009/POLITICS/05/26/soto mayor.princeton.yale/; accessed September 2010.

15. Stolberg, "Sotomayor, a Trailblazer and a Dreamer."

16. Stuart Auerbach, "Law Firm Apologizes to Yale Student," *Washington Post,*

December 16, 1978, D3.

17. Stephen L. Carter, *Reflections of an Affirmative Action Baby* (New York: Basic Books, 1991), 3.

18. Nina Totenberg, "Sotomayor: Tough Kid Turns Unintimidated Judge," National Public Radio, July 9, 2009. Available at http://www.npr.org/templates/story/story.php?storyId=106415875; accessed September 2009.

19. Sonia Sotomayor, "Statehood and the Equal Footing Doctrine: The Case for Puerto Rican Seabed Rights," *Yale Law Journal,* Vol. 88 (1978–1979): 825–849.

20. "At Yale, Sotomayor Was Sharp but Not Outspoken," *Yale Daily News,* May 31, 2009.

21. Sotomayor, "Statehood and the Equal Footing Doctrine," 826.

22. Sotomayor, "Statehood and the Equal Footing Doctrine," 829.

23. "History," *The Yale Journal of International Law.* Available at http://www.yjil.org/index.php?option=com_content&view=article&id=12&Itemid=13; accessed September 2009.

24. James D. Gordon III, "How Not to Succeed In Law School," *Yale Law Journal* 100, no. 6 (April 1991): 1704.

Chapter 5

1. Sonia Sotomayor, "Remarks on Receiving the Hogan-Morgenthau Award," New York City, January 17, 1995.
2. Ibid.
3. Jonathan Barzilay, "The D.A.'s Right Arms," *New York Times Magazine,* November 23, 1983, 118.
4. Ibid.
5. Michael Dorman, "Mr. D.A.," *New York Magazine,* May 16, 1983, p. 32.
6. Lee A. Daniels, "A Massive Crisis on Heroin in East Seen by Morgenthau," *New York Times,* September 23, 1980, B1.
7. "Sotomayor Confirmation Hearings, Day 2," *New York Times,* July 14, 2009. Available at http://www.nytimes.com/2009/07/14/us/politics/14confirm-text.html?pagewanted=all; accessed September 2009.
8. Barzilay, "The D.A.'s Right Arms."
9. Ibid.
10. Ronald Sullivan, "Steinberg Judge Hurt in Bicycle Crash," *New York Times,* December 16, 1988, B3.
11. Barzilay, "The D.A.'s Right Arms."
12. Ibid.
13. Ibid.
14. Benjamin Weiser and William K. Rashbaum, "Sotomayor Is Recalled As a Driven

Rookie Prosecutor," *New York Times,* June 8, 2009, A13.

15. Byron White, Opinion of the Court, Supreme Court of the United States, 458 U.S. 747, *New York v. Ferber.* Available at http://supct.law.cor nell.edu/supct/html/historics/USSC_ CR_0458_0747_ZO.html; accessed February 2010.

16. Joe Stephens and Del Quentin Wilber, "Gritty First Job Shaped Nominee," *Washington Post,* June 4, 2009, A1.

17. United States Senate Committee on the Judiciary Questionnaire for Judicial Nominees: Sonia Sotomayor, 2009, Page 30. Available at http://74.125.95.132/search?q=cache:od_ Zn0noK9UJ:graphics8.nytimes.com/ packages/images/nytint/docs/judge-sonia-sotomayor-confirmation-documents/origi nal.pdf+Hyman+Sotomayor+questionnair e&cd=9&hl=en&ct=clnk&gl=us&client=fi refox-a; accessed September 2009, March 2010.

18. "Two Men Imprisoned in Child Pornography," *New York Times,* April 5, 1983, B4.

19. Fred Kerber and Stuart Marques, "Cops: Swinger Is Killer & Thief," *Daily News,* January 30, 1982, 17.

20. *The People of the State of New York v.*

Richard Maddicks, Indictment No. 886/82, February 19, 1982.

21. Interview with Hugh H. Mo, August 26, 2009.

22. United States Senate Committee Questionnaire, 31.

23. "Sotomayor Confirmation Hearings, Day 2."

24. *The People of the State of New York v. Richard Maddicks,* 118 A.D.2d 437, 499 N.Y.S.2d 93.

25. Frank Faso and Stuart Marques, "'Tarzan' Testimony: He Wanted to Rope the Burglar Himself," *Daily News,* January 13, 1983, 14.

26. *The People of the State of New York v. Richard Maddicks,* 70 N.Y.2d 752, 520 N.Y.S.2d 1028 (Ct. App. 1987).

27. "Sotomayor Confirmation Hearings, Day 2."

28. *The People of the State of New York v. Richard Maddicks.* 118 A.D.2d 437, 499 N.Y.S.2d 93.

29. "Sotomayor Is Recalled As a Driven Rookie Prosecutor."

30. Ibid.

31. "Remarks on Receiving the Hogan-Morgenthau Award."

32. Ibid.

Chapter 6

1. Karen Sloan, "Sotomayor's Civil Practice Was with a Small, but Specialized, Firm," Law.com *National Law Journal's* Law.com, May 28, 2009. Available at http://www.law.com/jsp/nlj/PubArticleNLJ.jsp?id=1202431049336&slreturn=1&hbxlogin=1; accessed September 2009.

2. David Lipke, "Judge Sotomayor's Fashionable Past," *Women's Wear Daily,* Vol. 198, no. 1, July 1, 2009, 11.

3. United States Senate Committee on the Judiciary Questionnaire for Judicial Nominees: Sonia Sotomayor, 2009, Page 23. Available at http://74.125.95.132/search?q=cache:od_Zn0noK9UJ:graphics8.nytimes.com/packages/images/nytint/docs/judge-sonia-sotomayor-confirmation-documents/original.pdf+Hyman+Sotomayor+questionnaire&cd=9&hl=en&ct=clnk&gl=us&client=firefox-a; accessed September 2009, March 2010.

4. U.S. Trademark Act, § 15 USC 1116.

5. "Our Mission and History," International Anticounterfeiting Coalition. Available at http://iacc.org/about/mission.php; accessed February 2010.

6. Sonia Sotomayor, "Speech at the IACC (International Anticounterfeit-

ing Coalition) October 16, 1999 Luncheon." Available at http://judiciary.senate.gov/nominations/Supreme Court/Sotomayor/SoniaSotomayor-Questionnaire.cfm.

7. Nelson George, *Hip Hop America* (New York: Penguin, 2005), 159.

8. Sotomayor, "Speech at the IACC."

9. Dempster Leech, "Cracking Down on Trademark Counterfeiting," statement made at U.S. Senate Committee on the Judiciary, October 10, 1995. Available in 1995 WL 594257 (F.D.C.H.).

10. Joint Legislative Hearing on Trademark Counterfeiting in New York State, State of New York Assembly and Senate Codes Committees and Assembly Commerce, Industry & Economic Development Committee, August 21, 1991. Available at the New York State Library Digital Collections, http://nysl.nysed.gov/uhtbin/cgisirsi/sDMYe2APsL/NYSL/0/49; accessed September 2009.

11. Dempster Leech, "Cracking Down on Trademark Counterfeiting," statement prepared for the Senate Judiciary Committee, October 10, 1995, 1995 WL 594257 (F.D.C.H.).

12. *Fendi Adele S.R.L. v. Burlington Coat Factory Warehouse Corp.,* October 10, 2007.

2007 U.S. Dist. LEXIS 75812.

13. Michael Gross, "Notes on Fashion," *New York Times,* November 11, 1986, A16.

14. Martha Neil, "'Fendi Crush' Was Highlight of Sotomayor's IP Practice," *ABA Journal's* Law News Now May 26, 2009. Available at http://abajournal.com/news/ article/fendi_crush_was_highlight_of_ sotomayors_ip_practice; accessed September 2009.

15. Joint Legislative Hearing on Trademark Counterfeiting in New York State.

16. Ibid.

17. Ibid.

18. Ibid.

19. Ibid.

20. Ibid.

21. Ibid.

22. Ibid.

23. Interview with Heather McDonald.

24. Trish Donnally, "Fashion's Assault on Counterfeiters," *San Francisco Chronicle,* May 20, 1992, D3.

25. Sotomayor, "Speech at the IACC."

26. "Induction Proceedings for Judge Sonia Sotomayor," November 6, 1998. Available at http://judiciary.senate.gov/nomina tions/SupremeCourt/ Sotomayor/Sonia Sotomayor-Questionnaire.cfm.

27. Supreme Court Confirmation Ques-

tionnaire.

28. Michael Powell and Serge F. Kovaleski, "Sotomayor Rose on Merit Alone, Her Allies Say," *New York Times,* June 5, 2009, A1.

29. Ibid.

30. Ibid.

31. Ibid.

32. Ibid.

33. Sonia Sotomayor, "Yale Law School Preiskel/Silverman Speech," November 12, 1993.

Chapter 7

1. Jason Horowitz, "The Many Rabbis of Sonia Sotomayor," *New York Observer PolitickerNY,* May 26, 2009. http://www .observer.com/2009/politics/many-rabbis-sonia-sotomayor; accessed December 2009.

2. Michael Powell and Serge F. Kovaleski, "Sotomayor Rose on Merit Alone, Her Allies Say," *New York Times*, June 5, 2009, A1.

3. "Induction Proceedings for Judge Sonia Sotomayor," November 6, 1998, United States Court House, 500 Pearl Street, New York, NY.

4. Wayne King, "Now, No Hispanics Candidates for Federal Bench in New York,

New York Times, February 15, 1991, B1.

5. Ibid.

6. Ibid.

7. Jan Hoffman, "A Breakthrough Judge: What She Always Wanted," *New York Times,* September 25, 1992, B16.

8. Ina R. Bort, "Judicial Profile: Hon. Sonia Sotomayor," *The Federal Lawyer* Vol. 53, no. 2 (February 2006): 37.

9. Powell and Kovaleski, "Sotomayor Rose on Merit Alone."

10. Horowitz, "The Many Rabbis of Sonia Sotomayor."

11. Harry Pachon, Ph.D., letter dated March 12, 1991.

12. "Induction Proceedings for Judge Sonia Sotomayor."

13. Federal Judicial Center, *Your First Year on the Bench* [video], April 1994.

14. Confirmation Hearing on Hon. Susan Black, Sonia Sotomayor, Loretta Preska, and Irene M. Keeley, U.S. Senate Committee on the Judiciary, June 4, 1992. Available at www.scotusblog.com/wp-content/uploads/.../sotomayor-district-hearing.pdf; accessed November 2009.

15. Neil A. Lewis, "4 Women Delayed in Rise to Bench," *New York Times,* July 14, 1992, A20.

16. Federal Judicial Center, *Your First Year*

on the Bench.

17. Ibid.

18. Ibid.

19. "Induction Proceedings for Judge Sonia Sotomayor."

20. Hoffman, "A Breakthrough Judge."

21. Federal Judicial Center, *Your First Year on the Bench.*

22. Larry Neumeister, "Judge Finds Humility in Journey from Housing Projects to High Court," Associated Press, November 9, 1998.

23. TRAC Report.

24. *Dow Jones & Co. v. U.S. Dept. of Justice,* 880 F. Supp. 145 (SDNY 1995).

25. *Archie v. Grand Central Partnership, Inc.,* 997 F. Supp. 504 (SDNY 1988).

26. Murray Chass, "Owners Terminate Season, without the World Series," *New York Times,* September 15, 1994, A1.

27. *Daniel Silverman v. Major League Baseball Player Relations Committee, Inc.,* 67 F.3d 1054 (2nd Circ. 1995).

28. Ibid.

29. "Sports News," Associated Press, February 11, 1995.

30. Bill Madden, "Players, Owners Tell It to the Judge," *Daily News,* March 28, 1995, 45.

31. Ibid.

32. *Daniel Silverman v. Major League Baseball.*

33. Ibid.

34. Ibid.

35. Interview with George H. Cohen.

36. William B. Gould IV, "The 1994-'95 Baseball Strike and National Labor Relations Board: To the Precipice and Back Again," *West Virginia Law Review,* Vol. 110, no. 3 (Spring 2008): 983.

37. Larry Whiteside, "Baseball's Work Stoppage Is Over," *Boston Globe,* April 3, 1995.

38. Tom Verducci, "Brushback," *Sports Illustrated,* April 10, 1995, 60.

39. George Vecsey, "Hope Comes to Baseball Just in Time," *New York Times,* April 1, 1995, 29.

40. "Sotomayor Passes Judgment on Owners," *Boston Globe,* April 1, 1995.

41. Mike Mulligan, "Judge Delivers Wicked Fastball to Owners," *Chicago Sun-Times,* April 1, 1995.

42. Bill Madden, "And Now, Real Hardball Begins," *Daily News,* April 2, 1995, 4.

43. "Testimony of David Cone," U.S. Senate Committee on the Judiciary, July 16, 2009.

Chapter 8

1. Sonia Sotomayor, "Facing the Nineties As a Woman Lawyer in Corporate and Litigation Practices," remarks at a program of the Practicing Law Institute, n.d. Available at http://video.nytimes.com/video/2009/06/10/us/politics/1194840834851/practising-law-institute-panelist.html; accessed September 2009.
2. Catherine Lawton, "A Touch of Class," *Mademoiselle,* September 1986, p. 257.
3. Sheryl Gay Stolberg, "Court Nominee Manages Diabetes with Discipline," *New York Times,* July 10, 2009, A16.
4. "Induction Proceedings for Judge Sonia Sotomayor," November 6, 1998, United States Court House, 500 Pearl Street, New York, NY.
5. Ibid.
6. Lawton, "A Touch of Class."
7. Michael Powell, Serge F. Kovaleski, and Russ Buettner, "To Get to Sotomayor's Core, Start in New York," *New York Times,* July 10, 2009, A1.
8. Sotomayor, "Facing the 90s."
9. "Induction Proceedings."
10. Senator Patrick Leahy, "Delays in Senate Action on Judicial Nominations," Press Release, June 18, 1998.
11. "Hearings Before the Commit-

tee on the Judiciary, United States Senate, September 5, 30; October 28, 29; November 12, 1997." Available at Internet Archive, http://www.archive.org/stream/confirmationhear972unit/confirmationhear972unit_djvu.txt; accessed March 2010.

12. "Hearings Before the Committee on the Judiciary."

13. Ibid.

14. *Holmes v. Artuz* 1995 Westlaw 634995 (S.D.N.Y. October 27, *1995*).

15. Leahy, "Delays in Senate Action."

16. Ibid.

17. Paul A. Gigot, "Supreme Politics: Who'd Replace Justice Stevens?" *Wall Street Journal,* May 29, 1998, 1.

18. "Partisan Nonsense," *Times Argus,* June 15, 1998, an editorial quoted in Leahy, "Delays in Senate Action."

19. Neil A. Lewis, "GOP, Its Eyes on High Court, Blocks a Judge," *New York Times,* June 13, 1998, A1.

20. Jason Horowitz, "The Many Rabbis of Sonia Sotomayor," *New York Observer PolitickerNY,* May 26, 2009. http://www.observer.com/2009/politics/many-rabbis-sonia-sotomayor; accessed December 2009.

21. Larry Neumeister, "Judge Finds Humil-

ity in Journey from Housing Projects to High Court," Associated Press, November 9, 1998.

22. "Induction Proceedings."

23. John G. McCarthy, "A Practitioner's View of the Distinctive Practices of the Second Circuit," *Federal Lawyer* 53 No. 2, F 2006.

24. Daniel John Meador and Jordana Simone Bernstein, *Appellate Courts in the United States,* (St. Paul: West Publishing, 1994), p. 95.

25. Jo Becker and Adam Liptak, "Assertive Style Raises Questions on Demeanor," *New York Times,* May 28, 2009, A14.

26. *Shi Liang Lin v. United States Department of Justice,* 494 F.3d 296 (2d Cir. 2007).

27. Ina R. Bort, "Judicial Profile: Hon. Sonia Sotomayor," *The Federal Lawyer* Vol. 53, no. 2 (February 2006): 37.

28. *Ricci v. DeStefano,* 530 F.3d 88 (2d Cir. 2008).

29. Powell, Kovaleski, and Buettner, "To Get to Sotomayor's Core."

30. Shani Saxon-Parrish, "Her Honor: A Portrait of Justice Sonia Sotomayor," *Latina,* December–January 2009, 114.

31. Powell, Kovaleski, and Buettner, "To Get to Sotomayor's Core."

32. Joe Stephens and Del Quentin Wil-

ber, "Gritty First Job Shaped Nominee," *Washington Post,* June 4, 2009, A1.

33. Saxon-Parrish, "Her Honor," 114.

34. Lauren Collins, "Number Nine: Sonia Sotomayor's High-Profile Debut," *New Yorker,* January 11, 2010, 42.

35. Collins, "Number Nine."

36. Doug Gross, "Sotomayor Is Tough Judge with Breadstick Habit, Colleagues Say," CNN.com, July 17, 2009.

37. "Sotomayor in PAW: More About Sonia Sotomayor '76," *Princeton Alumni Weekly: The Weekly Blog* (n.d.). Available at http://blogs.princeton.edu/paw/2009/07/sotomayor.html#4; accessed March 2010.

38. Bort, "Judicial Profile: Hon. Sonia Sotomayor," 37.

Chapter 9

1. Ilana Seager, "Sotomayor LAW '79 Returns to Speak at Law School Reunion," *Yale Daily News,* October 19, 2009. Available at http://www.yaledailynews.com/news/university-news/2009/10/19/sotomayor-law-reveals-chaotic-nomination-process; accessed October 2009.

2. Bill Mears, "Analysis: Obama's First Judicial Pick Signals Fight for Control," CNN.com, March 18, 2009.

3. "Barack Obama before Planned Parenthood Action Fund," July 17, 2007. Transcribed by Laura Echevarria and available at http://lauraechevarria.com/?page_id=14; accessed October 2009.

4. Robert Barnes, "Over Ginsburg's Dissent, Court Limits Bias Suits," *Washington Post,* May 30, 2007, A1.

5. "Barack Obama before Planned Parenthood Action Fund."

6. Charles Babington, "Finding Clues in Obama's Senate Record on Justices," *Detroit Free Press,* May 18, 2009. Available at http://m.freep.com/news.jsp?key=463016; accessed October 2009.

7. "Transcript: Obama on Supreme Court Nominee," May 26, 2009. Posted by National Public Radio and available at www.npr.org/templates/story/story.php?storyId=104542818; accessed February 2010.

8. Ibid.

9. Shani Saxon-Parrish, "Her Honor: A Portrait of Justice Sonia Sotomayor," *Latina,* December–January 2009, 115.

10. Andrew J. Drexler, M.D., letter dated May 25, 2009; part of the U.S. Judiciary Committee's Sotomayor questionnaire materials.

11. Tom Watkins, "Sotomayor's Diabetes:

'She Overcomes It Every Day,'" CNN health.com, May 27, 2009.

12. Nina Totenberg, "How Obama's Nomination of Sotomayor Unfolded," National Public Radio, May 28, 2009.

13. "Remarks by President Obama in Nominating Judge Sonia Sotomayor to the United States Supreme Court," White House Office of the Press Secretary, May 26, 2009. Available at http://www.white house.gov/the_press_office/Remarks-by -the-President-in-Nominating-Judge -Sonia-Sotomayor-to-the-United-States -Supreme-Court; accessed October 2009.

14. Ibid.

15. "Transcript: Obama on Supreme Court Nominee."

16. "How Obama's Nomination of Sotomayor Unfolded."

17. "Remarks by President Obama."

18. Susan Swain, "Interview with Justice Sonia Sotomayor," C-SPAN, September 16, 2009. Available at http:// supremecourt.c-span.org/Video/Justice OwnWords/SC_Jus_Sotomayor.aspx; accessed October 2009.

19. Stephen L. Carter, *The Confirmation Mess: Cleaning Up the Federal Appointments Process* (New York: Basic Books, 1994), 58.

20. Ibid., p. 59.

21. Tom C. Korologos, "Obama Nominees, Take Note," *Washington Post,* January 5, 2009, A1.

22. Jeffrey Rosen, "The Case against Sotomayor," *The New Republic,* May 4, 2009. Available at www.tnr.com/article/politics/the-case-against-sotomayor; accessed February 2010.

23. Amanda Terkel, "Conservatives Blast Obama's Hispanic SCOTUS Nominee as 'Not the Smartest' and an 'Intellectual Lightweight,'" ThinkProgress.com, May 26, 2009.

24. Ibid.

25. "Partisan Confirmation Hearings Expected for Sotomayor," CNN.com, May 27, 2009. Available at http://www.cnn.com/2009/POLITICS/05/26/sotomayor.reax/index.html#cnnSTCText; accessed October 2009.

26. Jake Tapper and Sunlen Miller, "POTUS Interrupts Press Briefing to Announce Souter's Retirement, Announce Qualifications for Next Supreme," ABCNews.com, May 1, 2009.

27. Patrick Leahy, opening statement at Judge Sotomayor's Supreme Court Confirmation Hearing, July 13, 2009. Available at http://judiciary.senate.gov/hearings/

testimony.cfm?id=3959&wit_id=2629; accessed October 2010.

28. Jeff Sessions, Opening Statement at Judge Sotomayor's Supreme Court Confirmation Hearing, July 13, 2009. Available at http://judiciary.senate.gov/hearings/testimony.cfm?id=3959&wit_id=515; accessed October 2009.

29. Dianne Feinstein, Opening Statement at Judge Sotomayor's Supreme Court Confirmation Hearing, July 13, 2009. Available at http://judiciary.senate.gov/hearings/testimony.cfm?id=3959&wit_id=2626; accessed October 2009.

30. Tom LoBianco, "Sotomayor Vows 'Fidelity to the Law,'" *Washington Times,* July 13, 2009. http://www.washington times.com/news/2009/jul/13/sotomayor -hearing-opens-promises-transparency -spee/?feat=home_cube_position1; accessed October 2009.

31. Russ Feingold, Opening Statement at Judge Sotomayor's Supreme Court Confirmation Hearing, July 13, 2009. Available at http://judiciary.senate.gov/ hearings/testimony.cfm?id=3959 &wit_id=4083; accessed October 2009.

32. Charles E. Schumer, Opening Statement at Judge Sotomayor's Supreme Court Confirmation Hearing, July 13, 2009.

Available at http://judiciary.senate.gov/
hearings/testimony.cfm?id=3959&wit_
id=86; accessed October 2009.

33. Amy Klobuchar, Opening Statement at
Judge Sotomayor's Supreme Court Confirmation Hearing, July 13, 2009. Available at http://judiciary.senate.gov/hearings/
testimony.cfm?id=3959&wit_id=1202; accessed October 2009.

34. Al Franken, Opening Statement at Judge
Sotomayor's Supreme Court Confirmation
Hearing, July 13, 2009. Available at http://
judiciary.senate.gov/hearings/testimony
.cfm?id=3959&wit_id=8101; accessed October 2009.

35. "Sotomayor Confirmation Hearings, Day 2," *New York Times,* July 14,
2009. Available at http://www.nytimes.
com/2009/07/14/us/politics/14confirm-text
.html?pagewanted=all; accessed September
2009.

36. Ibid.
37. Ibid.
38. Ibid.
39. Ibid.
40. Ibid.
41. Ibid.
42. "Sotomayor Confirmation Hearings, Day 3," *New York Times,* July 16,
2009. Available at http://www.nytimes

.com/2009/07/15/us/politics/15confirm
-text.html?scp=1&sq=sotomayor%20
confirmation%20hearings,%20day%20
3&st=cse; accessed October 2009.

43. Ibid.

44. Nancy Northrup, "Center for Reproductive Rights on Nomination
of Judge Sonia Sotomayor to Supreme
Court, Center for Reproductive Rights,"
May 26, 2009. Available at http://repro
ductiverights.org/en/press-room/center
-for-reproductive-rights-on-nomination
-of-judge-sonia-sotomayor-to-supreme
-court; accessed October 2009.

45. "Sotomayor Confirmation Hearings,
Day 3."

46. "Sotomayor Hearings: The Complete
Transcript — Day 4, part 3," *Los Angeles Times,* July 16, 2009. Available at
http://latimesblogs.latimes.com/washing
ton/2009/07/sotomayor-hearings-the-com
plete-transcript-day-4-part-3.html; accessed October 2009.

47. "District Attorney of New York County
Robert Morgenthau Testifies at Judge Sotomayor's Confirmation Hearings," *Washington Post,* July 16, 2009. Available at http://
www.washingtonpost.com/wp-dyn/con
tent/article/2009/07/16/AR2009071602990
.html; accessed October 2009.

48. "Firefighter Criticizes Sotomayor," CNN.com, July 16, 2009. Available at http://www.cnn.com/2009/POLITICS/07/16/sotomayor.firefighters/index.html; accessed October 2009.

49. Dana Milbank, "Firefighters but No Brimstone," *Washington Post,* July 17, 2009, A2. Available at www.washingtonpost.com/wp-dyn/content/article/2009/07/16/AR2009071603767.html; accessed February 2010.

50. Ibid.

51. Swain, "Interview with Justice Sonia Sotomayor," C-SPAN.

52. Jake Tapper, "'Another Step Closer to a More Perfect Union,'" ABCNews.com, August 6, 2009. Available at http://blogs.abcnews.com/politicalpunch/2009/08/another-step-closer-to-a-more-perfect-union-president-obama-says-hes-very-happy-with-senate-vote-to-.html; accessed October 2009.

53. "Sotomayor Sworn in As Supreme Court Justice," *NBC Nightly News* transcript, August 8, 2009. Accessed on LexisNexis October 2009.

54. *Sotomayor Takes Oath, Becomes Supreme Court Justice* (video), CNN.com, August 8, 2009. Available at www.cnn.com/2009/POLITICS/08/08/sotomayor/

index.html#cnnSTCVideo; accessed February 2010

Chapter 10

1. Susan Swain, "Interview with Justice Sonia Sotomayor," C-SPAN, September 16, 2009. Available at http://supremecourt.c-span.org/Video/JusticeOwnWords/SC_Jus_Sotomayor.aspx; accessed October 2009.
2. Edward Lazarus, *Closed Chambers: The Rise, Fall, and Future of the Modern Supreme Court* (New York: Penguin, 1999), 31.
3. Shani Saxon-Parrish, "Her Honor: A Portrait of Justice Sonia Sotomayor," *Latina,* December–January 2009, 115.
4. Bill Mears, "Justice Ginsburg Ready to Welcome Sotomayor," CNN.com, June 16, 2009. Available at www.cnn.com/2009/POLITICS/06/16/sotomayor.ginsburg/index.html; accessed February 2010.
5. Devin Leonard, "The Jazz Mambo King in Exile," *New York Observer,* November 3, 2009.
6. Saxon-Parrish, "Her Honor," 110.
7. Jake Tapper, "'Another Step Closer to a More Perfect Union,'" ABCNews.com, August 6, 2009. Available at http://blogs.abcnews.com/politicalpunch/2009/08/another-step-closer-to-a-more-perfect

-union-president-obama-says-hes-very
-happy-with-senate-vote-to-.html; accessed October 2009.

8. William M. Landes and Richard A. Posner, "Rational Judicial Behavior: A Statistical Study," *Journal of Legal Analysis* Vol. 1, no. 2, (Summer 2009): 775–831.

9. Jeffrey Toobin, *The Nine* (New York: Doubleday, 2007), 11.

10. Landes and Posner, "Rational Judicial Behavior."

11. Ibid.

12. Swain, "Interview with Justice Sonia Sotomayor," C-SPAN.

13. "For a Justice, Sonia Sotomayor Is Low on Dough," Politico.com. Available at politico.com/news/stories/0509/23045.html; accessed February 2010.

14. Toobin, *The Nine,* 1.

15. *Hillary: The Movie,* DVD. Directed by Alan Peterson. Citizens United Productions, 2008.

16. *Citizens United v. Federal Election Commission* (Reargued) 08-205, oral argument session transcript, Supreme Court of the United States. Available at http://www.supremecourtus.gov/oral_arguments/argument_transcripts.html; accessed March 2010.

17. Swain, "Interview with Justice Sonia So-

tomayor," C-SPAN.

18. *Citizens United v. Federal Election Commission* transcript.

19. Swain, "Interview with Justice Sonia Sotomayor," C-SPAN.

20. Patrik Jonsson, "'Fighting' Obama Hits Supreme Court over Campaign Finance," *Christian Science Monitor,* January 23, 2010.

21. James Oliphant, "Supreme Court's Campaign Finance Ruling Could Bring Flood of Ads," *Los Angeles Times,* January 21, 2010. Available at http://articles.latimes.com/2010/jan/21/nation/la-na-campaign-finance-analysis22-2010jan22; accessed January 2010.

22. Swain, "Interview with Justice Sonia Sotomayor," C-SPAN.

23. Ibid.

24. Ibid.

25. Ibid.

26. Ibid.

27. Michael Powell, Serge F. Kovaleski, and Russ Buettner, "To Get to Sotomayor's Core, Start in New York," July 10, 2009, A1.

28. *Justice Sotomayor Throws out First Pitch* [video], New York Yankees, September 26, 2009. Available at http://newyork.yankees.mlb.com/news/article.jsp?ymd

=20090926&content_
id=7169594&cid=nyy&vkey=news_nyy;
accessed December 2009.

29. Swain, "Interview with Justice Sonia
Sotomayor," C-SPAN.

BIBLIOGRAPHY

ABC News. "Sotomayor's Brother Calls Critics: 'Derogatory and Insulting'" [Transcript]. *Good Morning America,* June 10, 2009.

"Alumni." *Yale Law Journal.* Available at www.yalelawjournal.org/alumni.html; accessed February 2010.

"Analysis: Obama's First Judicial Pick Signals Fight for Control." CNN.com, March 18, 2009.

"And Now, Real Hardball Begins." *Daily News,* April 2, 1995.

"'Another Step Closer to a More Perfect Union.'" ABCNews.com, August 6, 2009.

Associated Press. "Judge Finds Humility in Journey from Housing Projects to High Court." November 9, 1998.

Associated Press, "Sotomayor Adds Celebrity Element to High Court." November 18, 2009.

Associated Press. "Sotomayor's Speeches

Detail Life, Uncertainties." June 5, 2009.

Atkinson, Richard C. "Standardized Tests and Access to American Universities." The 2001 Robert H. Atwell Distinguished Lecture. Washington, D.C., February 18, 2001. Available at www.ucop.edu/news/sat/speech.html; accessed February 2010.

"At Yale, Sotomayor Was Sharp but Not Outspoken." *Yale Daily News,* May 31, 2009.

Ayala, César. "The Decline of the Plantation Economy and the Puerto Rican Migration of the 1950s." *Latino Studies Journal* 7, no. 1 (winter 1996).

"Barack Obama before Planned Parenthood Action Fund." Transcribed by Laura Echevarria. July 17, 2007. Available at www.lauraechevarria.com.

"Baseball's Work Stoppage Is Over." *Boston Globe,* April 3, 1995.

Bellafaire, Judith. "Puerto Rican Servicewomen in Defense of the Nation." Women in Military Service for America Memorial Foundation. Available at www.womensmemorial.org/Education/PRHistory.html; accessed February 2010.

"The Bias Question." *The Atlantic,* November 2003.

A Biographical Sketch of Sonia Sotomayor. Video from the Law School Admission

Council in 2004. Available at www.you tube.com/watch?v=yYjuS-d8PL8; accessed February 2010.

Bort, Ina R. "Hon. Sonia Sotomayor." *The Federal Lawyer* (February 2006): 37.

———. "Judicial Profile: Hon. Sonia Sotomayor." *The Federal Lawyer* (February 2006).

Bowen, William G., and Derek Bok. *The Shape of the River: Long-Term Consequences of Considering Race in College and University Admissions.* Princeton, NJ: Princeton University Press, 1998.

"A Breakthrough Judge: What She Always Wanted." *New York Times,* September 25, 1992.

"Brushback." *Sports Illustrated,* April 10, 1995.

Carson, Nancy. *Believing in Ourselves: A Celebration of Women.* Kansas City: Andrews McMell, 2002.

Carter, Stephen L. *The Confirmation Mess: Cleaning Up the Federal Appointments Process.* New York: Basic Books, 1994.

———. *Reflections of an Affirmative Action Baby.* New York: Basic Books, 1991.

Chavez, Linda. *Out of the Barrio: Toward a New Politics of Hispanic Assimilation.* New York: Basic Books, 1991.

"A City Gripped by Crisis and Enraptured

by the Yankees." *New York Times,* March 30, 2005.

Clark, Victor S. *Porto Rico and Its Problems.* Washington, D.C.: Brookings Institution, 1930.

Committee member statements posted on the United States Senate Committee on the Judiciary. Available at judiciary.senate.gov/hearings.

"Concepcion Alvarado Escobedo." U.S. Latino & Latina World War II Oral History Project. University of Texas at Austin. http://lib.utexas.edu/ww2latinos; accessed August 2009.

"Congress Balks at Baseball." *USA Today,* February 9, 1995.

Conn, Stetson, Rose C. Engelman, and Byron Fairchild. *Guarding the United States and Its Outposts.* Washington, D.C.: United States Army Center of Military History, 2000. Available at www.history.army.mil/books/wwii/Guard-US/ch16.htm; accessed February 2010.

"Conservatives Blast Obama's Hispanic SCOTUS Nominee as 'Not the Smartest' and an 'Intellectual Lightweight.'" ThinkProgress.com, May 26, 2009.

"Continually Defining What's Right and Just." *Princeton Alumni Magazine,* n.d.

"Cops: Swinger Is Killer & Thief." *Daily*

News, January 30, 1982.

"Court Nominee Manages Diabetes with Discipline." *New York Times,* July 10, 2009.

"Current and Former Editors." *Yale Law Journal.* Available at yalelawjournal.org/content/view/532; accessed February 2010.

"The D.A.'s Right Arms." *New York Times,* November 23, 1983.

Daniel Silverman v. Major League Baseball Player Relations Committee, Inc., 95 Civ. 2054 (S.D.N.Y. March 31, 1995).

Debenedetti, Gabriel. "At Princeton, Sotomayor '76 Excelled at Academics, Extracurriculars." *Daily Princetonian,* May 13, 2009. Available at www.dailyprincetonian.com/2009/05/13/23695; accessed February 2010

Drexler, Andrew J. Letter dated May 25, 2009. Part of the U.S. Judiciary Committee's Sotomayor questionnaire details.

Facing the 90s As a Woman Lawyer in Corporate and Litigation Practices. Video from The Practicing Law Institute. Available at http://video.nytimes.com/video/2009/06/10/us/politics/1194840834851/practising-law-institute-panelist.html.

Fair Test. "Schools That Do Not Use SAT or ACT Scores for Admitting Substantial

Numbers of Students Into Bachelor Degree Programs." FairTest.org, fall 2009. Available at www.fairtest.org/university/optional; accessed February 2010.

"Fashion's Assault on Counterfeiters." *San Francisco Chronicle,* May 20, 1992.

"'Fendi Crush' Was Highlight of Sotomayor's IP Practice." *ABA Journal* (May 26, 2009).

"'Fighting' Obama Hits Supreme Court over Campaign Finance." *Christian Science Monitor,* January 23, 2010.

"Finding Clues in Obama's Senate Record on Justices." *Detroit Free Press,* May 18, 2009.

"Fort Oglethorpe History." Catoosa County Chamber of Commerce. Available at www.gatewaytogeorgia.com/catoosa/ftogle.php.

"4 Women Delayed in Rise to Bench." *New York Times,* July 14, 1992.

"Friends Provide Glimpse into Nominee's 'Very Full Life.'" *Washington Post,* May 31, 2009.

"GED Testing Fact Sheet." General Educational Development Testing Service. Available at www.GEDtest.org.

Gerstein, Josh. "For a Justice, Sonia Sotomayor Is Low on Dough." Politico.com, May 28, 2009. Available at politico.com/news/stories/0509/23045.html; accessed

February 2010.

Gonzalez, Evelyn Diaz. *The Bronx*. New York: Columbia University Press, 2004.

"G.O.P., Its Eyes on High Court, Blocks a Judge." *New York Times,* June 13, 1998.

Gordon, James D. III. "How Not to Succeed In Law School." *Yale Law Journal* 100, no. 6 (April 1991): 1704.

"Grand Rapids Hispanics Proud of Sonia Sotomayor Nomination for Her Qualification." *Grand Rapids Press,* July 13, 2009.

"Gritty First Job Shaped Nominee." *Washington Post*, June 4, 2009.

Hanson, Earl Parker. *Transformation: The Story of Modern Puerto Rico.* New York: Simon & Schuster, 1955.

"He Is the Fashion Police." *New York Magazine,* March 6, 1995.

Henderson, Aileen Kilgore. *Stateside Soldier: Life in the Women's Army Corps, 1944–1945.* Columbia: University of South Carolina Press, 2001.

"Her Honor: A Portrait of Justice Sonia Sotomayor." *Latina,* December-January 2009, p. 115.

Hillman, James. *The Soul's Code: In Search of Character and Calling.* New York: Random House, 1996.

"History." *Yale Journal of International Law.* Available at www.yjil.org.

"History of YLS." Yale Law School. Available at www.law.yale.edu.

"Hope Comes to Baseball Just in Time." *New York Times,* April 1, 1995.

"Housing Project Part of 'Inspiring Life's Journey.'" National Public Radio, May 27, 2009.

"How Obama's Nomination of Sotomayor Unfolded." National Public Radio, May 28, 2009.

"In College Thesis, Sotomayor Appeared to Support Puerto Rican Independence." *Wall Street Journal,* May 26, 2009.

"Induction Proceedings for Judge Sonia Sotomayor." November 6, 1998. Available at http://judiciary.senate.gov/nomina tions/SupremeCourt/Sotomayor/Sonia Sotomayor-Questionnaire.cfm.

International Anticounterfeiting Coalition. "White Paper: The Negative Consequences of International Intellectual Property Theft." January 2005.

"It's a Young Families World." Unofficial Co-Op City Page. Available at http://home .comcast.net/~coopcity/ advertising.html.

Jaffe, A. J. *People, Jobs and Economic Development: A Case History of Puerto Rico.* Glencoe, IL: The Free Press, 1959.

"The Jazz Mambo King in Exile." *New York Observer,* November 3, 2009.

Joint Legislative Hearing on Trademark Counterfeiting in New York State, State of New York Assembly and Senate Codes Committees and Assembly Commerce, Industry & Economic Development Committee, August 21, 1991.

"Judge Delivers Wicked Fastball to Owners." *Chicago Sun-Times,* April 1, 1995.

"Judge's Journey to Top." *Daily News,* October 24, 1998.

"Judge's Mentor: Part Guide, Part Foil." *New York Times,* June 21, 2009.

"A Judge's Own Story Highlights Her Mother's." *New York Times,* May 28, 2009.

"Judge Sotomayor's Fashionable Past." *Women's Wear Daily,* July 1, 2009.

Justice Sotomayor Throws Out First Pitch. Video from the New York Yankees, September 26, 2009. Available at newyork.yankees.mlb.com.

Karabel, Jerome. *The Chosen: The Hidden History of Admission and Exclusion at Harvard, Yale, and Princeton.* New York: Houghton Mifflin, 2005.

Katyal, Neal Kumar. "Architecture as Crime Control." *Yale Law Journal* 11, no. 5 (2002).

Korrol, Virginia Sanchez. *From Colonia to Community: The History of Puerto Ricans in New York City.* Berkeley: University of California Press, 1983.

Landau, Elizabeth. "Cricket, Ivy League Classmates Startled Student Sonia Soto-mayor." CNN.com, July 15, 2009. Available at www.cnn.com/2009/US/07/15/sotomayor.college/index.html; accessed February 2010.

Landes, William M., and Richard A. Posner. "Rational Judicial Behavior: A Statistical Study (April 2008)." University of Chicago Law and Economics, Olin Working Paper No. 404. *Journal of Legal Analysis* 1, no. 2 (2009): 775–831. Available at http://ssrn.com/abstract=1126403; accessed February 2010.

LaRosa, Paul. *"Here Is New York,"* July 19, 2009. Available at www.paullarosa.com/blog/?s=Sotomayor.

"Latin Student Groups Assail University Hiring Performance." *The Daily Princetonian,* April 22, 1974.

"Law Firm Apologizes to Yale Student." *Washington Post,* December 16, 1978.

Lazarus, Edward. *Closed Chambers: The Rise, Fall, and Future of the Modern Supreme Court.* New York: Penguin, 1999.

Leahy, Patrick. "Delays in Senate Action on Judicial Nominations," Press Release, June 18, 1998.

Leech, Dempster. "Cracking Down on

Trademark Counterfeiting." Statement prepared for the Senate Judiciary Committee, October 10, 1995, 1995 WL 594257 (F.D.C.H.).

Leitch, Alexander. *A Princeton Companion.* Princeton University Press, 1978. Available at http://etcweb.princeton.edu/ CampusWWW/Companion/third_world _center.html; accessed February 2010.

"Long Hours and Hard Work Took a Toll on Sotomayor's Relationships." *ABA Journal* (July 2009). Available at ww.abajournal .com.

"The Many Rabbis of Sonia Sotomayor." *New York Observer,* May 26, 2009.

Márquez, Robert. *Puerto Rican Poetry: A Selection from Aboriginal to Contemporary Times.* Amherst: University of Massachusetts Press, 2007.

"A Massive Crisis on Heroin in East Seen by Morgenthau." *New York Times,* September 23, 1980.

Mauro, Tony. "Sotomayor's Law Clerks." *The BLT: The Blog of LegalTimes,* August 20, 2009. Available at http://legal times.typepad.com/blt/2009/08/soto mayors-law-clerks.html; accessed February 2010.

McCarthy, John G. "A Practitioner's View of the Distinctive Practices of the Second

Circuit." *Federal Lawyer* 53, no. 2 (2006).

"Vera E. McCraney," Flagler County Families. Available at www.flaglercountyfamilies.com/mil-mccraneyvera.html; accessed February 2010.

Meador Daniel John, and Jordana Simone Bernstein. *Appellate Courts in the United States.* St. Paul, MN: West Publishing, 1994.

Mears, Bill. "Justice Ginsburg Ready to Welcome Sotomayor." CNN.com, June 16, 2009. Available at www.cnn.com/2009/POLITICS/06/16/sotomayor.ginsburg/index.html; accessed February 2010.

Milbank, Dana. "Firefighters but No Brimstone." *Washington Post,* July 17, 2009. Available at www.washingtonpost.com/wp-dyn/content/article/2009/07/16/AR2009071603767.html; accessed February 2010.

"Mr. D.A." *New York Magazine*, May 16, 1983, p. 32.

Naison, Mark. "Sonia Sotomayor's Appointment Highlights a Time When Public Housing Was a Place of Hope and Possibility for Working Class Families in the Bronx." History News Network, May 30, 2009. Available at http://hnn.us/roundup/entries/88690.html.

"New York Retailers Face Fines for Selling

Fake Designer Goods." *Wall Street Journal,* December 6, 1991.

New York v. Ferber 458 U.S. 747 (1982). Opinion available at http://supct.law .cornell.edu/supct/html/historics/USSC _CR_0458_0747_ZO.html; accessed February 2010.

Northrup, Nancy. "Center for Reproductive Rights on Nomination of Judge Sonia Sotomayor to Supreme Court." Center for Reproductive Rights, May 26, 2009. Available at reproductiverights.org/en/press-room/ center-for-reproductive-rights-on-nom ination-of-judge-sonia-sotomayor-to -supreme-court; accessed February 2010.

"Notes on Fashion." *New York Times,* November 11, 1986.

"Now, No Hispanic Candidates for Federal Bench in New York." *New York Times,* February 15, 1991.

"Number Nine." *New Yorker,* January 11, 2010.

"Obama Announces Nomination of Sonia Sotomayor." *ABA Journal,* (May 26, 2009).

Obama, Barack. "Transcript: Obama on Supreme Court Nominee." National Public Radio, May 26, 2009. Available at www .npr.org/templates/story/story.php?story Id=104542818; accessed February 2010.

"Obama Nominees, Take Note." *Washington Post,* January 5, 2009.

"On a Supreme Court Prospect's Resume: 'Baseball Savior.'" *New York Times,* May 14, 2009.

O'Rourke, Meghan. "Nancy Drew's Father." *New Yorker,* November 8, 2004.

International Anticounterfeiting Coalition. "Our Mission and History." Available at http://iacc.org/about/mission.php; accessed February 2010.

"Over Ginsburg's Dissent, Court Limits Bias Suits." *Washington Post,* May 30, 2007.

"Owners Terminate Season, without the World Series." *New York Times,* September 15, 1994, p. 1.

Pachon, Harry. Letter dated March 12, 1991.

"Paging through Sotomayor's Open-Book Life." *Washington Times,* June 16, 2009.

Paradise, Paul R. *Trademark Counterfeiting, Product Piracy, and the Billion Dollar Threat to the U.S. Economy.* Westport, CT: Quorum Books, 1999.

"Partisan Confirmation Hearings Expected for Sotomayor." CNN.com, May 27, 2009.

"Partisan Nonsense." *Times Argus,* June 15, 1998.

"Players, Owners Tell It to the Judge." *Daily*

News, March 28, 1995.

Polk, Judd. "The Plight of Puerto Rico." *Political Science Quarterly* 57, n. 4, (1942).

"POTUS Interrupts Press Briefing to Announce Souter's Retirement, Announce Qualifications for Next Supreme." ABCNews.com, May 1, 2009.

"Prepping Sotomayor for Hearings: Get Your Game Face On." CNN, May 28, 2009.

Lee, Jesse (poster). "The President's Nominee: Judge Sonia Sotomayor." *White House Blog,* May 26, 2009. Available at www.whitehouse.gov/Sotomayor; accessed February 2010.

"Princeton Alumna, Trustee Confirmed as Supreme Court's First Latina Justice." *Princeton University News,* August 6, 2009. Available at www.princeton.edu/main/news.

"Prospect Hospital." *Wall Street Journal,* October 21, 1977.

Puerto Rican Legal Defense and Education Fund. "Report of Program Activities 1987." January 14, 1988.

Women in Military Service for America Memorial Foundation. "History Archive: Puerto Rican Servicewomen Answer the Call to Serve." April 2006. Available at www.womensmemorial.org/H&C/History/historypr.html; accessed February 2010.

"Puerto Ricans Find Bias at Princeton." *New York Times*, April 23, 1974.

"The Purse-Party Blues." *Time,* August 2, 2004.

"Recalling Sotomayor '76 at Princeton." *Princeton Alumni Weekly,* July 15, 2009. Available at http://paw.princeton.edu/issues/2009/07/15/pages/9033; accessed February 2010.

"Remarks Prepared for Delivery at the Lehman College Commencement, June 3, 1999, by Judge Sonia Sotomayor," part of Sonia Sotomayor's "United States Senate Committee on the Judiciary Questionnaire for Judicial Nominees." Available at http://judiciary.senate.gov/nominations/Supreme Court/Sotomayor/SoniaSotomayor -Questionnaire.cfm.

Rosen, Jeffery. "The Case against Sotomayor." *The New Republic,* May 4, 2009. Available at www.tnr.com/article/politics/the-case-against-sotomayor; accessed February 2010.

"San Felipe — The Hurricane of September 13, 1928, at San Juan, P.R." *Monthly Weather Review* 56, no. 9 (1928).

Sandis, Eva E. "Characteristics of Puerto Rican Migrants to, and from, the United States." *International Migration Review* 4, no. 2 (spring 1970).

Sanneh, Kelefa. "Review: Believe the Hype." *Transition* 80 (1999): 145–146.

"School Days." *New Yorker,* June 8, 2009.

Simon, Mallory. "Sotomayor Was Schoolgirl with Focus, Determination, Friends Say." CNN, July 14, 2009. Available at www.cnn.com/2009/US/07/14/sotomayor.childhood/index.html; accessed February 2010.

Sotomayor, Sonia. Interview by Susan Swain. C-SPAN, September 16, 2009.

"Sonia Sotomayor: From the Bronx to the Bench." *People,* August 17, 2009.

"Sonia Sotomayor Reflects on Her Success." *Hispanic Outlook in Higher Education,* November 4, 2002.

Sotomayor, Sonia. "The Genesis and Needs of an Ethnic Identity." Presented at The Latino Law Students Association, Columbia Law School, October 3, 2006.

Sotomayor, Sonia. "A Latina Judge's Voice." Judge Mario G. Olmos Memorial Lecture. Presented at the University of California Berkeley School of Law, 2001. [Reprinted, *New York Times,* May 15, 2009.]

Sotomayor, Sonia. "Letter to the Editor: Anti-Latino Discrimination at Princeton." *Daily Princetonian,* May 10, 1974.

Sotomayor, Sonia. "Reflections of a Latina Princetonian." Presented at The Princeton

Club, February 26, 2002.

Sotomayor, Sonia. "Remarks on Receiving the Hogan-Morgenthau Award." January 17, 1995.

Sotomayor, Sonia. Speech. Presented at the IACC (International Anticounterfeiting Coalition) luncheon, October 16, 1977.

Sotomayor, Sonia. "Statehood and the Equal Footing Doctrine: The Case for Puerto Rican Seabed Rights." *Yale Law Journal* 88 (1979).

Sotomayor, Sonia. Preiskel/Silverman Speech. Presented at Yale Law School, November 12, 1993.

"Sotomayor: 'Always Looking over My Shoulder.'" National Public Radio, May 27, 2009. www.npr.org.

"Sotomayor 'Always Willing to Speak Up' At Yale Law." CNN.com, May 26, 2009.

"Sotomayor Confirmation Hearings, Day 2." *New York Times,* July 14, 2009.

"Sotomayor, A Trailblazer and a Dreamer." *New York Times,* May 27, 2009.

"Sotomayor Is Recalled As a Driven Rookie Prosecutor." *New York Times,* June 8, 2009.

"Sotomayor Is Tough Judge with Breadstick Habit, Colleagues Say." CNN.com, July 17, 2009.

"Sotomayor Keeps Community Bonds

Tight." *USA Today*, December 28, 2009.

"Sotomayor LAW '79 Returns to Speak at Law School Reunion." *Yale Daily News,* October 19, 2009.

"Sotomayor Passes Judgement on Owners." *Boston Globe,* April 1, 1995.

"Sotomayor Rose on Merit Alone, Her Allies Say." *New York Times*, June 5, 2009.

"Sotomayor Sworn in As Supreme Court Justice." Video from MSNBC.com, August 8, 2009. www.msnbc.msn.com/id/32340419/ns/politics-white_house.

"Sotomayor Takes Oath, Becomes Supreme Court Justice." Video from CNN.com, August 8, 2009. www.cnn.com/2009/POLITICS/08/08/sotomayor/index.html#cnnSTCVideo.

"Sotomayor: Tough Kid Turns Unintimidated Judge." National Public Radio, July 9, 2009.

"Sotomayor's Blunt Style Raises Issue of Temperament." *New York Times,* May 28, 2009.

"Sotomayor's Civil Practice Was with a Small, but Specialized, Firm." *National Law Journal* (May 28, 2009).

"Sotomayor's Diabetes: 'She Overcomes It Every Day.'" CNNhealth.com, May 27, 2009.

Staudohar, Paul D. "The Baseball Strike

of 1994–95." *Monthly Labor Review* 120 (March 1997).

"A Steady Rise, Punctuated by Doubts." *Washington Post,* July 12, 2009.

"Students Complain about Selection of 'Minority Dean.'" *Daily Princetonian,* September 12, 1974.

"Steinberg Judge Hurt in Bicycle Crash." *New York Times,* December 16, 1988.

Suarez, Nydia R. "The Rise and Decline of Puerto Rico's Sugar Economy" [Sugar and Sweetener: S&O/SSS-224]. Economic Research Service, United States Department of Agriculture. December 1998.

"Supreme Change." *Washington Post,* June 16, 2009.

Sutton, John R. *Law/Society: Origins, Interactions, and Change.* Thousand Oaks, CA: Pine Forge, 2001.

Supreme Court Confirmation Questionnaire. http://judiciary.senate.gov/nominations/SupremeCourt/Sotomayor/Sonia Sotomayor-Questionnaire.cfm.

"Supreme Court Nominee Sonia Sotomayor Breaks Her Ankle at LaGuardia Airport." *New York Daily News,* June 8, 2009.

"Supreme Court's Campaign Finance Ruling Could Bring Flood of Ads." *Los Angeles Times,* January 21, 2010.

"Supreme Politics: Who'd Replace Justice

Stevens?" *Wall Street Journal,* May 29, 1998.

"'Tarzan' Testimony: He Wanted to Rope the Burglar Himself." *Daily News,* January 13, 1983.

"Testimony of David Cone," United States Senate Committee on the Judiciary, July 16, 2009.

"Testimony of Theodore Shaw," United States Senate Committee on the Judiciary, July 16, 2009.

"To Get to Sotomayor's Core, Start in New York." *New York Times,* July 9, 2009.

Toobin, Jeffrey. *The Nine.* New York: Doubleday, 2007.

"A Touch of Class." *Mademoiselle,* September 1986, p. 257.

TRAC Reports. "Supreme Court Nominee Judge Sonia Sotomayor: Tough on White-Collar Crime." Available at trac.syr.edu/tracreports/judge/213; accessed February 2010.

Treadwell, Mattie E. *The Women's Army Corp.* Washington, D.C.: United States Army Center of Military History, 1991. Available at www.history.army.mil/books/wwii/Wac; accessed February 2010.

"Two Men Imprisoned in Child Pornography." *New York Times,* April 5, 1983.

"Two Sides to Sonia Sotomayor." *Los Ange-*

les Times, May 31, 2009.

*WAC Handbook,*1944. From the Idelle Singletary Meng Scrapbook, Women Veterans Historical Collection. University of North Carolina-Greensboro. Available at http://library.uncg.edu/dp/wv/results28. aspx?i=4708&s=2; accessed February 2010.

Whalen, Carmen Teresa. "Sweatshops Here and There: The Garment Industry, Latinas, and Labor Migrations." *International Labor and Working-Class History.* 61 (spring, 2002): 51–52.

White House Office of the Press Secretary. "Remarks by President Obama in Nominating Judge Sonia Sotomayor to the United States Supreme Court." May 26, 2009. Available at www.whitehouse.gov.

"Your First Year on the Bench." Video from the Federal Judicial Center, April 1994.

Cases Cited

The People of the State of New York v. Richard Maddicks, 70 N.Y.2d 752, 520 N.Y.S.2d 1028 (Ct. App. 1987).

The People of the State of New York v. Richard Maddicks, 118 A.D.2d 437, 499 N.Y.S.2d 93.

The People of the State of New York v. Richard Maddicks, Indictment No. 886/82, February 19, 1982.

Clarett v. National Football League, 369 F.3d 124 (2d Cir. 2004).

United States v. Quattrone, 402 F.3d 304 (2d Cir. 2005).

Ford v. McGinnis, 352 F.3d 582 (2d Cir. 2003).

In re NYSE Specialists Securities Litigation, 503 F.3d 89 (2d Cir. 2007).

Farrell v. Burke, 449 F.3d 470 (2d Cir. 2006).

Fendi Adele S.R.L. v. Burlington Coat Factory Warehouse Corp., October 10, 2007, Documents Not Reported in F.Supp.2d, 2007 WL 2982295 (S.D.N.Y.).

Dow Jones & Co. v. U.S. Dept. of Justice, 880 F. Supp. 145 (S.D.N.Y. 1995).

Archie v. Grand Central Partnership, Inc., 997 F. Supp. 504 (SDNY 1998).

Daniel Silverman v. Major League Baseball Player Relations Committee, Inc., 67 F.3d 1054 (2nd Circ. 1995).

Shi Liang Lin v. United States Department of Justice, 494 F.3d 296 (2d Cir. 2007).

Ricci v. DeStefano, 530 F.3d 88 (2d Cir. 2008).

MISCELLANEOUS

2009 Questionnaire.

Supreme Court Confirmation Questionnaire.

Induction ceremony 1998.
U.S. Trademark Act, § 15 USC 1116.
TRAC Report.
"The 1994-'95 Baseball Strike."
C-SPAN interview.

ABOUT THE AUTHOR

Antonia Felix is the *New York Times* best-selling author of 15 nonfiction books including biographies of Secretary of State Condoleezza Rice, former NATO Commander Gen. Wesley K. Clark and First Lady Laura Bush. Her music biographies of Italian tenor Andrea Bocelli, musical savant Tony DeBlois and others grew out of her interest in classical music, as she is also an operatic soprano who performs throughout the United States and Europe. Felix studied music at the University of Wisconsin-Madison and Mannes College of Music in New York and holds an M.A. in English from Texas A&M University. She lives with her husband, opera singer Stanford Felix, near Kansas City.